Obama's
Wonder Years

Obama's
Wonder Years

2008 - 2016

(8 Years of Lower Unemployment & Rising Stock Markets)

James A. Vannes

Order this book online at www.trafford.com
or email orders@trafford.com

Most Trafford titles are also available at major online book retailers.

Print information available on the last page.

ISBN: 978-1-4907-4060-7 (sc)
ISBN: 978-1-4907-4062-1 (hc)
ISBN: 978-1-4907-4061-4 (e)

Library of Congress Control Number: 2014914828

Trafford rev. 02/28/2018

 www.trafford.com

North America & International
toll-free: 1 888 232 4444 (USA & Canada)
fax: 812 355 4082

Table of Contents

Introduction: This book is divided into 2 sections.

Note: During the 2008 - 2017 period, I kept routinely recording items I found interesting. It never entered my mind to publish same but looking back and reviewing the various entries proved to be a very enlightening exercise that I feel will be appreciated by discriminating readers. Unfortunately, most of the entries are not ascribed to the original source and as such I apologize to the original sources. As I had copied these items, the only errors are mine.

2008 - How Things Were

Since 2001: Gold up 239% & Oil up 267%

TIPS: Best to buy when the real yield being offered is over 2%. In Jan 08 it was 1.6%!

Private consumption in 2006: U.S. = $ 9 trillion (out of our 2006 GDP of $ 13T+) vs China's $ 1 Trillion

The U.S. had some 8 million companies with less than 100 employees.

The world consumption of aluminum is 100,000 tons a day.

In October 2007: The Russell 2000 Index was 24% in financial services!

Foreign Central Banks are recycling some $ 2 trillion into "Sovereign Country Funds" to convert U.S. treasury holdings into strategic assets!

Senior citizen's living sector: independent living communities, assisted living communities, nursing homes and continuing care retirement communities. The 11 REITS in the health care subsection have posted 22.8% annual average growth for the past 5 years. The Boomer wave will not hit for 10 or 20 years.

Amended 1099's: Since 2003, the number of amended forms has doubled to some 13% from the average of 5 to 8 percent. Schwab alone sends some 3 million 1099's.

Does your financial manger use rebalancing software?? Like 'iRebal'??

Typical Hedge Fund Organization: a quant fund, a commodities group, a long/short team, a private equity group, a distressed debt group which all means DIVERSIFICATION!

As an example of Public Sector retirement plan investments: There are 3.4 M Fed Govt employees in 'Thrift Savings Plan - TSP' which earned an average of 6.7% vs 1.6% in SS over past 16 years.

TSP has 2 fixed income and 3 equity index funds composed of:

	2004 Return	% of Funds
Gov Bonds	5.8%	43%
High Qual Bonds	7%	7%
S&P 500	12%	38%
SC 4500	11.8%	7%
Int MSC	6.%	5%

Teacher's Unions "reforms" are in their own interests - more spending, higher salaries, smaller class size, etc. with no evidence that these are important determinants in student learning. They oppose - no child left behind's performance measurements, school choice, charter schools, testing of teachers competence as threats to the status quo.

SS: Workers to elderly 1935: 41 to 1, 1950: 16 to 1, and 2004: 3 to 1. No concern about 'gambling' or Wall St. profiting. Teacher's have TIAA-CREF ($300B) Teacher Insurance & Annuity Assoc. - College Retirement Equities Fund. University & Foundation Endowments invested: 31% US equity, 18% Intl. Eqs, 14% Fixed, 5% cash and 32% alternate strategies. Calif has Calpers, a $140B public-employee pension fund also invested in equities. Life expectancy 1935: 62 yrs, 2004: 78 yrs. 1st baby boomer retires 2010 and SS benefits will exceed payroll tax revenue in 2018.

The arts do NO measurable good! Can raise test scores in non-arts way. Propaganda has moved to "enriching people's lives" by "expanding capacity for empathy", "creation of social bonds", and "Expression of communal meaning". Unfortunately there is no evidence that any of this occurs. In fact art can be divisive - Mapplethorpe, NAZI art, Communist art etc. The traditional 'high' arts: classical music, painting and sculpture, theater, dance, novels and poetry are being displaced by film, graphic design, photography, pop music and TV.

According to the Tax Foundation as of 2004, 55% of the public employee pension plans were invested in corporate equities. But deemed "risky" for individuals by Unions.

Audited Tax returns of people with incomes over $ 1,000,000: 2006 = 17,015 vs 2007 = 31,382.

Massachusetts has the 5th largest percentage of household millionaires @ 6.26% with 156,208 in a household population of 2,493,707. #1 New Jersey = 7.12%

Median new home price December 07 = $ 219,200 vs December 2006 = $ 244,700.

5Mar08 - Gold hits record $ 986.20 but below inflation adjusted $ 2,239.67 from Jan 1980.

Oil hits record $104.52, above its inflation adjusted 103.76 set in 1980.

Euro hits high against dollar @ 1.5305

Profit colleges charge as much as 10 times as much for an associates' degree as a local community college.

The poor's share is shrinking but the "pie" has grown enormously. Current GDP = $14T, 3 times 1970. Poor share 181B to 476B = poor incomes UP 36%!

*Households: 1970 = 71% married (3.14 persons) vs 2008 51% (2.57)

1970 = 17% one person household's vs today's 27%

The US has 103 operating nuclear reactors generating electricity. There is only one steel company in the world today that can cast the reactor vessels (the 42-foot, egg shaped container at the core of a reactor): Japan Steel Works.

Modern Portfolio Theory (MPT) uses historical date to estimate future returns, risk and correlations of different asset classes in order to maximize a portfolio's return for a given level of risk. (InvestmentNews - 10Mar080

Problems with Modern Portfolio Theory (MPT): Misleading 'return' data based the use of the period starting in 1926 showed an average nominal return for stocks of 10.2%. Going back to 1849, the average falls to 8.9%.

This is due to the 1926 start period having lower price-earnings ratios. The 10.9% figure used in MPT misleads the asset allocation program.

Investment returns do NOT follow normal distribution curves as MPT assumes.

Risk as measured by the mean variance of returns is understated.

MPT portfolios are too diversified and end up as indexed portfolios.

In a long term bear market it is difficult to find opportunities that will produce absolute returns.

A Secular bear market started in March 2000: We are approaching the 8th year of what has been historically a 13 year cycle.

From 1948 to 1999, the percentage of women in the work force climbed from 32.7% to 60%. In January 2008 it was down to 59.2%. Restaurant meals purchased per person in 2007 = 207 vs a peak of 211 in 2001. Meanwhile Americans prepared 861 meals at home in 2007 vs 817 in 2002 - NPD Group

On 13 March 2008, the DJIA swung nearly 340 points, the 12th time in 2008 where the index range exceeded 300 points.

12Mar08 Nominal peeks: Inflation adjusted = Gold's 21 Jan 1980 to $ 2,239.67. Silver's $ 48.70 of January 1980 to today's $ 132.13. Oil hit record $110.33.

In Germany, there were 500,000 employed in call centers = 1% of the work force.

In Jamaica, due to government involvement: in 2003, some 5,000 liters of milk was dumped daily whereas in 2007, only 14 million liters were produced domestically of the 140 million liters consumed.

In Germany, the cost of acquiring a degree in Philosophy is 67,500 euro.

2007: Medicare spending $ 367.5Billion or 13% of the fed budget and is growing 6.5% a year

17Mar08: European share prices fell to 2005 levels.

Goldman Sachs and the market (18Mar08): Outgoing Abby Joseph Cohen sees the S&P 500 at 1675 Dec 08. Her replacement David Kostin sees the S&P 500 down to 1160 and by Dec 08 @ 1380!

Bear Market Histories:	percent decline	S&P 500 P/ E ratio
June 1948-June 1949	-21%	10
Aug 1956 - Oct 1957	-22	14
Nov 1968 - May 1970	-36	18
Jan 1973 - Oct 1974	-48	18
Nov 1980 - Aug 1982	-27	9
July 1990 - Oct 1990	-20	17
Mar 2000 - Oct 2002	-49	28

Of the 10 recessions since 1945, seven were accompanied by the above bear markets - down 20+%. As per above, these recessions began at the above P/ E ratios.

Student-Loans: Some 27 lenders have stopped providing loans due to unprofitability. The Federal Family Education Loans program (FFEL) will provide loans to some 8 million students and parents in the amount of $ 109 billion in the coming fiscal year.

Bear Markets - REITS

Total return	# of Months	return	following bear
9/72-12/74	-37%	27	19.3%
8/79-4/80	-15%	8	40%
6/81-7/82	-10%	13	54%
2/87-10/87	-10%	8	21%
8/89-10/90	-30%	14	36%
12/97-12/99	-30%	11	34%
Average	-26%	16	34%
2/7/07-1/17/08	-33%	11	

From 1999 to 2008: the US stock market's S&P index was 1352.99 on 25Mar2008 vs 1362.80 in April 1999. After dividends and inflation, The S&P 500 has risen an average of 1.3% a year.

Natural Gas Resources in trillions of cuft: Russia 1,082, Iran 993, Qatar 895, Saudi 250, UAE 214, US 209

Business vs Government: Business incentives that force efficiency and cost controls are financial reward, competition and fear of extinction. All of these are missing in the public sector

Check public sector spending: inefficient operations, inflated overhead costs, poor administration, questionable procurement policies, and the usual fraud and abuse.

Employer total compensation cost per hour of work Dec 2007 - Per US Labor Department: Union wages/salary $ 22.34 + Total Benefits $ 13.75 = $ 36.09 vs

Nonunion w / s $ 18.24 + TB $ 7.05 = $ 25.29

In 2007, US food prices had their largest gain in 17 years - WSJ 1Apr08

Bush reduced capital gains tax rate to 15% in 2003. Capital gains realized were $ 269B in 2002 and $ 729 in 2006!

Total wealth held by the world's millionaires = $ 50 trillion.

World grain and oil seed production in 2007 was a record 2.5 billion tons but stocks fell by 39 million tons for the year.

March 2008: US consumer price index inflation = 4.3% and 6.4% in the producer price index!

California Public Employees Retirement System or CALPERS authorized as much as 3% of its $ 240 billion portfolio to commodities.

1Apr08 WSJ - Corn futures rise, Soybeans fall: Per Dept of Ag acreage release: Soybeans planting up 10% to 74.8 million acres while corn down 8% to 86 M acres.

1st quarter 2008: India -29.2%, China -26.8%, Germany -18.4%, US -10%

US Health Care Spending in 2006 = $ 2.1 trillion. Of this, hospital care was 32% or $ 648 billion. 33% of all Medicare spending was for the final two years of life for patients with chronic illnesses (including congestive heart failure, dementia and kidney failure).- national average $ 46,412.

US cropland price for average acre rose 13% in 2007 to $ 2,700 or double the $ 1,340 of 1998. Nebraskan corn belt acreage up 88% since 2003 to $ 1,425.

In 2007, the 50 million SS beneficiaries received $ 585 billion.

REITS: short interest a record 10.3%, some 6.1 points above the 4.2% short interest in the NY Stock Exchange

Stock market recoveries: The S&P 500 stock index rose 24% on average in the six months following 10 of the last 11 recessions - the exception was in 2001!

Recession: Judged by the Business Cycle Dating Committee of the National Bureau of Economic Research and commonly defined as two consecutive quarters of decline in GDP. Actually based on four monthly indicators: employment, industrial production, constant dollar income and wholesale-retail trade.

With only the 1990-92 recession exception - when the yield curve returns to normal - as it did in March 2008 - during a recession, it has invariably indicated that the economy is poised to resume expansion within a few months. The question - are we in a recession?

Trade deficit cured by cheaper dollar? In 2002, the Euro averaged 94.6 cents and our deficit with Germany was $ 36B. In 2007 Euro = $1.37 and deficit $45B. Same story with Canada; 2002 C$ = $.64 with a $ 50B deficit vs 2007 $C = $.93 and deficit of $64B.

Jobless rate: Between 1948 and 1983 it varied from 2.5% to more than 10%. In the last 10 years it has been between 4% and 7.5%. This moderation may be due to the shift from a volatile manufacturing economy to a more stable services economy.

Per the International Monetary Fund - in 2007, China was the biggest contributor to world growth with growth of 11% followed by India #2 and the US #3.

Buy and Hold: From 1985 to 2008, this NYSE listed stock beat Warren Buffet's Berkshire Hathaway by over 450 basis points a year! The company: Bear Stearns

Memory lane: In 1980 gold was just under $900, DJIA was below 900 - lower than in 1966 and inflation was in the double digits as was interest on long government bonds.

Electronic trading dominated by speculators now classified as "noncommercial" and consisting of 3 groups: commodity funds (aggressive short term traders), hedge funds ((ultra-aggressive traders) and index funds (net long as a hedge against inflation). There is now an 80% correlation between what the noncommercial group is doing and the direction of the underlying market.

The bull run in commodities started in 2000 as the dollar came under pressure.

Open contract growth: Corn: Jan 05 - 645,000 to Jan 08 1.429M. Soybeans from 253K to 564K and wheat 315K to 642K.

American's debt on housing exceeds the actual equity of their homes. Year end 2007, home equity declined to 47.9% Some 8.8 million homeowners will have 0 or negative equity by April 2008

DJIA under Dems & Repubs presidents & congress: Dems (Gain per annum) up 7.2% vs Repub 3.8%. But After inflation: Dems 2.5% and Repubs 2%

Median price of a new home Dec 2007 $ 219,200 down 10.9% from 2006

Foreclosures in 2007 = 2.2M up 75% from 2006

Total US unemployment March 2008 = 7,800,000

Capital gain distributions expected to be a record $ 581bllion in 2007, up 39% from 2006's $ 418 billion. Mutual fund investors expected to pay a record $ 33.3 billion in taxes on CG's surpassing previous record of $ 31.3 billion in 2000.

US federal Budgets: 1989 = $ 1 T, 2002 = $ 2T and 2009 = $ 3T

Deficits: FY 2007 est $ 426B, actually $ 163B or 1.2% of GDP, 1/2 its average of the past 40 years.

Tax rates affect the amount of income reported.

SS: FY 2007 transferred some $ 80 B of surplus SS taxes to General Government expenses. That surplus is projected to drop to zero during the next ten years!

The US pays out $ 100 million every hour for imported oil!

The US consumes 87 million barrels of oil daily!

Emerging Markets: On 31Dec07 some $ 17B invested. In the first quarter 2008 some $ 1.85B was redeemed (11%) and the category lost 12%.

Stock and commodity cycles tend to have a reverse coincidence. Current commodity cycle started in 2000?

The world population living in cities is projected to grow from the current 50% to 75%.

51% of US electricity comes from coal.

US backed student loans this year 07/ 08 = $ 68.2Billion

Holding $ 2,436.5B US treasuries: Japan 586.6B (24.%), China 486.9B (20%), UK. 180.7B (7.4%) Brazil 146.6B (6%), Oil Exporters Algeria, Bahrain, Ecuador, Gabon, Indonesia, Iran, Iraq, Kuwait, Libya, Nigeria, Oman, Qatar, Saudi Arabia, UAE and Venezuela 146.1B (6%)

The US will graduate some 1.5 million from college in May 2008

Digital information creation, capture and replication growth: 2006 = 173 billion gigabytes to 1,773 bgbytes. The rate is 60% annual growth! UP 10 times in 5 years

Economic reality: The 1980s "windfall Profits" tax on oil companies resulted in reduced domestic oil production and increased imports. Every time the capital gains tax has been raised, federal revenue from it has declined and every time it has been reduced, federal revenue has increased.

The combined oil consumption of India, China, Russia and the Middle East will surpass that of the US in 2008.

S&P500 weightings, 26May08 - WSJ
    Financial Sector 16% Down 30% since Oct 07, vaporizing some $ 814 billion
    Technology 16.4%, Peak in March 2000 at 34.9% to 13% in Oct 2002
    Energy 15%, In the 1980's peak of 30%, March 2000 = 5%

Sell in May and go away??

Foreigners hold over $ 4 trillion US = 1/4 the value of all our public traded businesses, or 80% of our commercial real-estate or 7% of our estimated national wealth!

The rate of annual dollars spent in the US for gasoline went from $ 340 billion in 2007 to $ 450 billion in 2008.

Since 2002, the US dollar has dropped about 25% against the currencies of our major trading partners with another 15 to 20% required to correct our trade imbalances.

Canada's natural gas reserves in 1985 were 99.2 trillion cuft. In 2005 56.3 trillion cuft! Canada currently exports 50% of its gas to the US.

In 2000, commodity mutual funds and natural resources funds and exchange-traded funds held $ 5 billion vs 2008's $ 105 billion!

Since 2000, operating earnings for the S&P 500 are up 63%, dividend yields are up 86% and 10 year treasuries are down from 6.2% to 4%.

When the Fed has stopped cutting rates: the market has typically gone up 5% in the first 3 months and 12% after 6 months.

The past never fails to offer trustworthy guidance about what you should have done.

A carbon tax as a de facto consumption tax? Could be used to offset labor and capital taxes that discourage work and investment.

Current injection of light, sweet crude into the US Strategic Petroleum Reserve is 60,000 barrels a day or 0.3% of US consumption. (June 2008). Only 10 million of the 87 million barrels the world produces daily is light, sweet! The US does not 'buy' reserve oil - the government gets 185,000 barrels of royalty oil from Gulf of Mexico leases which it sells and swaps the rest (mostly sour & heavy) for sweet.

The Altamount Pass, Calif wind farm has killed some 130,000 birds in the past 27 years including between 75 and 116 golden eagles

With the US planting more corn and thus less soy beans, Brazilian farmers are clearing more of the Amazonian rain forest to plant soy beans.

The 10 Republican inaugural years since 1925 averaged a 0.5% loss with only 3 positive. All but 1932 and 1940 have been positive for democrats.

US oil reserves: We consume 7.5 billion barrels a year. Our 21 billion of 'proven reserves' would last less than 3 years. We had 700M barrels of crude in our Strategic Petroleum Reserve at the end of March 2008.

Obama pushing requirement that 25% of electricity to come from renewable sources by 2025 - currently less than 1%. Quoting Sen. Obama - "We can't drive our SUVs and eat as much s we want and keep our homes on, you know, 72 degrees at all times and then just expect that every other country's going to say OK. That's not--that's not leadership"

Commodity speculation: When Exxon buys crude, it is a business expense to be sold in the process of making a profit. When Calpers buys crude oil futures, it is speculation! Commodities of them selves do not create value. Over time, stock prices go up in real terms because of the value creation process, commodity prices do not.

Foundations: Why do foundations spend only 5% of assets on philanthropy and grow at 13% every year. (answer - the IRS requires the 5%)

The Euro Zone: Austria, Belgium, Cyprus, Finland, France, Germany, Greece, Ireland, Italy, Luxembourg, Malta, The Netherlands, Portugal, Slovenia and Spain with conversion states Slovakia (2009), Lithuania (2010), Estonia (2011), Bulgaria, Hungary, Latvia, Czech Republic, Poland, and Romania (2012)

Honest money is the bedrock of democratic capitalism. Why work if financial rewards are destroyed by inflation. Push tax payer's into higher brackets - per the old communist aphorism - "They pretend to pay us - we pretend to work."

Since 2005, US manufacturing exports are up $ 200 billion with service and agriculture trade surpluses soaring. (June WSJ)

The 1931 Davis-Bacon law requires a 'prevailing-wage" be paid on government construction projected. This inflates federal construction costs from 5 to 39%.

Oil demand: China & India forecast to account for 70% of new global oil demand by 2030 and at 20mbd in 2030 will overtake combined US & Japan use. China will become the largest automotive market in the world by 2015. The UK & Indonesia have switched from oil export to oil import with Algeria, Malaysia, Mexico and Iran to follow. Country managed oil reserves = 83%, only 3.8% by integrated oil companies.

Investing takes a positive attitude. A positive long term view of the American and international economic growth. If you do not believe - do not invest.

June 2008 - The DJW index of US financial stocks doubled from Oct 2002 to March 2007 and since fallen 37% giving up some $ 1 trillion in market value.

P/ E vs Inflation: Since 1950, when inflation is between 2% and 4% the average P/ E has been 17.4, vs a P/ E of 14.7% when inflation is between 4% to 6%. Summary - lower inflation makes future earnings growth more valuable and leads to higher multiples on earnings and vice versa.

Diamonds: The US accounts for half the worldwide sales and sales are slow. Diamond prices up 3.6% over the past 2 years vs S&P GSCI commodities benchmark up 73.5%.

The past 12 months retail food prices per the CPI: April 2007 - April 2008 = UP 10.3%, the highest increase in 83 years.

Buying GOLD can be tricky: In October 1986, Gold at $ 424. $100,000 would buy 231 Kruggerrands @ 432 each = $ 99,792. or 37 MS-64 $ 20 St. Gaudens (37 @ 2,700 each = $99,900. June 2008, Gold @ $ 868. The 231 Kruggerrands @ $ 855 = $197,505 vs the MS-64 Saints @$1,020 = $ 37,740.

China's consumption of meat has increased from 44 pounds per capita in 1980 to 110 pounds today. It takes 7 pounds of grain to produce one pound of beef or 4 to 1 for pork.

Since 1950, manufacturing jobs have gone from 30% of all jobs to 10% with industrial production up 120%!

US petroleum distillates are primarily Diesel 65% and heating oil 30%

Government run oil: Iran: under the Shah = 5 mbd vs 2008 = 3 mbd. Venezuela down 1mbd since Chaves. Nigeria down by 25%.

SS taxes: Obama's plan to raise SS taxes results in more taxes paid in to the government, with an increased overpayments (Income less benefits = surplus) being spent on current government expenditures resulting in more treasury bonds that must be redeemed at some future date which means more taxes now and more taxes in the future!

June 2008 - 53 countries, mostly emerging, with 3 billion population (42% of the world) having double digit inflation.

In the US, the top 20% of income earners spend more than the lower 60% combined.

Buffet's cycle of three 'I's: Innovator, imitator, Idiot.

Why emerging markets are the only area for equity diversification:

Current correlation of US stock Mkt indices with World stock Mkt indices = .83

US Mkt is 42% of the world mkt capitalization

US = 5% of world population and 25% of world GDP

Cause of World Food Problems? Developed countries legislate price supports to enrich farm voters. Lobbies extort tariffs to block cheap food imports and subsidies to underwrite food export at prices that destroy competitors in poor countries. (see milk in Jamaica). Conservationists push to set aside productive land and pay farmers not to grow (36 million acres at a cost of $ 2 B) and now green energy advocates push ethanol quotas ($ 7 B subsidies and 1/3 of the corn crop)and tax credits to divert food into fuel. Developed Countries spend 15% on food while poor countries spend 75%. One-third of the world's population live under food price controls. US food aid of $ 2B in grains distributed free destroys local grain sales and drives farmers in recipient countries out of business.

The former 750 million people living in Western affluence have been joined by 3.5 billion now seeking a similar standard of living ie autos, meat, medical etc.

2007 Global Luxury Markets: Japan = 34%, Emerging Markets = 30%, US >20%

OIL 1997 - Consumption to Production to 2007

Global	up 16% (31.1BBLS)	up 12.9% (29.BBLS)
Asia/Pacific	up 27% (9.2BBLS)	up 2.1% (2.9BBLS

China	up 88% (2.8BBLS)	
India	up 50% (1 BBLS)	
E Union	up 2%	Down 30%
USA	up 11.1%(7.5BBLS)	
Mid East	up 40% (2.2BBLS)	up 15.8% (9.2 BBLS)
Japan	(1 BBLS)	

Reserves: Proven Global oil reserves = 1.2 trillion barrels = 40 years @ 40BBLS/yr. In addition, the US has 81 BBLS of heavy oil, 80 BBLS of 'oil sand", 293 BBLS of "light oil" and 2 trillion barrels of extractable shale oil, mostly in Wyoming, Colorado and Utah. (42 gallons per barrel)

Energy History: In 1850, 90% of America's energy supply was wood based. By 1910, coal supplied almost 80% of our energy requirements. By 2000, coal was 25%, oil 40%, natural gas 20% with the remainder nuclear, hydro, renewable etc.

Wind-generated energy: It accounts for less than one-hundredth of on percent of total US energy consumption. Solar power accounts for even less.

Definitions of Democracy: Two wolves and a lamb voting on what to have for dinner. or The poorest 51% of the population tyrannizing the better off 49%.

US areas off limits to drilling for known hydrocarbons: 62% on shore, 85% offshore.

Ethanol: While the 5 First-Growth, 2005 Bordeaux wines go for $ 1,000 a bottle, some 18 million liters of less-prized Bordeaux wine was distilled into ethanol due to no market.

When short covering is obvious - if it ends around 11 to 11:30 AM and the market again heads down - "Lookout" could be a very bad day.

sub-prime has become sub-crime

Currency cycles, the dollar: 1979 - 1984 declined 50%+, 1999 - 2000 declined 29%, 2000 - 2004 up 64%

Seven states have no income tax including Florida, Texas, Washington and Nevada while Tennessee and New Hampshire do Not tax wages an salaries but do tax investment income, such as interest and dividends.

Americans spend $ 3 billion on chiropractors and $ 1.5 billion on homeopathy,

1% of US taxpayers pay 40% of all income taxes while the top 10% pay 71%.

The bottom 40% of income earners pay no income taxes, the bottom 60% pay less than 1% of federal income taxes on net.

"Misery Index" back to life after 25 years - election coming. as of 31 May 08 - Inflation rate of 4.2% and unemployment of 5.5% 1 Jul = 9.7% vs Carter's 1980 high of 21.8%.

Nearly 70% of taxpayers use form 1040A or EZ. The 30% minority complaining about the complexity of the 1040 are viewed as another laughable grievance of rich people.

The income tax is a tax selectively imposed on cash receipts, rather than a tax on economic income.

Tax Freedom day (assumes every penny of income earned before that date has been used to pay Fed, state & local taxes combined): 2008 = 29 April. The worst was 4 May 2000. This only addresses money collected by the Governments

vs

Tax Friedman Day (The day that the American's earn enough money to pay for government spending - includes borrowed money) 2008 = 19 May

We pay less but the government spends more via borrowing!!!!!

Taiwan's foreign exchange reserves = $ 270 billion, 4th largest in the world.

China has 600 tons of gold reserves = 1% of its total FERs

Harvard Management's $ 38B allocations: US equities = 12%, Developed Foreign equities = 12%, Emerging market equities = 10% (22% total foreign equities), Real assets including commodities 33%, fixed income 9%, Private Equity 11% and Hedge funds 18%. total = 105%

Buy and Hold? Per Citi, a portfolio should hold 25 to 30 stocks. Only 1 in 10 stocks consistently outperformed the S&P 500 index over the past 20 years in any 3 year period. 1/ 3rd of stocks underperformed the overall market by at least 15% or more at any given year.

Every 100,000 payroll jobs lost takes some $ 3 billion in disposable income away from consumers.

World sugar consumption = 155 million tons per year. In 2006, the market hit a high of 19 cents a pound. In 2007, output jumped 19 million pounds!!!!! Massive overproduction in very short order. Commodities are hard to predict year to year.

Vietnam is the 2nd largest producer of coffee in the world and they are now focused on cocoa.

By Oct 3rd 2008: US stocks down 24%, Foreign 32% and Emerg mkts 40% since 1 Jan

On 3 Oct 2008 the five year treasury yielded 2.68% while the DJIA dividend yield was 3.14%. After some 20 years, stocks out yield bonds!!!!!!!!!!!!!!

Heating Oil: January 2007 low = $1.453 vs July 2008 high = $ 4.1586

October 2008: Gold's highest drop since 1980, Oil's worst month in history- down 1/ 3, copper down 36%, UK's FTSE down 11% and DJIA down 14% - both the worst drops since 1987.

Convertible Bonds: down 36% in 2008 up to 4 November mostly from hedge fund sales

China unveiled a $ 586 billion economic stimulus program in Nov 2008

Our current crisis is financial not economic! Core inflation (long term) = wages

The 2 trillion barrels of shale oil in the western US is not economically recoverable until the price reaches $ 200 per barrel according to T. Boone Pickens - Nov 08.

Tax returns filed in 2008 = 155 million, up 15 million with an extra 8 million 1040A's. There were 117 million economic stimulus payments.

In the past 10 years, there have only been 3 months when ALL the major assets classes:

> US Stocks (Russell 3000), Foreign Stocks (MSCI
> EAFE), Emerging Markets
> Stocks (MSCI EM), US
> Bonds (Lehman Aggregate), Foreign Bonds (Citigroup
> WGB) non $), Emerging Markets Bonds (Citigroup
> ESBI), US Inflation linked
> Treasuries (Lehman Treasury TIPS), Citigroup High Yield Bond Index,
> Commodities (DJ-AIG Commodity), REITs (DJ
> Wilshire REIT) posted losses: April 2004, Oct 2005
> and Sep 2008 = 2.5% failure rate

In October 2008, the 100 largest corporate pension funds lost $ 120 billion and are now only funded for 76% of obligations.

Calpers 2007 portfolio of $ 236B has $ 1.3B in commodities to be increased to 1.5% by the end of 2010 or up to $ 3.5B.

If a household worker is paid over $ 1,600 per year - paper work required + SS & medicare payment of 7.65% of gross pay, fed unemployment insurance 0.8% state unemployment insurance 2 to 4%. Add employers 7.65% SS & medicare etc

Per the NY Times, 19Oct08: the traditional 60/40 stock-bond mix outperformed an all stock portfolio only 3 years in the past 100 years!

Per technicians: when 9 stocks are up for every 1 down, a bottom is at hand. Unfortunately this has occurred 8 times so far up to November 2008

Per Laszlo Birinyi: Over the past 42 years had you missed the 5 best days of each year, your $1 investment, without dividends, would now amount to $ 1.11. Had you missed the 5 worst days of every year, your dollar would be worth $ 2,696!

People don't change when the see the light. They change when they feel the heat!

Global oil production is 31 billion barrels per year vs annual new discoveries of 10 billion barrels. Peak year for oil discoveries = 1964.

A projected $ 2 trillion deficit for 2009 would equal 12.5% of GDP, more than twice the record 6% in 1983.

The US absorbs 85% of world savings to finance its deficit.

Estimated cost of repair US infrastructure = $ 1.6 trillion

On October 13, 2008, the S&P 500's dividend yield was 3.74% - the first time since 1958 that exceeded the yield on the ten-year Treasury note!

From 10 September to 25 November 2008, the MSCI World Index fell 31.5%.

Jan-Nov 2008: Warren Buffett's Berkshire Hathaway down 30%. Ken Heebner's CGM Focus down 53%, Bill Miller's Legg Mason Value down 58% and the 'Oracle of Maitoba', Randolf McDuff 's Global down 65%!

Congress was horrified in 1954 with the projected 1955 budget deficit of $ 4 billion. The 2009 budget deficit is projected at $ 482 billion excluding bailout funds.

Hyperinflation: Hungary July 1946 - prices doubled every 15.6 hours, Zimbabwe Oct 2008 - pde 24.7 hrs, Yugoslavia Jan 1995 -pde 1.4 days, Germany Oct 1923 - pde 3.7 days, Greece Nov 1944 - pde 4.5 days and China May 1949 - pde 5.6 days.

US railroads employed 2 million in 1920 vs 2004's 177,000

DJIA: 9 Oct 2007 = 14,164 vs 10 Oct 2008 = 7,882

Stocks go down 3 times faster than they go up.

The 1938 New England hurricane felled some 2 million trees, enough lumber to build 200,000 homes.

When you are having hard times: 90% of the people do not care and the other 10% are glad.

On 20 November 2008 the DJIA hit 7552.

In 2008, ETF funds attracted $ 180 B while open-end Mu Funds had a $ 320 B outflow

In 2008, 4 of the 5 largest one-day point gains in the DJIA (all in Oct & Nov) and 4 of the 5 worst one day point declines (2 in Oct)

Due to 2008 market collapse, DJIA 500 qualification reduced from $ 5Billion worth to $ 3 b!

Barack Obama elected president

4 October 2008

Investment Wisdom 2009

OIL: In 1995 the US Geological Survey estimated that the Montana and North Dakota Bakken held a mere 150 million barrels of recoverable oil. With todays technology, the survey's estimate is up 20 times to 3.6 billion barrels of recoverable oil!!!!!!

Autos - made in America: The Jeep Patriot is only 66% US vs Toyota's Sequoia at 80%. The BMW X5 is more American than the Pontiac G8 an Australian import. The Ford Crown Victoria has the highest percentage of US/Canada content at 90% and is assembled in Canada.

January 2009 the worst in the Dow's 113 years - down 8.84%. The Russell 2000 down 11.2% - worst since creation in 1984

Per Ken Fisher 2/09 - categories of stocks that fared better than the market in a bear market's 1st half but lagged badly in its later stages tend to lead the next bull market bounce and for a long time = energy, materials, industrials and consumer discretionary.

Treasuries: In 1990 of the $ 14T in household assets, $300B was in treasuries vs of the $45T in 2008, less than $ 100B was in treasuries.

18Feb09 - Natural gas prices are down 70% from the 2 July peak of $ 13.694 MBTU

Helmerich & Payne has sidelined 42 of its 192 land drill rigs

In 2008 there were 650 surgical fires in US hospitals

California's budget 2003 = $ 104B vs 2008 at $ 145B

> State Sales Tax: California 8.25% vs National
> Median of 5.5 % - Feb 09
> State Income Tax: California 10.56% vs National
> Median of 6%
> In the past 10 years, 1.4 million nonimmigrant
> Americans have left Calif

The New York Philharmonic paid $ 2.9M to its music director and $ 864,000 to the CEO.

21Feb WSJ: Savings accounts + money market funds up 14% in a year to $ 9.35T = 83% of US stock market value from 43% a year ago and the average of 66% since 1960. Since the Oct 2007 high the S&P excluding financials is down 43%. Per the AAII, in Jan08 63% stocks, 23% cash vs Jan09 48% stocks & 30% cash.

Debt: Junk rated bonds and bank debt maturing in 2009 =

$ 26B vs 2011 = $ 120B

Gold at $ 1,000/ oz is behind the inflation adjusted 1980 record of more than $2,200

Bank of America down 14 cents or 3.6% to $ 3.79!

Total household debt vs disposable (after-tax) income: In 2000, households owed debts of $ 6 trillion or 85% of their income. By 2008, their debt had more than doubled to $13T and the debt ratio had soared to 125%.

Regulatory Problems: SEC's 'mark to market', during the past century if required during severe economic contractions would have rendered all financial institutions insolvent.

"uptick rule" eliminated by SEC. Created by Joseph Kennedy to end his bear raids.

SEC rule change in 2004 that allowed broker dealers to be leveraged 33 to 1 when 12 to 1 had been the rule for years.

March 6, 2009, the S&P 500 index bottoms at an intraday low of 666.79.

March 2009 - 144 million Americans have jobs!

Hedge Funds correlation with the S&P 500 = 95%
Government spending represents 38.5% of GDP
US stocks current value $10 trillion vs Oct 2007 $19 trillion.

In the 30 years since Jimmy Carter and economist Alfred Kahn deregulated the airline industry, 9 major and 100's of minor airlines have gone bust.

Iron Ore concentration: Brazil = 40%, Sweden = 24%, German = 12% and China = 9%.

2008 Production: Platinum 6,000,000 Oz, Gold 107,000,000 Oz (2,400 metric tons)& Silver 889,000,000 Oz. 75% of platinum demand from autos, 25% jewelry and vaults. Copper 18 million tons - China bought 300,000 tons by April 2009 headed for a1.2 million ton stockpile?

The SPDR Gold trust (NYSE: Gold) owns 82,000 - 400 troy Os gold bars worth $ 31B

The US Congressional effect: Over the past 44 years, Congress in session 7,244 days = S&P up average annual rate of 0.3% vs Out 3,821 days = S&P Avg. Annual rate 16.1%.

In 2008, 1,471 hedge funds closed!

By March 2009, Avg. billionaires net worth $3B, down 23% in 12 month with 793 vs 1,125 a year ago.

Over 41 years ending in 2006 - alcohol (Brown-Forman), tobacco (Altria) and gambling stocks (Intl. Game Tech) returned about 3.5% a year more than other stocks.

Per Moody's: over the past 10 years annual increases: Education 5.91%, Health care 4.16%, wages and income 3.7%.

Per Fed Reserve: U.S. Household net worth dropped $ 11 trillion (18%) during 2008!

As of March 2009 - annual returns over the past 30 years: Bonds 9.4% and Stocks 8.8%

Actively managed bond funds typically have expense ratios of 50 basis points or more. In an efficient market, this forces managers to own riskier bonds in order to equal the performance of a passive portfolio. Owning an actively managed bond fund requires a belief that the market is sufficiently inefficient to allow managers to overcome the expense ratio and outperform a passive portfolio.

Fees: Typical tech mutual fund 1.74% vs tech ETF's 0.58% In 2008 nearly $ 6B was in tech ETF's with $12.5B in QQQQ which is 60% in tech.

International equity funds: 2008 down 45%+, emerging Market stocks Down 50%+

Ethanol: takes up to 1,000 gallons of water to manufacture 1 gal of ethanol. If all 300 million acres of cropland in the US was used to produce ethanol, it would displace only 15% of our oil demand.

The US rich: in 2007 to be in the top 1% of wealth = over $ 8.272M, Top 5% = over $ 1.87M, top 10% = over $ 894,000. Share of national wealth remained the same: in 1995 the top 1% had 33.9% while in 2007 = 33.8% equal to $ 21.8T.

Avoid the financials?: In 2006 Citigroup was the 4th largest US company by stock-market capitalization, Bank of America was 5th and AIG 10th and thus held by virtually every Mu Fund / Pension fund etc. We were all in the same boat! Unfortunately the boat was sinking.

In 2008 the US consumed 138 billion gallons of gasoline, avg cost $3.33/ gal. This years $ 2 per gal equals a saving of $ 195 billion or $ 639 per everyAmerican.

In 2008, household net worth fell $ 11.2 Trillion

In 4th quarter 2008, Americans saved $ 337 billion

A metric ton of gold equals 2,204.62 pounds. China has increased it gold holdings from 454 metric tons in 2003 to the present 1,054 tons currently valued at $ 30.95 billion

@ $ 913.60 per ounce on 24April2009.

The IMF holds 3,217 metric tons (103.4 million ounces) of gold and is the world's 3rd largest official holder.

H.J.Heinz, the largest purveyor of baked beans in the U.K. has cut the tin plating on its cans by 10% resulting in a saving of 1,400 tons of tinplate annually in the U.K.

Risk does not mean volatility: If a stock goes down exactly 10% per year for 5 years, the volatility is 0. I would not consider this a risk-free experience.

To deviate from a carefully considered allocation plan is folly, and the cost of straying is highest when the temptation to do so is the greatest.

The current average recovery rate for oil is 35%. Raising it to 50% would increase the world's recoverable oil by about 1.2 trillion barrels equal to today's proven reserves.

The US consumes 1 billion pounds of popcorn annually.

US carbon emissions: 34% electricity generation and 28% transportation.

Bet the tide, not the boats

The spread between interest rates on junk bonds and Treasury debt historically leads new unemployment claims for benefits by about three months.

International Country fund ETF's are cap weighted (weighted according to the total market value of their outstanding shares) making Banks, Insurance and oil companies their major holdings.

China's population increases by 2 million annually.

The US consumes 140 billion gallons of gasoline annually. A $1 increase diverts $140 B away from "discretionary" spending. In 1980, 9% of consumer spending went for energy while it was 5.1% in the 1st quarter 2009, the lowest in 5 years.

Past real estate bear markets ended when the average time it took to sell a new house dropped to 3.5 months. Currently (May09) it takes almost a year.

European CO_2 price per ton = 13e in 1000 ton lots

Russia: Has $ 600B in reserves with energy = 65% of gross exports. Government is the only source of credit = take over of energy and now the banking sector. Current infrastructure sited for the needs of a centrally planned economy. Population down 6M (4%) since collapse. Women ages 20 - 29 will fall 33% in next decade. 30-40% of Men die during their working years with working age population down 10M by 2020.

Inflation coming: Fiscal stimulus by Governments flood economies with cash - US allocated $ 11.4T with $ 2.4T spent, China $600B, Russia $ 290B, UK $ 147B, Japan $ 155B.

Money supply in line with Bull & Bear markets: Down in the late 80's prior to the 1987 crash, up in 1995 with major bull, down in March 2000 - market down, Up in 2001 ending in 2006.

Liquidity links: In 1998 cash into economy led to tech stock boom and bust. More liquidity in 2001 led to residential real estate boom and bust.

China has over US$1.6T in cash & US Treasuries. With 1.3B people it is the most cash rich country in the world. In 2008 the US bought $340B of Chinese goods.

Options: The inverse relation between time (theta) and volatility (gamma). Time is always working against you while volatility is always working for you. Regarding a call: As the underlying asset rises, the call gains in value at an increasing rate and vice versa. This is called curvature.

Corn: Takes much more fertilizer to maximize corn yield than soybeans. Corn is a high cost high risk potentially high profit crop. Price of fertilizer is important

The investment grade bonds backed by mortgages = $ 5T. The FOMC is buying 10% ($ 500B) between Nov08 and Jun09

Stochastic indicator: below 20 = oversold, above 80 = overbought

The 'future auto technology' of the 70's was turbines - sounding like vacuum cleaners. In 2001, President Bush said we would all be driving hydrogen fuel cell cars.

There are 100 countries in the world that can export ethanol vs 10 that can export oil.

There are 240M vehicles on US roads today.

Annuity: You do not need one if your annual retirement expenses (including income taxes) come to less than 3% of your assets.

Bull or Bear - WSJ 15Jun09: In 2008 the DJIA fell 33.8%. This week it was up 34% from its March 9 2009 low. Bull market definition: a 20% gain from a low point. Bear market definition: a 20% decline from a high. The DJIA is currently 38% below its record close in Oct 2007. Ned Davis considers this the 4th secular bear market since 1900. The last 1966 - 1982.

TIPS basket consist of: Housing costs 43%, Food 16%, Transportation 15%, Health care and recreation 6% each, apparel 4% education, communication and 'other' each 3%.

Deflation does not persist for long periods. Longest 1930 through 1932.

Exports percentage of GDP: US 13% of $14T+, Japan 17.4% of 4.5T, China 36.5% of 4.2T, Germany 47.2% of 3.7T

July2009 - the average US gas field requires a gas price of $ 7.79 per Million BTUs to earn a 10% return. Qatari LNG costs approx '0' and can be shipped to the US for $ 2 per MBTUs.

Since 1949, bear markets bottomed a median of 5 months before the recessions have ended and 8 months before corporate earnings hit a trough and unemployment peaked.

Sell in May and go away? 1929 - 2008 (80 periods, 1June - 30 Sept) S&P 500: down 28 times (35%) avoiding 13 double digit loss years vs 18 double digit up years. Total of 195% appreciation and missed out on dividends. Stay the course!

Dividends? In the first 6 months of 2009, more than 40 companies in the S&P 500 cut their dividends by $ 41B!!! more than in all of 2008! Currently, the S&P500 yields 3% vs a 2.6% yield of the 10 year Treasury - the first time since 1958 that stocks yield more than treasuries.

Do NOT sell a slow market

A European style welfare-entitlement state requires European-style levels of taxation on the middle class and will result in European-style low growth and high unemployment rates.

The liberal dream: yoking the middle-class to cradle-to-grave government entitlements.

In 1990 the American banking system's reserves were 2.5 times greater than Chinese reserves. In 2009, China's reserves are 25 times the American Federal Reserves!

In 1945, 100% of the world's currencies reserves were the dollar. Today, 19% of the world's money supply is dollars. When the dollar is no longer the world's reserve currency: all products in the US will cost more do to currency adjustment costs.

Ben Graham's dollar cost averaging, investing based on forecasts, predictions and fundamentals only works if you plan to live forever.

The 10 largest stock funds collected $ 21.40 billion in advisory fees during the period 1999-2008 and ended up where they started. Some performance!

Currently the top 20% of taxpayers pay 80% of taxes vs 40% of householders who pay no income tax. Under Obama's plan the top 20% will pay 90% of all taxes and the no tax crowd will be 50%.

In 1969, Richard Nixon raised the capital gains tax from 28% to 49%. Reported gains from the sale of capital assets fell 34% - even the government lost!

Although Franklin Roosevelt's attempt to tax municipal bond interest failed, Obama will try again and assuming he has a sympathetic Supreme Court, it could pass!

To pay less capital gains tax you can either hold or never buy.

The purpose of trading is to produce profits, not to be right.", Robert Pardo

We can not undo the past or predict the future.

July 2009: The US Government owns or controls our largest automaker (GM), our largest insurance company IAIG) and our largest suppliers of mortgages (Fannie Mae and Freddie Mac).

The proposed new financial regulations are going to increase capital adequacy standards and decrease the amount of credit available to lower and middle class borrowers.

America's challenge is to get the private sector to produce products that can be sold around the world.

In 1991, the biggest bank in the U.S. was the 22nd largest in the world. To financially support our largest company's in world competition, you need world size banks.

Question: Will the government's cures be worse than the disease itself?

The global nature of the textile industry is its concentration in newly industrialized countries which has put a long term downward pressure on textile prices.

The U.S. dollar index leads the price of cotton by 8 months on average. Cotton's competitors in the U.S. are soybeans and corn. When Soybean acres switch to corn for ethanol, cotton acres could switch to soybean acres.

S&P after recessions: 5Aug09 - excluding the current downturn, since 1960 there have been 7 recessions. In the 12 months from the mid points of the contractions, The S&P 500 rose 17% on average. In the following 12 months - only 4% rise on average. If the recession ended in June 09, the midpoint of the downturn was September 08. In the 10 months since then, the S&P500 is actually down 14%.

TIPS: China has $ 2 T in foreign exchange reserves with $ 800 B in TIPS and requiring the U.S. to issue more TIPS.

5Aug09 - TIPS: The inflation gap between TIPS and comparable nominal notes: currently 1.88% = expected annualized inflation over the next 10 years. In the past 3 weeks it has swung between 1.52 to 1.90

European auto makers make 80% of their profits on 20% of their autos. Low end autos make virtually no profits so when incentives to buy low priced autos increase the number of autos sold, it does not result in proportionally increased profits.

The US's monetary response to the financial problems have been 3 times more (adjusted to today's dollars) than the US spent to fight WWII and 12 times more (relative to GDP) than the total committed to fight the Great Depression. In June 2009, Import prices soared at a 19% annualized rate.

Fat-Tailed Models: Normal distributions that emerge in finance generally do so because the factors influencing an asset's value or price are mathematically "well-behaved", and the central limit theorem provides for such a distribution. A 60/40 portfolio down 20% would occur once in 111 years by this bell-curve distribution. However, traumatic "real-world" events (such as an oil shock, a large corporate bankruptcy, or an abrupt change in a political situation) are usually not mathematically well-behaved. Under the fat tail assumption, a 20% decline would occur every 40 years. Fat / Heavy tails in market return distributions also have some behavioral origins (investor excessive optimism or pessimism leading to large market moves) and are therefore studied in behavioral finance. Hedging against extreme market events may cost 0.5% to 1% of assets a year. (see Aston Dynamic Allocation Fund - heavy in treasuries and cash) and reduce returns in up markets

Since people fear losses more than value gains = "value at risk" measure. A focus on extreme risk uses "conditional value at risk".

Summary: It is virtually impossible to forecast extreme events. Focus on their consequences rather than the probability they will occur.

US gasoline accounts for 10% of world-wide crude oil consumption

1st Qtr 2009 US consumer debt was 124% of disposable income vs 131.5% end of 2007, 90% early 1999 and 61% in 1984. Consumer spending is 70% of US economic activity.

S&P 500 long term P/ E is 16. March 2009 = 13! June 09 = 16. Aug 09 = 17.7!

The only thing that goes up in a market crash is correlation. In Sept 2008, every one of the 16 different asset classes were down.

WSJ 2Oct09 - September car sales: GM down 45%, Chrysler down 42%%, US down 23%. 'Clunker' rebate hangover!!!! Shocking, just shocking

Seasonal cycles: Gold, since 1975 - down from Oct 10 thru mid November. A high in March. Soybeans, Harvest low November into early December with seasonal highs in late May to early June. (Monsanto, Archer Daniels Midland, Bunge Potash, Mosaic or Terra Ind along for the ride)

Euro, Two peaks: July and after Jan 1. Low 3rd week in October and up thru the end of December and a 2nd in late Feb early March

Reality: For China to become the world's leading economy it will have to increase its GDP by 5 times while the US stands still! US net worth is $339 T.

The monetizing of debt by the Government hurts people in trade and investors - a relatively small class of society.

Major long term threat to economies = Population shrinkage as capitalism requires growing everything!

The capitalist system is based on the limited stock company with a concept that personal wealth can be protected while engaged in business - a political concept.

Greenspan Put: The systematic lowering of short-term interest rates to inflate the stock market bubble in the late 1990's and then the real estate bubble in the early 2000's.

Wealth: defined by Adam Smith as the capacity to consume.

Wealth is distributed unevenly by its nature. Skewed toward concentration. The young have none vs the old who have accumulated some for their old age. It is also more of a relative than absolute concept.. We live better than any Roman Emperor.

Were the years 1995 - 2006 the American 'Belle Epoque' as was 1900-1914 to Europe?

WSJ 7Oct09 - Russian oil production of 10M barrels a day is 25% more than Saudi. US distillate inventories at a 27 year high and there are between 71M and 92 M barrels in tankers in the Atlantic headed our way

Household Net Worth: Down 18% in 2008, or $11T with stocks down 41% = $8.5T and real-estate down $ 2.5T. In 1999-2002 stocks down 38% and in 1972-74 stocks down 48% and it took 8 years to fully recover.

Consumer spending vs GDP: US 70%, China 30%. Income by GDP-per Capita: US $46,946, China $3,160 & Brazil $8,209.. China with 4 times our population is buying 1M autos per month - 70% 1st timers.

December S&P is 88% correlated with the change in holiday sales. In 2008, S&P down 27.9% vs holiday sales down 23.7%.

The shift from the G-8 to the G-20 highlights the rising importance of emerging market nations.

Regulatory stringency is counter cyclical, declining in good times and rising in bad. Banks by the Fed, the office of the comptroller of the currency, the federal insurance corp. and state banking agencies.

US gas reserves in 2000 = 177 TcF and produced 165 TcF from 2000 to 2008. We now have 245 TcF reserves, a 90 year supply!!!!!.

China buys $ 20 B a month in US Treasury paper! Global GDP shares: US 25% vs Chinas 10%. China is the largest emitter of greenhouse gas on the planet.

Doctor's earn: U.K. $58,000 vs Poland's $ 4,300!!!

Bill Gates's $ 50B net worth exceeds the GDP of 140 countries including Costa Rica, Bolivia, El Salvador and Uruguay.

The 'Greens' practice a crude form of religion - pantheism, the worship of the earth and all its manifestations

Commodities: 6Nov09-WSJ So far this year $50B into commodities. 1st Qtr $ 22B, 2ndQ $ 17B, 3rdQ 11B and Oct $2.2B. Crude up 79%, Gold up 23%!

Housing prices after inflation: from 1975 to 2000 up 1.4% annually. From 2000 to 2006 up over 7% annually. Thus would have to drop 40% to return to the historic trend line!!!

By mid 2009: 10% of Americans were in foreclosure or default.

An elevated VIX usually means that options premiums are higher. Time to sell covered calls!

U.S. Commercial real-estate debt = $ 3.4 trillion. Too big a problem for the Govt. ?????

Fed Raising Rates: In 2004 - stocks weakened about 6 months before rate increases.

2-year treasury note yields shrank - a sign that markets expected a slower economy.

Gold Reserves in metric tons: US 8,133.5, Germany 3,408.3, IMF 3,217.3, Italy 2,451.8, France 2,445.1, SPDR Gold (GLD) 1,117.5. - WSJ 23Nov09

CALPERS, the California Teachers pension fund has $ 200 billion and took a 43% loss on its real estate March 2008-9

Unemployment in the construction industry 19.1% in Oct09

Coal Glut!!! WSJ 30Nov09 - US production: Central Appalachian 20% down from $111 / ton last year to $54, Powder River, Wyoming 40% down from $14.50 to 8.25.

Switch to gas. Electric utilities stockpile = 200M tons up 37%. Coal mining employment down 7.5% to 79,600. Australia to increase output for China by 15% in 2010

Oil Glut: Southwald, England - 2Dec09WSJ- 40 tankers with hundreds of thousands of barrels or crude and oil derived products anchored off shore thanks to contango.

75% of stocks follow the markets direction. Sell when down 7%. Sell when going below 50 day moving average.

The world's 10 largest banks account for 70% of global banking assets vs 59% in 2006

7Dec09 - VIX index at 21.25. Historic average = 20.28. At Lehman crisis = 80

Oil's correlation with the dollar is almost 70% in Dec 09. Fundamentals do not count!!!!

Gold's last high $ 825.50 in January 1980 equivalent to $ 2,300 today. In June 82 $298!

Estimated cost to generate a megawatt hour 1Jan09: Gas plant $60, Geothermal $60, Nuclear $67, Wind, onshore $81, Coal, thermal $87, Solar photovoltaic $ 407.

Drilling deep: it takes 24 hours to pull and change a drill bit from 6,000 feet.

Gold / Silver 14Dec09: Ratio of Gold divided by silver = since 1970 @ 54, today @ 66, Oct 08 @ 84. Gold's Dec 3 record = $ 1,217.40. Palladium up 97% this year!!

Estate Tax: The 3rd time tax. The first on earnings taxed by fed and state personal income taxes, the 2nd the portion of the after-tax earnings that is accumulated and invested in assets, taxed a 2nd time as capital gains and dividends (both of which are taxed previously with the corporate profits tax).

Savers and high earners are taxed more times and at higher progressive rates placing a disproportionate burden of taxation on those who save and accumulate capital.

16Dec09 - Banks: In 2000 the top 4's $ 2T = 35% of the U.S. banking sector's total vs today's $7.4T = 56%

Federal Deposit Insurance Corps. to add 1,600 staffers to handle 2010 projected increase in bank failures

As 2009 closes - Greece and California have the same credit rating!!!!

The 2000 decade: the worst performance in the history of the New York Stock Exchange - down an annual 0.5% for each of the 10 years!!!!!!

8Dec09 WSJ - Banks and mortgage investors have 639,000 foreclosed homes. Concentrated in Florida, California, Arizona and Nevada. 10% of 09 home sales.

Communists accuse capitalists of practicing 'conspicuous waste'. Capitalists call it "Destructive Creation", the deliberate introduction of new, perhaps improved generations of durable goods that destroy, directly or indirectly, the usage value of units previously sold inducing consumers to repeat their purchase. Hitler called it "Fordism".

Investment Wisdom 2010

Per Benjamin Graham, the price of every stock consists of two elements: One, "investment value" measures the worth of all the cash a company will generate now and in the future and Two, the "speculative element" driven by sentiment and thrill seeking in bull markets, fear and regret and revulsion in bear markets.

In 2009, Mu fund investors sold all year and during the March low - $25 B.

Gold supply: central banks hold nearly 1 billion ounces while investors hold 1.2 billion ounces equal to 20 years of annual demand vs base metals that measure their inventory in weeks of demand.

Ethanol: in 2010 we have 180 refineries with 50 under construction which takes 6 months and needs only 20 people to operate. 4 billion bushels of corn or 1/3rd of the corn crop will produce 12 billion gallons.

January 2010 - $ 3 trillion is in money market funds while equity mutual funds are at a record low of cash-to-assets of 3.6%

We need to create the "binding experience" of a common culture in and increasingly diverse society.

Per Ibbotson, Since 1926, U.S. stocks have earned an annual average of 9.8% but after inflation, fees and taxes, under 4%! All other major assets earned less!!! Historically, inflation has eaten 3% of return a year.

William Bernstein of Efficient Frontier Advisors advises 51% global stocks, 26% bonds, 13% cash and 5% each commodities and real estate - Jan 2010.

Water: 70% of water consumed is for crops. By 2050 there will be 3 B more people on earth. Treated water from sea water is now 60 million cubic meters a day or 1% of global consumption. In 2009 up more than 12% over 2008. See ERI and Flowserve

Platinum PPLT & Palladium PALL ETFs: 20Jan10 WSJ - since July each has over 100,000 ounces. Platinum is a 6 million ounce market with a small surplus in 2009.

Stillwater Mining is the biggest palladium producer @ 500,000 ounces. The amount of palladium going into ETF holding exceeds production!!!!

Beware of: 'primacy bias' - the extrapolation of present circumstances too far into the future.

'home bias' - a preference for local companies

The Global investor: 42% US, 45% developed foreign, 13% emerging (MSCI Barra all country) and 70% large cap, 20% mid sized and 10% small cap. (the average US investor has 72% in US stocks.)

Why Health Insurers like Obama care: Humana 4th quarter profits. Medicare Advantage plans enrollment up 5% - government related pretax income up 69% to $452M from $ 267M vs 6% drop in commercial business and its $ 53.6M loss.

Housing: Jan 2010 - Home prices down 35% = bottom? Housing starts Jan = 357,000 down 80%. Mortgage rates at 40 year low. Housing affordability at a 20 year high.

	2008	2009
U.S.Stocks	- 38.5%	+ 31.3%
International	+ 41.8%	
MSCI Emerging Markets	- 54%	+ 74.5%

85% of immigrants to the U.S. are non-European (Asia, Latin America or Caribbean. Immigrants and their children = 65 million or 23% of U.S. population

Since 1960, Zug, Switzerland has used low taxes to entice corporations to relocate their headquarters. Names such as Johnson & Johnson, Burger King Holdings and Siemens AG have done so! Yahoo Inc. in Vaud. Kraft and Google also in country + 150 other US

Oil exploration & production expenditures: In 2004, 327 energy firms spent $ 167B vs 2009 when 387 firms spent $ 395B. Note, deep water production can take 10 years.

Adjustable Rate Mortgages: COSI = cost of savings index (tied to the bank's own deposits is longer term and slow to respond to dips in interest rates), CODI = certificates of deposit index (based on the price of 3 month CODs which are short term) and COFI = certificate of federal index (overseen by the Federal Home Loan Bank of San Francisco).

Oil Drilling: In the past 2 year, drilling technology has reduced the time required to drill an average well from 56 days in 2006 to 24 days in 2009 which makes wells profitable at $ 50 a barrel vs 2006's $ 80 break even.

Feb 2010 - since the start of the recession, education and health care have added 839,000 jobs (primarily in healthcare). These can not be outsourced to other countries.

Gold in exchange-traded funds surged by 595 metric tons to near 1,800 tons in 2009!

Barrick's forecast for core operations is between $425 and $455 per oz.

Feb 2010 S&P Weightings: Consumer Discretionary	10%
Consumer Staples	11%
Energy	11%
Financial	14%
Health Care	13%
Industrial	10%
Materials	4%
Technology	23%
Utilities	4%

Feb 2010 - Oil now 60% correlated with DJI or 8.2 times the 5 year average!

The Norwegian Government Pension Fund with an internal staff of 249, hundreds of external money managers and a time horizon measured in generations still fell 23.3% in 2008 highlighting "structure explains performance".

Spring Oil Rally? Oil futures normally begin a steady climb around Feb/ Mar as large fuel consumers lock in supplies at cheap winter prices before heavy summer gasoline demand starts. Every year since 2004 oil prices have increased from 34% to 119% from winter lows to summer peaks.

E-Recycling (recycling electronic equipment) per ABI Research, consumers and industry discarded 53 million tons of electrical and electronic equipment in 2009 and expected to grow to 71 million tons by 2014. World wide value of electronic scrap recovery 2009 = $5.7B and 2014 = $14.7B!

March 09 to March10 the U.S.issued some $ 7 trillion in debt and national debt increased by $ 4T.

GM selling more vehicles in China than the U.S.

Global Stocks: U.S. stocks = 45%. Small caps = 15%.

The average price of existing U. S. homes in Feb 2010 = $ 165,100

The Greek Public Sector = 40% with retirement at age 53 on 70% of salary

Americans have lost their sense of evidence

Obama's advisers estimated a multiplier effect from government spending (stimulus) of up to 1.55 or for every dollar the government spent, the economy would grow by as much as $1.55. The International Monetary fund study shows a multiplier of .7 or for every $ spent, the economy see just 70 cents in activity.

Stimulus results: The government spent $480 B to increase the GDP by $355B or an increase in debt of $1.35 for every dollar increase in GDP, a multiplier of .74.

The Precautionary Principle: The government should attempt to prevent any risk - regardless of costs, however minor the benefits and even without understanding what those risks actually are. The EPA is set up on this 'principle'.

IBD 6July2010 - Federal Income Taxes paid =

Top 10% of US household:	1980	2007
	48.1%	71.2%
Bottom 60%	14.8%	>1%

Jobs lost 2008 recession: Large companies 3M, small companies 5M = 8M private

Every month in the US, 125,000 people enter the work force.

Obama administration engaged in a set of policies that turned a market correction into an economy-wide crises.

China vs USA energy consumption. In 2000 china consumed 1/2 of USA. In 2009 it consumed more. Coal: US 22%, China 66%. Energy equivalent in oil per person: US 2000 8 tons and 2009 7.1 ton vs China 1.7 tons.

Tax Rates 2011?

Current rate	% Filers	Range	2001 rate
10%	19.7	to $16,750	15%
15	36	16,751-68,000	15%
25	16.4	68.001-137,300	28%
28	3.0	137,301-209,250	31%
33	1.2	209,251-373,650	36%
35	0.7	over 373,650	39.6%

Per WSJ: Top Income Tax rate 41%, Cap Gains rate 20%, Top Dividend rate 39.6% and estate to 55%

The US rich: The top 5%, by income, account for 37% of all consumer spending, which includes consumer spending, interest payments on installment debt and transfer payments. The bottom 80% account for 39.5%. The top 10% of earners take about half of all income in 2007.

Is the US becoming a plutonomy? an economy dependent on the spending and investing of the wealthy.

Fiscal multiplier below 1 - - due to rising government debt which makes individuals and companies reduce spending as they fear future tax rises? Does government austerity boost private-sector confidence??

Yield Curve 'Recession Forecast'? An inversion = short term US Govt. yields exceed long term yields = recession. Problem: US Govt. artificially holding short yields at '0'!

The US's top 5% of income = 30% of consumption.

Rare-Earth: China has 95%!!! of the worlds output. Dysprosium, neodymium etc. Cuts 2nd half 2010 shipments by 72%!!!! = global shortage of 20,000 tons.

To pay for Obama's children's health-insurance program in 2009, taxes on a pound of roll your own tobacco went to $ 24.78 a pound vs pipe tobacco at $ 2.83 per pound.

U.S. beef consumption per capita: 1976 = 94.3# vs 2009 = 59.1#. We have the lowest herd ever @ 100.8M but export 2 billion #s of beef & veal in 2010.

In 3 years, the world's stock market values went from $ 60T to $ 40Trillion!

Stock Market summary: Oct 2007 14,100, Oct 08 8,400 & March 2009 6,600! US stock losses from Sept 08 to March 09 = $ 3.9T

"Death Cross" = when the 50 day moving average moves below the 200 day moving average = lower prices ahead?

Largest banks by assets: US = Bank of America, J.P. Morgan Chase, Citigroup, Wells Fargo and Goldman sacs. Global = BNP Paribas, Deutsche Bank, Barclays, Royal Bank of Scotland, Mitsubishi UFJ Financial, HSBC, Bank of America, Credit Agricole, J.P Morgan Chase, Citigroup.

We are at the end of a 30 year interest rate cycle: January 1981 short interest rates were 19.08% - now 0.14%. Thirty year mortgages in October 1981 were 18.45%- now 4.28%. Over this period the stock market rose tenfold! Wall Street does not do well in a rising interest rate environment.

October 2010 - Dow made a "golden cross" where the 50 day moving average crosses above the 200-day moving average. Since May 1999, the DOW has crossed 11,000 a record 37 times!

Quantitative easing: trigger core price inflation drive up real economic activity?? or just inflate the price of financial sector assets and commodities???

This dollar debasing strategy has resulted in: Money into Emerging Market funds $ 60B, Precious metals and commodity funds $ 19B and US equity funds DOWN $50B. Low interest rates encourage capital intensive investment rather than labor intensive capital expenditure. Our manufacturing sector of 11.6M (1/3rd fewer than 10 years ago) added 114,000 workers this year vs Trade, transportation and warehousing with 29M workers, up 176,000 this year.

Gold being a 'gold trap; routing funds into a nonproductive asset.

Retirement Plans: 72 million workers in 483,000 plans!

Social Security: Nearly 58 million get SS checks. SS currently running a deficit and the $ 250 bribe would add $ 15B to the 2011 deficit (now estimated to be $1.4T)!

WSJ 15Oct2010: 30 year mortgages at 4.19%

Ethanol bailout: EPA ok's 15%!! for this fuel that is more expensive than gas, increases carbon emissions more than gas, gets worse mileage than gas and that few consumers would willingly buy unless required by law. The rule is to absorb the industry's extra capacity to produce. = corn belt pandering.

In 1848, Alexis de Tocqueville wrote that the French knew a lot about politics and understood nothing about economics. The leftist unions represent the public sector, a quarter of the active population!

Japan's Quantitative easing: Over the past 20 years Nikkei has gone from 40,000 to 9,500. Although public debts funded at rock bottom rate of 1.5% on its bonds, interest payments consume 27% of tax revenue. Bank of Japan will have to fire up the printing presses. The analogy is Israel 1972-1987 high government spending drove up consumer prices by a factor of 10,000 and stock prices by a factor of 6,500.

US Growth metric: Population growth = 1% + Improvements in efficiency = 2% therefore must grow 3%, otherwise unemployment goes up!!!

Fiscal Policy: Moving some taxes or elements of public spending up or down to either propel or restrain total spending - these decisions are political and made by congress

Monetary Policy: lowering or raising short-term interest rates to either speed or slow growth - these decisions by the technocratic Federal Reserve.

Oct 2010: National unemployment 9.6%, Blacks 16.1%, black teens 41%. 70% of black children born to single mothers, only 35% live with two parents.. The tea party does not threaten the interests of blacks, it threatens the interests of the democrat party.

The NAACP tries to discredit the tea party for political reasons.

In October 2010, long term unemployment (27 weeks or more - due to structural changes in the economy) exceeded short term unemployment (under 5 weeks - due to business cycle fluctuations) for the first time in history.

In 2006, in the construction sector some 7.7M were employed building 1.8M new housing units vs 5.6M building 600,000 units in 2010.

World's most profitable company? Federal Reserve Bank at $ 52.3B or $7.1B more than Exxon and more than GE, Microsoft and Walmart's combined $48B.

Adults 65 and over with home mortgages: In 1989 one in five with median debt of $15,000. In 2007 one in three with median debt of $60,000.

GOLD 3Nov2010: Gold supply 2010 = 115.7M Oz. 39.8M into investment demand vs 15.5M in 2000. Jewelry 2000 = 104.3M Oz vs 66.9M in 2010. India's imports thru September down 9% at 212.6 metric tons (1 Metric ton = 2,204.62 pounds). Gold 4 Nov @ $1,392 up $55! In the US 3rd qtr - 28.3 tons into ETFs for a total of 2,070.1 metric tons in ETFs.

How some of every $1,000 of fiscal year 2009 Federal taxes was allocated: Prepared by the left leaning Third Way, it leaves out a figure for the national debt and multiple overlapping entries regarding Defense.

Social Security	192.65
Medicare	120.76
Medicaid	71.32
Interest on National Debt	53.16
Non-Iraq/Afghanistan military operations and maintenance	50.91
Iraq & Afghanistan Operations	41.43
Military personnel	35.71
Military weapons purchases	28.68
Food Stamps	15.38
Central Intelligence Agency	14.16
Veteran's benefits	13.82
Federal highways	11.83
Veterans health care	11.42
National Institutes of Health	8.55
Foreign aid	8.53
Department of Energy	6.81
Housing subsidies for the poor	6.63
Military retirement benefits	6.04
Pell Grants for low-income college students	5.51
NASA	5.05
Border security & immigration enforcement	4.47
IRS	3.27
Agriculture subsidies	3.24
Coast Guard	2.65
FBI	2.09
Head Start	2.02
Fed Emergency Management Ag	1.99
Ctr for Disease Control & Prevent	1.81

Federal prisons	1.75
National parks	0.79
Food & Drug Administration	0.59
Congress's salaries & benefits	0.04

World Energy: In 2007 10% from renewables, mostly hydro vs 2035's projected 14%.

Energy Department forecast for 2035: Oil & Nat gas 52%, Coal 28%, renewable 14%.

Electricity: 31% from coal. Natural Gas: Produces electricity at 53% of the cost of on-shore wind and 21% of photovoltaic solar!

Congress mandates the Fed to strive for "maximum" employment and "stable" prices. Interpreted to be 5% to 6% unemployment and about 2% core inflation. "Quantitative Easing" is viewed as costly, risky and unlikely to have an immediate or major effect on growth in gross domestic product. Per economist Melchior Palya: universal home ownership would fix the population to the ground and overburden them with housing costs that combined would limit the mobility of American workers. Too much credit always turns into too much debt which eventually destroys the economy via the burden of escalating interest payments.

Oil: Every 1 cent rise in the price of gasoline costs the economy $4M per day or $1.46B per year. Historically, when oil triples, a recession occurs. Dec 08 oil was $ 33/bbl

Wood pulp used for making toilet paper hits all time high in 2010, the response

Size of Scott 1000 toilet paper sheet:

1995	4.5" X 4.5"
1999	4.5" X 4.1"
2006	4.5" X 3.7"
2010	4.1" X 3.7"

2010	Width	Sheets per roll
Cotonelle Double Roll	4.2"	to 260 from 308
Angel Soft Double Roll	4" from 4.27"	to 300 from 352
Charmin Ultra Soft Big Roll	4.27"	to 176 from 200
Quilted Northern Soft	4" from 4.5"	to 242 from 286

Air and wind compete with coal. Oil is overwhelmingly a transportation fuel.

Natural gas carbon dioxide emission: 71% of oil and 56% of coal. 51% of gas reserves are outside OPEC vs 23% for oil.

Gas prices: 10Nov10 - $4.21 per MBTU's. Down 73% since the all time high in 2005!

Commodities: Over the past 200 years, commodities have peaked every 30 years. Most recent: 1920/21, 1950/51 and 1980/81 with next 2010/11? Currently (Nov10) undervalued: Cocoa iPath DJ-UBS Cocoa ETN = NIB, Coffee iPath DJ-UBS Coffee ETN = JO, Lumber iShares S&P Global Timber & Forestry Index = WOOD and Guggenheim/Beacon Global Timber Index = CUT.

US jewelry sales: Down 2.7% in 2008 and another 1.6% in 2009. Jewelry Gold demand down from 73% in 2005 to 52% in 2010.

Tech Winter takes its name from the four-month period of cold weather outperformance we've observed in tech stocks over the past 25 years, annually stretching from November through February. Vanguard's Primecap?

Inflation is a tax on wealth!

Creditor rights laws have become wishy-washy and vulnerable to politics. see GM

Options: 75% of all options and 83% of put options expire un-exercised and worthless.

Moral: Sellers are the winners!

Oil ETF's have historically been penalized by roll over penalties (when funds sell out of expiring futures and pay a premium for the next month contract): USO shares are down 11.6% in 2010, thru November while oil prices are up 3%. Greenhaven Continuous Commodity Index Fund (GCC) has a work around.

Value of U.S. real estate dropped $698B in the 3rd Quarter 2010! The first drop in 2 years and whipping out the previous 5 quarters gains. Leaves U.S. real estate at $18.3T, a 26% drop from the 2006 peak and the lowest since 2003.

From 2009 to 30Sep2010: $474B has gone into U.S. taxable bond mutual funds vs $84B out of U.S. equity mutual funds.

A strong dollar redirects capital to worthy entrepreneurs and out of ruinous commodity speculation.

Governance precedes philanthropy.

Cap weighted indexes are significantly slanted toward the performance of the top 10 holdings.

ETF's reduce company specific risk.

Taxes & the top 1%: Usually incorrectly reported as "the wealthiest 1% of U.S. households now take home more than 20% of all household income." the flaw is; it is not 'take home' but income including CG's before taxes. In 2004, the top 1% earned 19.4% of total income before taxes and paid 41% of individual federal taxes. No other country is so dependent on so few taxpayers. Per the OCED's 2008 study of 24 countries, "Taxation is most progressively distributed in the United States." Per OECD study, top10% ratio of taxes paid to income received U.S. 1.35, France 1.1, Germany 1.07.

Dividend taxes reduced from 38.6% to 20% 2002. From 2002 to 2007 average dividend income reported by top 1% tripled. Business income reported by top 1% increased significantly when individual tax rates were brought down to corporate rates in 2003.

Lesson: Higher tax rates cause the top 1% to report less income. Dividend paying stocks exchanged for tax-exempt bonds etc.

US strategic oil reserve is full at 726M barrels!

Investment Wisdom 2011

Gold: Global dollar currency reserves = $ 10T. Central banks diversifying into Gold!

Gold is 70% correlated to inflation.

8Feb - Junk Bond yield below 7% approaching 2004 low of 6.976%

Uranium: All time high price + $ 135/pound. In 2010 up from $ 40.50 to $ 62.50. There are 59 Nuc reactors under construction. Russia's Mega tons to mega watts program ends in 2013 = BUY 'URA' @ $ 21.75????

FY 08: Interest payments $ 412B. Only Defense and income redistribution (HUD & Food Stamps) are higher.

Retired Municipal Teacher's (RMT) Division of Group Insurance Commission: Natick, MA's school system will assume a portion of your total premiums and term life at minimal cost. $40M unfunded. Active teachers 584 and retired 367 with avg. benefit of $ 17,400.

Ethanol Effect: In 2007 US farmers planted 15.2 Million more acres with corn, a jump of 19% at the expense of soybeans and cotton. - - cotton its all time high in 2011!

US conventional gas production up 6 fold in the last 20 years to 32BCFt/ day. New technology has gas global resources at 33,000 TCuFt or about 5 times 2009 estimate!

Wisdom of Crowds?

	DJIA	Stock Fund Money Flows
1 Nov 2010	11,007	Nov outflow 6.4B
1 Dec 2010	11,578	Dec outflow 12.9B
1 Jan 2011	11,891	Jan outflow 4.2B
1 Feb 2011	12,130	
14 Feb	12,391	Wk of 16 Feb inflow 5.2B

Stock market: First 5 trading days of month typically up while last 5 days are down

Risk free rate of return = 2%

US 2010 coal exports: Steam Coal 40M tons and Met coal 42M tons

From 1926 to 2010, average annual return for micro caps (Market cap under $500M) was 12.8%, small caps (less than $2B), 12.2%, mid caps 11.4% and large caps 9.4%.

vs

March 2011: SC P/E = 21, LC P/E = 14. SC only off high by 4%, LC off 16%.

The China Nuclear Energy Association said China plans to add 60 reactors by 2020 with each requiring 400 metric tons of uranium to their current 13 working reactors. China's 2010 uranium import of 17,136 tons was triple that of 2009. Cameco to ship 23M pounds through 2020. Uranium demand 2011 and (planned reactors): US 19,427metric tons (9), France 9,221 (1), Japan 8,195 (12), China 4,402 (50) with China expected to surpass the US

17Mar11 - Uranium tumbles on Japan Crisis. In Feb, uranium hit a 3 year high of $73 a pound, on 16Mar it was $49.25. Per Nuclear Energy Institute - 65 nuclear units are currently under construction and there are 400 operating reactors consuming about 180 million pounds of uranium a year. Nuclear accounts for 14% of global electricity

70% of Income Tax submissions come from AGI's under $58,000

Jobless recoveries: 1991 unemployment went up, after 1992 it took 2 1/2 years to return to pre-recession level. After 2001 the pre-recession rate of 4.3% unemployment has yet to return

In 2008, net national saving turned negative for the first time in history

P/E ratio: now 13 vs avg of 19 over past 20 years. For past 5 years = 15. For past 10 years = 23.7 vs avg of 16. Using the 10 year avg during the 90's tech bubble = 40

2010 REIT performance: Apartment +47%, Hotels +42.8%, Regional Malls +34.6%, Shopping Centers +30.8%, Office +18.4% vs Health care +19.2%

U.S. ice-cream market = $ 9.3Billion

18Mar11 - Coal: shipped coal 805 Mtons vs demand 823 Mtons. Japan imports down 4%, price per ton $ 123,50 Germany suspending 7 reactors = coal imports up 3 Mtons @ $ 145/ton? from todays $ 122? US EPA reduced mercury to close 18% of coal plants = 60 gigawatts? Less nuclear = more coal. Indian & Chinese coal demand to increase.

Steel: Iron ore price down 3.4% to $147 ton from $ 170.

Fed funds rate has been between 0% and 0.25% since December 2008.

Soak-the-Rich: Income tax revenues have been remarkably stable at 8% of GDP regardless of tax rates:

	1952-1979	1993-1996	1988 - 1990
Individual tax paid as % of GDP	7.8	8	8.1
Range of top tax rate	70% to 92%	39.6%	28%

Raising the individual tax receipts above 9% of GDP has always failed. The only times it occurred was 1944 @9.4%, recessions of 69, 81 & 91 and tech stock boom 98.

The top 400 paid lower CG tax rates 1995 @ 28% vs 2000 @ 20% their taxes paid doubled from $5.2B in 95 to $11.8B in 2000

Foreign bank holders disclosed in 2009 = 15,000. In 2010 9,500 were settled!

Gas prices & retail sales: per ConvergEx Group - "during the past 8 periods of gains and declines in gasoline prices over the past two decades show that rising gas prices coincide with periods of healthy retail sales."

Fund performance vs S&P 500: over the past 10 years the S&P500 annual average yearly gain was 0.72% without dividends but 2.81% with dividends. Since 2005 without 12.5%, with 28.1%. Make sure the fund states S&P 500 with or without dividends.

Biofuel production now absorbs 20% of the world's sugar cane, 9% of oilseeds and coarse grains and 4% of sugar beets - and 40% of U.S. corn production.

Growth Energy, the ethanol lobby run by retired General Wesley Clark supports the 45 cent blender tax credit on ethanol as well as the 54 cent tariff on imported ethanol. Current mandate calls for annual production of 36 billion gallons of ethanol by 2022. The artificially high prices for biofuels causes farmers to divert from wheat (which people eat) to feedstocks like corn.

The average cost of Treasury borrowing over the last 20 years was 5.7%. Present average cost = 2.5%. A return to 'normal' = higher interest expense in year 2014 of $420B!!! Over 10 years = $4.9T!!!!!!!!! Government Growth forecasts = 4%+ per year vs actual 2.5%. Each 1% for one year = $750B lost revenue.

2011 daily world oil demand averages more than 89 million barrels.

Containers and packaging generated about 72 million tons of trash in 2009, nearly 1/3 of that years total municipal solid waste.

1July2011: S&P up 29% in past year, 8% year to date. DJIA up 6% since 23 June low of 11874 to 12583.

US coal exports over 90M tons per year. US oil production bottomed in 2008 at 5.4M barrels per day - projected to increase to 7.4M by 2019.

The average annual return for the S&P500 from 1999 to 2009 (including dividends reinvested) was -0.86%. Since the March 2009 nadir - up almost 100%.

The so called endowment approach to investing that divides assets equally between domestic and overseas stocks, government bonds, real estate investment trusts and commodities has outperformed the conventional mix of 60% stocks and 40% bonds over the past 30 years.

A risk diversified portfolio (dollar weights): Stocks 51%, Bonds 37%, Commodities 3%, REITS 3% and Hedge Funds 6%

Problem solving ability peaks at age 20. Ability to make financial management decisions peaks at age 53. All has to do with mental capacity!

Cognitive impairment: At 80 years old = 16%, 80 - 89 age group 29.2% and 90 and older 38.8%. Mild dementia has 2 M new cases every year.

August and September rank among the worst two months for the major stock market indexes according to The Stock Trader's Almanac.

Low S&P 500 PE? 13.3 in Mar 2009, 6.6 Aug 1982, 8.3 in Dec 1974 & 5.6 in Jun 1932.

On 2 August 2011 the Dow Theory (DJIA and DJTA in tandem, crossed their June lows) gave a 'sell' signal. DJIA = 11,870. Close 8 Aug = 10,809. Down -1,061 / -9%

10Aug11 - Dividend yield on the S&P500 rose above the yield on the 10-year Treasury for the first time in almost 50 years.

Per Catholic University, as of 2007 the U.S. Code contained some 4,000 offenses with criminal penalties. Dodd-Frank adds 24 more new offenses.

Aug 2011 - A death cross means the average price for the last 50 days is less than the average price for the last 200 days, a sign that the short-term trend in stock prices is negative.

Mining accounts for 60% of Australia's exports.

Global Financial Assets (stocks, bonds & mortgages) = $200T. Above ground gold = $3T (1.5%) with half in central banks. Gold ETF's increased 2011: April $500M, May $21M, June $314M and July $257M.

46% of the sales of the S&P500 companies come from foreign countries.

QE2 reduced the value of the dollar, raised the cost of living and the cost of production = reduced U.S. competitiveness.

Per Berkeley economist Brad DeLong: When central banks shift expected inflation upward they make households fear holding risky debt and equity less because they fear dollar devaluation more. Quantitate easing caused the dollar to fall, inflated industrial commodities, reduced profitability for U.S. firms shifting more work overseas thus turned out to be an anti-stimulus, stimulating nothing but the domestic cost of living and the cost of production.

Per Goldman Sach's Alan Brazil (Aug11) - "Here we go again...solving a debt problem with more debt has not solved the underlying problem....can the US continue to depreciate the world's base currency?"

Since 1962, the S&P 500 has on average gained 19% in the 3rd year of a presidency. Only 1 of the last 19 times have stocks ended down. Will 2011 be the 2nd?

There are no companies and no jobs without investment first, and policy of dollar weakness have made the U.S. a bad place to commit growth capital over the last 10 years. Gold is the single best measure of the U.S. dollar.

Last 10 Years

	1970's	1980's	1990's	
Gold	+ 595%	+1,355%	-52%	- 29%
vs				
S&P 500	+ 2.9%	+ 16%	+ 222%	+ 314%

Gold/Silver margin activity: In April & May 2011, CME raised Silver margins 5 times in 15 days for a total of 84% = 25% drop in price. No margin change for gold which dropped only 1%. On 23 Sept 11, CME announced margin increases for gold up 21% and Silver up 16% effective 27 Sept

S&P avg. quarterly changes since 1990: 1st +.8%, 2nd +2.45%, 3rd -.9%, 4th +4.7%.

According to the IRS, the top 1 percent of income earners—those earning more than $380,000 in 2008—paid more than 38 percent of all federal income taxes while earning 20 percent of all income. The top 10 percent ($114,000 and above) earned 45 percent of income and paid 70 percent of all taxes. At the same time, the bottom 50 percent of income earners— those earning less than $33,000—earned 13 percent of all income and paid less than 3 percent of federal income taxes.

IBD 12Oct11 - S&P 500 12% below its 52 wk peak of 1,370.50 and 24% off its all time high set in 2007.

U.S. Pay phones: 2000 = 2,200,000 vs 2011 = 425,000

Inflation protection: Principal Diversified Real Asset Fund = 30% in TIPS + MLPs, commodities and real estate natural resource shares. or buy Alerian MLP ETF, Vanguard REIT Index Fund & Power Shares DB Commodity Index Tracking Fund.

Euro zone oil consumption: 2005 = 11.5M barrels a day vs 2010 = 10.6M down 13.6%. The oil decrease of 850,000 BLS a day is equal to the daily consumption of California! Euro zone steel consumption down 14.4% from 2000 to 2010.

GOLD: Up under two conditions. 1. When up with bonds, the dollar and the yen = the "flight-to-quality" money is moving in. 2. When gold is up and down with riskier assets like stocks and commodities it has to do with investors response to changing crises views. When long-term bond yields fall, the opportunity cost of holding Gold is reduced.

Central Banks BUY GOLD! CB's became net buyers in 2nd Qtr 2009. 3rd Qtr 2011 - central banks doubled gold buys in the 3rd Qtr to 148.4T over the 2nd Qtr's 66.5T and 7 times from a year ago's 22.6 tons. Total buy for first 3 Qtr's 2011 = 348.7T

During the 2000's, U.S.based multinational corporations added a total of 2.9M employees abroad with 1.5M to payrolls in Asia, 477,500 in Latin American while cutting 864,000 at home. They spent $2.40 for every $1 spent overseas on capital spending. Canada +1M, Mexico +904,300, U.K. + 1.1M, Germany -614,500, France +529,900, China +943.900 & India +453,300.

U.S. copy paper is a $ 3B annual business declining about 3% a year due to reduced workplace printing due to PDF documents and email.

Fed 2011 bank stress test scenario: Unemployment @ 13% in 2013, GDP shrinks 8%, Home prices down another 20% by 2014, stock market down 50% over next year.

U.S. Energy: In 1973 imports of oil = 37% and by 2005 60%. In the last 12 months = 46%. NatGas: 1973 = 4%, 2007 = 16% and last 12 months = 9%. Imported oil 2006 = 13M barrels/day vs 9M now. (demand down 2.5M Bl/d and imports of refined oil products down from 2.5M b/d to exporter). Exports of value added refined products cuts the trade deficit. Note: Europe has lower productivity, the key to offsetting energy import costs and is already highly dependent on energy imports.

Too-Big-To-Fail: In the past 5 years the 4 biggest banks have grown their share of total commercial bank assets from 54% to 62%!

Over the past 5 years, 64% of broad U.S. Stock funds and 92% of high yield bond funds have been beaten by their bench marks.

Oil vs Corn: West Texas, It takes 407 million gallons of water to irrigate 640 acres and grow $ 200,000 worth of corn on the arid land. The same amount of water could be used to frack enough oil wells to generate $ 2.5 billion worth of oil. Each well takes 6 million gallons to frack a well.

When Congress raises top tax rates on capital gains and dividends, the highest income earners will report less income from capital gains and dividends and hold more tax-exempt bonds.

Venezuela Oil Company = 1st half 2011, price up 35% but cash flow from $4.8B in 2010 to negative. Production down 24% in decade. Oil company payments to Government tripled to $18.5B for social programs. Mexico's Oil Co. = tax rate 115% = NO investments in oil production!

Financial repression: The Feds purchase of long term treasury securities camouflages the true cost of capital. (Every 1% increase in interest rates above the current base line = $1 Trillion of debt service over 10 years!!!!!!) This repression hides indications as to when our debt burden is intolerable.

From 1929 to 1940, from Hoover to Roosevelt, government intervention helped make the Depression Great". Drained investment capital from the system, top income tax rate: 1929 = 25%, 1932 = 63% and then to 79%.. Corporate taxes from 11% to 12% in 1931, 13.75% in 1932, 15% in 1936 with a 27% surtax on undistributed profits. Inheritance tax raised from 20% to 45% in 1932, to 60% in 1934 and 70% in 1935.

Gift tax reinstated in 1932 to 33.5%, 1934 to 45% and 52.5% in 1935. All led to enduring stagnation. The Dow did not return to 1929 levels until nearly a decade after Roosevelt's death" per Amity Shlaes.

Dec 2011 - More than 60 billion euros moved out of Greek Banks since 2009 with 14B from September to early November.

Hedge funds cut commodities exposure be 50% from May to December with commodities index falling 19%.

Department of Agriculture: Budget $ 57 billion (includes $9B for crop supports). Employees 105,000 or 1 for every 11 farms. Average income including benefits $123,000 vs average farm employee's $28,000.

Investment Wisdom 2012

Obama scuttles Keystone XL, Department of Interior bans uranium mining on one million acres of federal land in Arizona.

Food Stamps: Under G.W. Bush up 10.9M. Under Obama 2009 - 2011 up 11.2M or in 2008 28.2M = $ 37.6B to 2011's 44.7M @ $ 75.3B. Texas 4M, CA 3.7M, Fl 3.1M.

Of 20 major commodities, seven peaked before 3 July 2008 - the day the S&P GSCI index of commodities set its all time record. Baltic Dry Index high May 2008 now down 90%. Nickel up 754% from Jan 2002 and May 2007 - now down 67%. NGas up 700% by December 2005, now down 80%.

S&P500: Peaked on October 2007 and with invested dividends, has lost 8% since. - WSJ 21Jan2012. Equal weight 500 - up 52% since Aug 2000.

The U.S. Total Stock Market Index returns for 10 years = 3.9% and for 20 years = 8% annually.

U.S. cattle herd: smallest (90.8M) in 60 years due to drought in the southern Plains.

Japan has it first trade deficit ($ 32B) in 31 years (2011). Japan's overseas assets are valued at $ 3T producing enough interest and dividends to put the current account in surplus.

U.S. manufacturing has increased by 33% in the past 10 years but employment has gone down due to automation.

Bernanke promises 6 years of zero interest pushing investors into more risky investments.

Where did the middle class ($35,000 to $105,000) go? In the past 30 years the percentage of households making more than $ 105K in inflation adjusted dollars doubled to 24% from 11%. Households making less than $ 35K remained the same

The Great Expansion of 1980 - 2007 from Reagan's reverse of high taxes, loose money, big government. Developing countries under free market, deregulation, trade agreements etc. grew 2 and 3 times faster and their GDP increased to 22% of world GDP from 13%. U.S. GDP held steady at 26%. Now being reversed by Obama - leading to stagflation like the 70's??

Low Rate Risk: In the U.K. low interest rates boosting inflation in higher commodity and import prices squeezing real wages and crimping consumption and debtor credit-worthiness.

GOLD: Are the sheep getting in? December 2011 - highest sales ever of gold American Eagle coins (114,500) and Silver American Eagle coins (5.697million ounces).

December: gold down 10%, silver down 15% vs January: gold up 11%, silver up 21%.

Federal Reserve's 'operation twist', a price-insensitive buyer, sopped up 5 year and longer securities to the level of $920B up from $171B in December 2007.

Natural gas: Japan will have closed its 54 nuclear reactors by May 2012. Now importing 78.5M tons of liquified natural gas as they produce only 4% of consumption.

Liar Loans = $ 16.4T. The U.S. collects $2T in taxes and spends $ 3.5T. 36% of Gov debt is less than 1 year.

Gold: Buyers for 2011 - China 18%, India 10% and U.S. 5%.

We pay China $ 119 million every day in interest

The US consumes 10,000 tons of aspirin yearly.

Commodity Super Cycles (coinciding with ultra loose U.S. monetary policy)? - Per Longview Economics's Chris Watling there have been 3 cycles in the past 80 years: 30's-40's, late 60's-70's and since 1999 which coincide with equity bear markets. SHOULD START TURNING IN 2014!!!!

Silver 4Apr12 WSJ: Margin 13% vs gold 6%. Industrial applications 2011 = 86% of demand. Europe & China down = silver down!

U.S. oil is 20% below world price and natural gas 80% below world price

Gold sinks - March/April 2012 = India doubles import taxes on gold = retailers strike for 20 days! Gold is India's 2nd largest import after oil. India is the world's top consumer of gold! Akshaya Tritiya festival is a big gold buying event

31May 2012 - 10 year treasury has lowest yield in 200 years @ 1.53%! Gold down 6% in May and off 19% since Sept high of $1,920

Cortisol levels jump when the brain senses uncertainty. If cortisol stays elevated for extended periods, it can inhibit rational decision making and "produce a tendency to find threat and risk where none exists." This can lead to probability neglect.

Lest we forget: Long Term - Small Caps & value easily outperform LC & Growth!

Technology: QQQ & XLK with lots of Apple! Also IYW!

29June2012: Gold hits $1,603! and silver $27.48

Dow 10,000 = March 1999, December 2003, October 2009

Since the start of 2007, a cumulative $350B has flowed out of stock funds with $1T into bond funds. Consumer holding mix: 2011, 45% in stocks and 25% in bonds

2005, 55% in stocks and 15% in bonds.

Platinum: 45% used in tailpipes of which 75% in diesel vehicles while 24% is used in jewelry. Only one third of producers can produce profitably at $ 1,546 / Oz.. (Light vehicle sales in Europe down 7% in 2012!!) Palladium commonly used in gasoline vehicles.

Steel: China produces 2 million tons a day = half of the world's steel.

Net outflow from U.S. stock mutual funds for 12 months 1Jul11-1Jul12 = $129B. In July - another $7B.

Market all time high = 9Oct2007 at 14,164.

Jargon like "alpha", "beta" or 'proprietary algorithms' are based on mathematical models of past performance - an assumption constantly rebutted by history.

Non-traded REITS typically estimate share value annually, typically pay higher yield although may come from borrowed money or out of investor's original capital. Upfront commission typical 8%.

Portfolio Theory defines risk only as volatility, or the extent to which returns can vary from average. But that isn't the only source of risk. "Conventional portfolio theory says not to hold all your eggs in one basket If you margin your account is like piling eggs on top of eggs until the pile becomes unsteady. Borrowed money can make even the most diversified "safe" portfolio risky. Leveraged accounts can be wiped out in the short run!

Gold: China imported 67 tons in June 2012 vs June 2011's 25 tons. QE1 = Au up 35%, QE2 Up 21%. From June 11 to June 12 Au up 14% vs gold-mining costs up 25%.

Platinum typically costs 20% more than gold and is historically a buy now at 8% below.

American families who own stocks or stock funds: 2001 - 53%, 2011 - 46%. Since Mar 2009 investors pulled $138 billion from mutual & ETFunds and put $ 1T into bond funds.

DJIA secular bear markets:

19 Jan 1906 - 24 Aug 1921 =	15 years - 1.1% annualized
3 Sep 1929 - 28 Apr 1942 =	13 years -10.6%"
9 Feb 1966 - 12 Aug 1982 =	17 years -1.5%"
14 Jan 2000 - 2 Oct 2012 =	12 years +1.1%"

Switch to REIT: Total market value of REITS 1990 = $ 9B vs 2011 = $ 451B. In 2011, reported profits of $ 25 billion, must pay out 90% but avoids federal taxes!!

To see real DOW performance you have to weight with the TWEXB (Trade Weighted U.S. Dollar index.

Week of election 6 Nov 2012 - $ 488M out of Funds! Money Market funds = $2,556T

Cheap money and record low interest rates promote over investment in the longest-term alternatives

Inflation: SS 2013 COLA = 1.7%. AIER's Everyday Price Index (EPI) more applicable to Seniors is up 5.2% y-t-d. with prescription drugs +3.2% y-t-d.

AMT in 2011 = 4 M paid

From the beginning of 2009, investors have added $1 trillion to bond funds with 3/4 ($752B) into actively managed funds

Dec 11 to Dec 12 - $132 billion out of actively managed stock funds and $57B into passive funds

An actively managed fund's process: 1. analysis - how the manager assembles the portfolio 2. behavior - how the manager responds to the emotional extremes in the market 3. organization - how the business is structured to ensure that investor's interests come first. 4. How the portfolio differs from average - if indistinguishable from average, do not use.

unemployed	+ discouraged	+ Seeking full	time employment
March 2007	4.4%	4.6%	8%
Dec 2012	7.9%	8.4%	14.6%

In Nov 12 the share of the available labor force that is working fell to 63.6% down from 65.7% when the recession ended in June 2009 - the lowest level since 1981. The number of non-working, working age worker was 89.2M possibly due to the hugh increase in government benefits for not working - food stamps, disability payments and unemployment insurance. Welfare payments that redistribute income from workers to mostly non-workers now exceed $1 trillion a year.

Money manager window dressing: the bidding up of shares just before quarter-end, may explain why unusual numbers of stocks beat the market the final day of each quarter.

The Government printed more $100 bills than $1 bills during Oct 11 to Oct 12. Does this indicate a move toward an increased underground economy? One million dollars in $100 bills = 22 pounds and fits into an aluminum attache case.

Dec 2012 - Correlation of individual sectors to the S&P500: Energy & Industrials 93%. Financials 92%, Tech 91%, Emerg Mkts 89%, Health 88%, Materials 86, Utilities 34%

Long Term Mutual Fund Assets in Trillions:

	Bonds	Stocks	HiQual Corp Bond
Dec 2007	1.68	6.52	6.40%
Oct 2012	3.38	5.81	3.57%
	+101%	-11%	

Shipping oil by rail: Loading and unloading rail cars can add $ 4.50 to a barrel. Per Marathon Petroleum, to move oil from N. Dakota to the East Coast adds $10 a barrel. Warren Buffett owns the railroad.

Silver: Since 2008, price has tripled! Silver paste used in photovoltaic solar panels has declined from 60 million ounces of silver in 2011 to 40M (1,244 metric tons) in 2012 as silver now accounts for 20% of production cost. Solar panel sales up 8% in 2012 to 30 gigawatts.

U.S. Household debt as a percentage of personal income: September 2009 = 114%, June 2012 = 97% Pre 2000 = 79%.

Investment Wisdom 2013

From 1996 through 2006 $ 1.5 Trillion flowed into equity mutual funds, 6 times the investment in bonds.

2007 - 2012: $400 B has been redeemed and $750B into bonds.

Private investment is not attracted into basic science or education as they do not provide the potential for near term profit.

Over the past few years and with taxes rising, the private sector has and may continue to reduce capital spending possibly creating supply shortages, particularly in energy and commodities into 2016.

From 1947 to 1980, the average annual inflation rate was about 4%. By the end of 1980, prices were 4 times as high as in 1947, wiping out 3/4 of the war debt.

January 2013 - $41B into stocks vs Dec -23B. Since 2008, $ 1T into bonds with $41B in Jan 13. Bank deposits down $114B in 1st wk of 2013. Unemployment 7.8%

Market too high????? From Aug 1982 to Aug 1987 the S&P500 closed at all-time peak prices 152 times. From Oct 1990 to March 2000 there were 308 record high day closings. This Bull market started on 9 March 2009 and the S&P has yet to close at a new high. It is 2% below its March 2000 high while the PE has gone from 28 to 15. and earnings have doubled. Bull markets are at least up 20% - the average is 56 months and up 122%. The 1966-68 Bull was 26 months up 48%, the biggest 1990 - 2000 was 113 months up 417%.

This Bull market is up 160%. in 47 months. Markets typically go UP 25% from a new all time high.

Money Flow: Nov 12 - Stocks = + 1.8B & Bonds   + 12B,
            Dec 12 - Stocks = + 10.0B & Bonds - 169M
            Jan 13 - Stocks = + 34.2B

Cyclical markets = short term + / - 20% vs Secular markets = 10 years and Avg Bull + 18%/yr, Avg Bear+1%

Secular Bear Markets
1902 - 1921
1921 - 1942
1969 - 1982
Secular Bull Markets

1982 - 2000 up 19% / year with p/e from 7.7 to 28.6,

Mar 2000 - (March 2009 Secular bear market bottom????)
Long term S&P 500 PE = 15.

WSJ 12Feb - Employee compensation at 54.7% (vs 58.2 in 2000) of gross domestic product is the lowest since 1955. When this goes up, profits go down. The value of the U.S. stock market equals 133% of GDP vs the 60 year average of 82%.

Collectible U.S. coins: Per Coin World magazine - coins vs DJIA 2011 +5% vs +8.4% & 2012 - .5% vs +10.2%

Market timing per "Rebel Without a Cause" and James Dean as Jim and Buzz do a 'Chickie Run' - hold on tight to the wheel and keep an eye on the door.

Since 1986, silver from $5.74 to a high of $48.70 in 2011

In 2009 Bill Gross and Mohamed El-Erian predicted: several years of economic stagnation with below average equity returns. Jan 2009 - Jan 2013 S&P 500 up 55.3% (15.3% annual) vs Bonds up 22.8% (6.9% annual).

Over the past 87 years the S&P 500 has provided an annualized inflation adjusted total return of 6.9% well over twice the bond return.

Dow 5Mar2013 = 14,253.77 - adjusted for inflation since 9Oct2007 = 12,900. vs equal weighted Dow at 16,683.44 - - some 2,518.91 points or 17.8% higher than the 2007 high of 14,164.53

2012 performance: Hedge Funds 5.5%, Dogs of the Dow 5.7%, Dow 30 7.3%

Globally 2010-2012: 700B into Bonds = up 7%/year vs -300B in stocks up 9%/year

Nasdaq Composite record high of 5048.62 hit on 10 March 2000.

S&P 500 hit a 12 1/2 year low on 9 Mar 2009 of 676.53. Its all time high =1565.15 on 9 Oct 2007.

Per AARP MA poverty 65+ with SS = 7.5% vs without SS = 40.7% and over the past 10 years a 60% stocks, 40% bond portfolio = +7% annually

Less Government Spending = More prosperity

	Gov share GDP	GDP Growth	S&P 500
1983 - 1989	23.2% to 21.4%	4.3% per year	253 to 508
			= 100% increase
1993 - 2000	22.6% to 18.8%	3.9% per year	569 to 1488
			= 162% increase
2000 - 2010	18.8% to 25.5%	1.6% per year	1488 to 1133
			= 24% decrease

Buffett's rail line BSNF transports 500,000 barrels of oil a day from the Bakken shale as a result of no pipeline.

Railing oil from Alberta to the West coast = $8 to $14 a barrel. Going East = $ 20 a barrel vs pipeline (now non existent) of $8. To tanker it to East Asia = another $5 per barrel.

U.S. net oil imports in 2005 = 60% of consumption vs projected 2014 = 32%.

January 2013 Stock and bond funds and ETF's attracted $51.7B - largest 4 week inflow in 17 years.

IBD 28Mar13 - Russia & S. Africa try to organize platinum cartel. SA mines 70% of the world's Platinum & Russia 10% while Russia also mines 40% of world palladium.

The average dividend focused fund lost 9.27% in the 2000-02 bear market and 41.52% in 2007 - early 2009.

2013 projected sales: personal computers 350M, Smartphones 919M, tablets 200M.

11Apr13 WSJ: Seven day yield for taxable money-market funds yield steady at 0.02% for the 22nd straight week.

MM fund assets down $8.38B in latest week to $2.605T.

NYSE short interest ratio on 10Apr13 = 18.61. The five year high was 22.29!

Cyprus to sell $500M gold! Goldman Sacks 12 month forecast = $ 1,390

IBD 8Jul13 - June jobs report = "solid"? Part time positions up 360,000 and full time positions down 240,000!

Year to date: 130,000 full time jobs and 557,000 part time jobs. Full time job underemployment rate up from 13.8% to 14.3%. 45% of college grads in jobs that do not require college degrees.

At Time Of Death - Federal estate tax law allows a 2013 decedent to pass onto his or her heirs $5.25 million estate tax-free. Under the "American Taxpayer Relief Act" signed by President Obama on Jan. 2, 2013, the amount that can be passed estate-tax free onto the heirs of a decedent in 2014 and beyond will be increased according to the rate of inflation. The federal estate tax exemption was $1 million in 2003 (source: Treasury Department, BTN Research).

Bull Supercycle? A supercycle lasts 12 to 15 years. A normal bull run lasts 3 3/4 years. A bear market (down 20%) lasts 8 to 9 months. NASDAQ low 1265 in March 2009. Down 20.2% July to Oct 2011.

The Fed and the Treasury are aware that for every 1% interest rates increase, it may cost an extra $160 billion-plus in interest charges to the federal budget.

80% of stocks owned by 5% of people

2013: Small Cap Growth = 40.31%,

SCValue	= 35.77%,
Mid Cap Growth	= 34.30%,
MCV	= 34.65%,
LCG	= 33.25%
LCV	= 30.72%

Per John Templeton: the 4 phases to a bull market are "born on pessimism, grow on skepticism, mature on optimism and die on euphoria."

The S&P 500's averaged an annual 11.87% since 1971

Date	Milestone	Gain	Days
2/23/1995	4,003.33		
11/21/1995	5,023.55	25.5%	189
10/14/1996	6,010.00	19.6%	226
2/13/1997	7,022.44	16.8%	85
7/16/1997	8,038.88	14.5%	105
4/6/1998	9,033.23	12.4%	189
3/29/1999	10,006.78	10.8%	240
5/3/1999	11,014.69	10.1%	24
10/19/2006	12,011.73	9.1%	1882
4/25/2007	13,089.89	9.0%	128
7/19/2007	14,000.41	7.0%	59
5/7/2013	15,056.20	7.5%	1460
11/21/2013	16,009.99	6.3%	139

Investment Wisdom 2014

Obamacare to focus on "important sub groups" per Dr. Donald Berwick - (running the Centers of Medicare and Medicaid) rather than the individual patient. The Federal Government must get between the doctor and the patient to facilitate "social justice."

Dr. Ezekial Emanual says that doctors take the Hippocratic oath too seriously "as an imperative to do everything for the patient regardless of cost or effects on others."

As long as doctors are in charge, cost control would not be possible.

To recap, during 2013, the Dow Jones Industrial Average returned 29.7%, posting its largest annual gain in 18 years. The broader S&P 500 went up 32.4%, its best calendar-year return in 16 years. The MSCI EAFE index, a measure of developed international stock markets, returned 22.8%. The yield on the Barclays U.S. Aggregate Bond index ended the year at 2.48%, up from 1.75% at the end of 2012. On a total return basis, the U.S. bond market lost 2.0% for the year—its first calendar year with a negative total return since 1999, and just the third since the benchmark was developed in 1976.

17Jan14 IBD - The Shanghai Gold Exchange delivered 2,197 metric tons of gold to buyers in 2013 vs 1,139 in 2012. In 2013 China imported 1,066 metric tons vs India's 975 with another 200 MetT smuggled in. (MT = 2,240 pounds.)

Solar tax credits: Go not to consumers but to companies that get the consumer to sign away tax credits and accelerated-depreciation tax savings in exchange for "free" solar installations and a long-term agreement to buy the solar power at just below market prices.

Natural Gas Production: U.S. 2013 hit an all time high of 25.3 trillion cubic feet and by 2015 is expected to export 100 million metric tons of LNG.

German bank deposits hit an all time high of $4.6T in June 2013

U.S. household debt hits largest quarterly increase since before recession!

By one account, there were 400,000 individual investor clubs in 1998 vs 39,000 in 2012.

WSJ 22Feb14: Dec13 margin debt at all time high $444.93B, up 35% from year earlier. Daily trades up since last year: E Trade 27%, TD Ameritrade 28%, Schwab 17%!

IBD 7Mar14: Last? bullish confirmation date: 12 March 2009. Is the market approaching a 5 year mark? On May 2011 the Nasdaq and S&P 500 hit peaks and then declined for five months, eventually falling 20.4% and 21.6% respectively off their highs. By traditional measures, the 20% drawdown confirmed a bear market had been or was under way. After 2 1/2 months a NEW bull market was confirmed on 20 Dec 2011. So the current bull market is about two years and three months old.

Market Alert: when the 10 year bond rate exceeds the 30 yr = inversion = watch out!

Palladium: World production: Russia 42% & South Africa 37%

IBD's market Trend: "Confirmed Uptrend" went to "Uptrend Under Pressure" on 13 March 2014. On 26 March to "Correction". On 3 April "Confirmed Uptrend" all in 20 days. On 5 April to "Market in Correction" - sell everything. Same reversals in January and February. Wash sales anyone???

From Baron's 2014 annual review: Currencies are not intended as a "store of value." They are used to buy things. Historically, the dollar has lost about 50% of its purchasing power every twenty years. On average, the dollar loses about 3-4% of its buying power every year. Stocks have doubled in price approximately every ten years for the past century. This represents compounded annual growth of about 7% per year. U.S. stocks median value for the past 100 years = 15.5 times earnings. "Nominal economy growth = 6.8% (2-2.25% real + 3-4% inflation.) Stocks are your "hedge" against the loss of purchasing power of our currency.

Large cap domestic index funds have outperformed managed funds about 90% of the time for decades - David Dreman Forbes June 2014. VFINX or SPY

Since 2008, the U.S. population aged 16 and over (and not in the armed forces, prisons, nursing homes etc.) increased by 15 million.

Saving disposable income: Germans 10%, U.S. 5%. Only 14% (8.9M) of German's invested in shares or equity funds in 2013.

Germany: In 1919 one Oz of gold cost 170 mark. In 1923, 50 billion mark!

In seven of the past 11 years, the S&P 500 index's calendar year high has occurred during the month of December.

Readings of 1.0 or greater in the put-call ratio have come just before short-term market bottoms.

In 2001 the U.S. produced 50% more electricity than China. In 2011 China produced 25% more than the U.S. Almost 80% of China's electricity comes from burning coal and China consumes nearly half the world's coal.

Diversify:	2013	1st 6 months 2014
Russell 2000, Growth	+43.3%	2.22%
MSCI US REIT Index	1.26%	17%
MSCI EM Growth	.1%	6.52%
S&P Natural Resources	16.49%	16.43%

WSJ 2Sep14: Best Bull Markets

4Dec87-24Mar00, 13Jun49-2Aug56, 3Oct74- 28Nov80 and the latest 9Mar09 to today 2,000 days, up 196%. Today trading @ 15.6 PE above 10 year average 14.1 vs 25 at tops.

Averages were up in 4 of the past 5 Septembers.

Schiller's CAPE (cyclically adjusted price earnings) over 25! = SELL???. 1st over in Dec 1985 - but dot com top not till April 2001 and again in Sept 2003 with top 4 years later. CAPE has indicated the stock market overvalued 97% of the time since 1989.

From 1900 to 2013, the spread between an average year's highest and lowest close was 23 percentage points with stocks returning an annualized 6.5% after inflation and dividends.

Benjamin Graham: An emergency fund renders unnecessary an accurate estimate of the future.

Three vs. Nine - In the past 20 years (1994-2013), the S&P 500 has gained more on a total return basis during the fourth quarter (i.e., the months of October, November and December) than the index has gained during the other three quarters combined. Over the past two decades, the final three months of the year have gained 165.1 percent (total return) vs. a gain of 120.1 percent for the first nine months of the year. The S&P 500 consists of 500 stocks chosen for market size, liquidity and industry group representation. It is a market value weighted index with each stock's weight in the index proportionate to its market value (source: BTN Research).

S&P 500 Highlights: Gains = 1933 +53.99, 1935 +47.67% & 1936 +33.92%

Losses = 2000 -10.14%, 2001 -13.04%, 2002 -23.37% & 2008 -38.49%

	Gold vs	S&P
1970's	+1,355%	+16%
1980's	-52%	+222%
1990's	-29%	+314%
2000's	+595%	+2.9%

There are no companies or jobs without investment first, and policies of dollar weakness have made the U.S. a bad place to invest growth capital.

Silver: Annual production = 800 M Oz. Average solar panel = 20G, Laptop = 1.25G/$1, cell phone = 200-300 milligrams/25cents. Solar consumes 52MOz today.

Historical Treasury Department Interest rate 1990 - 2013 = 5% and from 1971-2013 = 7%. Currently 2.4%. At 5% Treasury interest payments would double from $416B.

to $867B. At 7% = $1.2T!!!!!!!!!!!!

Recent Global money printing = $10T

Sell on Rash Hashanah - - Buy on Yom Kippur

Per Warren Buffett 2Oct14 - He has NO bonds and will have NO bonds, even in his Berkshire Hathaway managed retirement accounts!!!!!

7Oct2014 Almost all of gold's weakness has been a strong dollar move. From December 2008 to June 2011, gold jumped 70%. August 2011 high of $1,888.70.

In 1945, the yield on 10-year T-notes embarked on a long, steady climb from 1.7% to 15.8%, the highest ever in U.S. history, in 1981.

Buybacks: Per Warren Chiang, managing director at Mellon Capital - "Executives are compensated on EPS - the primary reason they do buybacks."

Hypermarkets (Costco, Wallmart etc.) operate 3% of gasoline stations but do 13% of nation wide gasoline sales.

2014 mortality estimates for 65 year olds: women 88.8 years, men 86.5 years.

Company Buy backs: Per Goldman Sachs - They are NOT free to buy back shares in the 5 weeks before earnings are released. Since 2007, 25% of corporate buybacks occurred in the last 2 months of the year.

WATCH for Happiness Letters from brokers: Never sign and return a happiness letter. Nor should you speak to your broker about it. Call the compliance officer or branch manager who sent the letter and politely insist on seeing the internal data that prompted it. Do not discuss anything else or answer any questions seeking to establish how satisfied you are with the account's performance. Take everything (happiness letter, account statements and internal data) to your accountant for an objective second opinion.

Nov 2014 = Valuations are fairly high - The S&P 500 traded at 25.7 times its average inflation-adjusted earnings of the previous decade in October, compared with an average of 16.5 times since 1880.

Signs everywhere point to a major market correction. The average time between 20% price drops is 635 days. We're currently at 1,358 days. The Shiller Index – a measure of stock prices versus corporate profits – is above 25. It's only passed that level three times: 1929, 1999, and 2007. Massive crashes followed each time.

Market timing: On 31Dec2008, the stock market was DOWN 42% from its 9Oct2007 high. During that period, $250billion was taken out of stock mutual funds. Time to buy? from 31Dec08 to 9Mar09 the S&P fell another 25%.

DJIA Record Closes: From 1Jan2008 to 31Dec2012 = 0

2013 = 52, 28Nov2014 = 31

Copper Demand is highest in a consumer driven economy: U.S. household spending = 70% of economy vs China's 35%. Copper demand should grow with China.

Nov 2014: S&P 500 @ 16.2 times next 12 months earnings vs 10 year average of 13.9.

Cash lives: Oct 2012: Cash payments 40%, Debit cards 25%, Credit cards 17%, Checks and all other electronic-payment techniques made up the rest.

Apple (AAPL) makes up 8% of Nasdaq - Dec 2014

U.S. Treasury buyers? Due to Government changes in bank liquidity rules, banks bought $71B in 3rd Qtr 2014 bringing treasuries to their highest portion of total bank assets in this century equal to 20% of bank total assets. Even though treasury yields are low and will weigh on bank earnings.

Small caps: In 2013 the S&P600 was up 39.7%. 5Dec14 IBD: Small caps have lagged in this uptrend. The S&P600 is up 12% from its mid-October low vs a 16% gain in the Nasdaq.

Dec 2014: Britain's market has yet to recover the high set in 1999 and Germany's has been flat since midyear. Gold is down 36% from its September 2011 peak and oil has fallen more than 50% from its July 2008 record price.

Home prices across the United States (based upon new and existing home sales) at the end of September 2014 were at the same level that they first reached at the end of September 2005 or nine years ago (source: Office of Federal Housing Enterprise Oversight, BTN Research)

26Dec14 WSJ: Through November 2014, stocks had best 5 years at 19% compound annual return. 5 year cycles - Since 1930 there have been 10 5year up runs followed by major up's for 5 years - 3 times with starting Schiller P/E 12.3, 5 times up 4%/year with Schiller P/E 26.8. Schiller P/E currently 27!

Investment Wisdom 2015

Gold Price cycle: Typically run up for Chinese Lunar New Year (2015 - 2nd half of Feb). Chinese and Indians are half the global gold buyers.

Vanguard Balanced Index Fund (60% stocks, 40% bonds) returned 6.95% over past 10 years (04 - 14) vs S&P500's 7.7%. From (Oct07 to 9Mar09 lost 36% vs S&P500's -55%.

For every 1% increase in interest rates, the U.S. Government's interest payments will go up between $150-$175 billion.

57% of U.S. tech sales are overseas.

In 2014: Companies in the S&P500 paid $350B in dividends and made $553B in buybacks. U.S. company new share sales = $300B.

Oil: Global daily market = 93,000,000 barrels! Brent field after 40 years = 1,000BL/day

The Mystery Cycle

Years ending in 5 that coincide with the election cycle. Average annual returns since 1935:

S&P 500 index	=	11%
Year 3 of the election cycle	=	20.7%
Years ending in 5	=	28.4%
Year 3 + years ending in 5	=	42.4%

The Currency Effect - Over the past 12 months

iShares MSCI EMU ETF Lost 4.6% including dividends vs WisdomTree Europe Hedged Equity Fund Up 19%

They both have the same top 10 holdings

Since end of 2010 S&P500 companies increased earnings by 6.8% per year (30.3%) while EPS has grown 7.4% due to share buybacks (32.9%)

Thanks to fracking: February 2015 = produced 49% of Oil and 54% of natural gas.

2014 Taxes: The 3 million in the top 1% earned 17.1 % of total U.S. income and payed 45.7% of the total income tax.

May Day - The average total return for the S&P 500 during the month of May since 1990 has been a gain of 1.22 percent the sixth best performing month over the 25-year period.

Container shipping, a $6 Trillion industry that moves 95% the world's manufactured goods. Break even cost to move a 20 foot container from Asia to Europe = $1,300. 1 June 2015 rate was a record low of $ 342. Ships can now carry 18,000 containers and cost $ 185 million and are 1,309 foot long.

WSJ 5Jun15 - Swiss Re estimates Fed policy cost U.S. savers $470 billion in interest income through 2013.

June 2015	6months	1 Year	5 Years
Russell 1000 - LC	6.55%	12.73%	14.73%
" 2000 - SC	14.46%	8.21%	14.57%
" 3000 "	7.13%	12.37%	14.71%

2015 - S&P 500 is at its highest percentage of the GDP at 72%. The push to get more of the GDP into LC's so as to better be able to control them by the Government?

WSJ/15Jun15 - Warren Buffett's single best measure of stock market valuation: the ratio of the value of publicly traded companies in the U.S. to the countries gross national product. Currently company valuation is at 150% of GNP. The historic norm over the past 20 years = 119%. Buy when 70% to 80% and sell as it approaches 200%.

Since 1927 a 60/40 portfolio has been 99% correlated to the stock market. Bonds do not fluctuate enough relative to stocks to effect the stocks effect.

Swoon June: Down 9 of the last 11 years.

S&P 500 down on 30 June 2015 - the 9th consecutive month and a record for end of month down days.

Japan has an enormous national debt that leads the world as a percent of its GDP (226% of GDP versus 161% for Greece and 80% for the United States).

Data Point: IBD 10Jul15 - The Nasdaq and S&P500 are trading under the 50-day and 200-day line.

Arch Coal's stock is down 99.7% in the past 5 years.

Corporate buybacks: Not allowed in the 5 weeks leading up to their quarterly reports.

2nd Qtr reports started week of 6 July with 68. Number of S&P reporting in following weeks: 45, 132, 146 and 109.

AIER June15 - Total consumer debt relative to household income remains unchanged since 2007. Reduced credit card debt and car debt have been counterbalanced by greater college debt. And mortgage debt remains a serious problem. It has fallen a little bit, relative to household income, since 2007, but remains nearly double the level of 1989.

Moving forward, the big problem is that the Federal Reserve has hinted it will begin raising interest rates later this year. This would increase household debt payments, and make it even harder for them to de-leverage. Even worse, more than 1 million HAMP mortgages are starting to reset at higher rates, resulting in higher mortgage payments for these homeowners.

WSJ 27Jul15 - Six companies (Amazon, Google, Apple, Facebook, Netflix and Gilead) account for 53% of the Nasdaq's $664 billion market value gain through July 24!

IBD 30Jul15: S&P 500 in March 2009 = 666 vs 30Jul15 at 2,108 or 20% compound annual average return. Nasdaq from 1265 to 5111 good for 25% rate.

IBD 5Aug15: Apple at the end of June 2015 - nearly 4,900 mutual funds owned the stock plus 175 hedge funds, 2,600 advisors, about 176 banks etc. Apple accounted for 7.2% of the Nasdaq's total weighting.

WSJ 10Aug15 - Electricity from existing coal plants costs $38 per megawatt-hour; from new wind facilities, $106.

WSJ 26Aug15: China buys 1/8th of the world's oil, 1/4th of its gold, 1/3rd of its cotton and up to 1/2 of the major base metals.

24Aug15 - combined new lows hit 1,765, an astounding number. 25Aug - NYSE stocks above their 200 day line = 13%. 26Aug - major indexes up 4%.

Fairholme trailed more than 99% of peers in 2011, beat 99% in 2012 and then lagged behind 97% in 2014, according to data compiled by Bloomberg. This year, it's ahead of 97% of rivals. Since the fund was created at the end of 1999, it has returned 11% a year, compared with an annual gain of 3.9% for the S&P 500.

Commodities: The average broad based ETF has lost an average of 7.9% a year over the past 5 years. Aug 2014 to Aug 2015 - S&P GSCI down 43.1%, RJI down 33.4%,

Only need 4% or 5% to be covered.

From 24Mar2000 to 10Sep15: Vanguard Wellington +7.54/year = $10,000 to $32,000, S&P 500 ETF + 3.49%/year = $10K to $17K.,

AQR Managed Futures Strategic Fund @ 4%

Volkswagon emissions scandal: 23Sep15 - Platinum used for diesel engines hits near 7 year low @ $929.70/Oz vs Palladium used for gasoline engines up $34.15/Oz to $645.

Tax Data - The 5.56 million tax returns from 2013 that reported at least $200,000 of adjusted gross income (AGI) represent 3.8 percent of all returns filed, received 31.4 percent of all AGI nationwide and paid 55.2 percent of all the federal income tax that was paid in 2013 (source: Internal Revenue Service, BTN Research).

August 2015: Investors took out $9.22B from stock funds and $22.97B from bond funds.

Oct 2015: Financials make up 21.6% of the world market and 16.5% of the S&P500

Erosion: IBD 28Oct15 - AT&T's dividend = 5.6%! Over the past 20 years the S&P500 is up 256% vs AT&T's 19%.

A good starting point is Mebane Faber and Eric Richardson's Ivy Portfolio. In "The Ivy Portfolio: How to Invest Like the Top Endowments and Avoid Bear Markets" (John Wiley & Sons, 2011), they show that the world of endowment returns can boil down to five core asset classes, all of which are equal-weighted at 20%:

- Domestic equity: S&P 500 Total Return Index
- International equity: MSCI EAFE Total Return Index
- Real estate: FTSE NAREIT All Equity REITs Total Return Index
  Commodities: Goldman Sachs Commodity Index
  Bonds: Merrill Lynch 7–10 year Government Bond Index

Wealth is created by concentration, wealth is preserved via diversification.

The 7 Year Shemitah Cycle of the Jewish calendar.
7 years ago in 2008 = Financial crisis
14 " " "   2001 = terrorist attack with a recession & bear market
21 " " "   1994 = bond market panic

28 " " " 1987 = stock market crash
35 " " " 1980 = Gold & Silver prices peaked.

Will precious metals bottom in 2015?????????????

1901-1902 Shmita Year - 46% U.S. Stock market value wiped out.

1916-1917 Shmita Year - 40% U.S. Stock market value wiped out. German, Austro-Hungarian, Russian and Ottoman Empires collapsed. Britain, the world's greatest empire was almost bankrupt. The beginning of American to rise to world power. All during this one Shmita year.

1930-1931 Shmita Year - 86% U.S stock market value wiped out in the worst financial crisis in modern history.

1937-1938 Shmita Year - 50% U.S. Stock market value wiped out. Global recession.

1944-1945 Shmita Year - End of German Reich and Britain's hold on territories. Establishment of America as the world's super power.

1965-1966 Shmita Year - 23% stock market value wiped out.

1972-1973 Shmita Year - 48% U.S. Stock market value wiped out. Global recession. U.S. Voted to kill its unborn children (Abortion legalized). U.S. lost its first war - Vietnam...

1979-1980 Shmita Year - U.S. and global recession.

1986-1987 Shmita Year - 33% U.S. Stock market value wiped out.

1993-1994 Shmita Year - Bond market crash.

2000-2001 Shmita Year - 37% U.S. stock market value wiped out. 9/11 and Global recession.

2007-2008 Shmita Year - 50% U.S. Stock market value wiped out. Global recession.

2014-2015 Shmita Year - Rebellion/same sex marriages...very severe judgment coming (See 7x7 Shmita Harbingers)

U.S. stocks (S&P 500) are +2.4% YTD with international equities (ACWI ex-U.S.) -3.9%YTD.

The largest 50 companies in the S&P 500 are +7.7% YTD, while the smallest companies (451-500) are -8.4% YTD

The Last Six Months - The current bull market (ongoing since reaching a bear market low on March 9, 2009) is the 11th bull for the S&P 500 since 1950. In the previous 10 bulls, the final six months of the bull market produced an average 13.3 percent gain (source: BTN Research).

U.S. corporations have been paying a smaller and smaller share of federal taxes! The reason is that there a fewer and fewer corporations. For the past few decades the number of pass-through businesses have greatly increased in number. They pay through the individual income tax code.

The Last Month - Of the last 25 Decembers, 21 have produced a positive total return for the S&P 500. The average December performance since 1990 is a gain of 2.0 percent, the best of any month (source: BTN Research).

Above Average - The ongoing bull market for the S&P 500 is the 11th for the index since 1950 and has reached 6.7 years in length. The average length of all 11 bulls since 1950 is five years (source: BTN Research).

Almost All Seniors - Of Americans age 65 or older, 88 percent received a monthly Social Security benefit payment during fiscal year 2015 (i.e., the 12 months ending Sept. 30, 2015), either in the form of a monthly retirement benefit, a survivor benefit or a disability benefit (source: Social Security Administration, BTN Research).

Not Big Earners - Of the 52.8 million tax returns filed in 2013 that did not pay any federal income tax, 85 percent reported less than $30,000 of adjusted gross income (source: Internal Revenue Service, BTN Research).

IBD 8Oct15: Business investment deemed lackluster by Jason Furman, WhiteHouse chief economist. In 2014 business invested $2.2 Trillion with AT&T $21.2B, Verizon $16B and Exxon $12.4B.

The Impact of Inflation - An adjusted gross income (AGI) of $80,580 was required to rank in the top 1 percent of U.S. taxpayers in 1980. An AGI of $74,955 was required to rank in the top 25 percent of U.S. taxpayers in 2013 (source: Internal Revenue Service, BTN Research).

Ten Years, No Growth - The median sales price of existing homes sold nationwide during the month of October 2015 was $219,600. The median sales price of existing homes sold nationwide during the month of October 2005 (i.e.,10 years ago) was $229,000 (source: National Association of Realtors, BTN Research).

Outside the United States - For the average company within the S&P 500, 48 percent of the revenue is derived from sales made to foreign buyers. Of the technology companies within the S&P 500, 59 percent of the revenue is derived from sales made to foreign buyers (source: S&P Dow Jones Indices, BTN Research).

Middle Class defined: Top 20%, Bottom 20% and the middle class the middle 60%.

Calculated in this manner, the middle class will never shrink!

Its 2015 income spread = $21,000 to $106,000. The NY Times $35,000 - $100,000.

2015: Last 12 months (Nov to Dec) gasoline sales decline 10.9% = $100B not spent.

Third Quarter 2015, Americans Lost $1.2 Trillion in wealth (mostly stock market)

15Dec2015 - England closes its last coal mine. From 1954's 217M tons (1,330 deep mines) to 2014's 3.7M tons, Left below is some 30M tons. Demand for coal is projected to rise until 2040. UK production cost $ 65 per ton vs $45 for imported coal!

U.S. stocks posted their worst annual performance since 2008, closing out a rocky year that tempered investors' expectations for gains in 2016.

The Dow Jones Industrial Average, a basket of 30 stocks, lost 2.2% in 2015, while the broader S&P 500 fell 0.7%.

The S&P's loss ended three years of double-digit gains for the index, but was far from the nearly 40% dive it took in 2008.

Sell when down 7% or goes below 50 day average.

VIX above 20, sell covered calls

The S&P 500 is market cap weighted: Apple, Microsoft, Facebook, Amazon, JNJ while the DJIA is price weighted: Boeing, Goldman Sachs, 3M, UNH, Apple.

2016 - Investment Wisdom

The 2015 / 2009 page $1.1T consolidated omnibus spending bill violated every promise that Republicans made to the voters who rewarded them with landslide victories in 2010 and 2014.

2015 the worst year for the S&P 500 since the start of the bull market in 2009

From March 12, 2009 through 2015: compounded annual returns Nasdaq 20.5%, S&P 500 16%.

Distorting the U.S. economy: Federal Reserve' s balance sheet went from $905 B in Sept 2008 to $4.5T or 1/4th of the U.S. economy by 2015. Via QE the Fed bought 61% of all treasuries issued, peaking at close to 80% in 2014! This has led to the miss pricing of the true cost of credit below its natural level and distorts the integrity of prices and exchange rates.

Lack of business confidence is what economists call "regime uncertainty". Low interest rates for borrowing money have companies using cash and cheap borrowing to buy back shares (not to invest in new ventures). Stock buybacks have been the key to the bull market.

Crude oil prices dropped 46% in 2014 and 30% in 2015. Further drop could signal a recession and a bear market.

Apple sales in China: In 2009 2% of Apple's revenue vs 25% in 2015. Growing middle class!!!

10-year Treasury yields bottomed at 1.43% in July 2012. Since then, rates have meandered irregularly higher as economic growth advanced and the Fed continued to make slow moves toward normalization."

For the first time in almost 40 years, U.S. equities experience a single-digit percentage change for the second year in a row. "It is especially rare for equities to deliver single-digit returns in consecutive years 2014 and 2015. This last happened in the U.S. in 1977 and 1978. A large upside move or large downside move is unlikely given the crosscurrents."

Stocks outperform bonds for the fifth consecutive year. Overweight in equities versus bonds, and would be especially wary of U.S. Treasuries."

Information technology, financial and telecommunication services outperform energy, materials and utilities.

The federal budget deficit rises in dollars and as a percentage of GDP for the first time in seven years.

2013 was a great year for stocks and still saw two down months. 2008 was a terrible year and still saw four up months.

Apple Computer comprises about 3.7 percent of the S&P 500. Microsoft and Exxon, the next two largest companies as of this writing, comprise about 2 percent of the Index each.

A look at nine funds from a 2011 article titled "Best Large Blend Funds for the Long Term" from U.S. News. Ending November 2015, those funds had returns that averaged 11.29 percent. Compare that with S&P 500 index funds that returned 14.36 percent (Vanguard), 14.27 percent (SPDR), and 14.30 percent (Fidelity Spartan). Investors are going to continue to recognize the underperformance of actively managed funds.

"Supply Side" reforms, include corporate tax cuts, shutdown of over capacities, and elimination of "zombie" corporations. These reform measures—if implemented—would be very bullish for the Chinese economy over the long term, although short-term pains could be possible. History has shown that stock markets usually embrace supply-side reforms with rising prices. This is because supply-side reforms usually lead to a more efficient economy with improving corporate profitability, stronger growth, and increasing resilience. 10Jan16 - So-called Chinese H-shares, which are Chinese companies that are listed in Hong Kong, trading at a P/E ratio of 5-6 times.

Jan 2016 - Canadian heavy oil @ $14 a barrel!

Home ownership at 50 year low, 22% unemployment, velocity of money never lower

College education cost up 1,134% since 1978 / 10 times COL, only 37% of loans up to date, 1/2 of graduates in jobs that do not require degree.

Saudi set lowest prices strategy for their oil on 27 November 2014.

Gold mine production dipped by 1% in the third quarter 2015. Globally, mines produced 827.8 metric tons of gold. That was below 2014's record third quarter production of 836.1 metric tons. It's also the first dip in production since 2008.

USA Today, 11Jan16: Percent down from 52 week high; Large cap -21.3%, Mid cap -25.3%, small cap -29.2% and overall -25.5%

Avoid the Worst - The total return for the S&P 500 was a gain of 1.4 percent (total return) in 2015. If you avoided the three worst percentage days last year, the 1.4 percent gain rises to 12.3 percent gain (source: BTN Research)

	VIX	Down
2008 / 9	80	38%
2011	50	15%
2015 Aug	40	10%
2016 23Jan	27	10%

Last crash was in 2008 = 8 Yrs
PUT on S&P 500 SPY?

In the last five years the growth of credit to government has gone up thirty-seven percent, growth of credit to corporations thirty-two percent, growth of credit to small businesses and households only six percent. As you know, small and new enterprises are where the bulk of the jobs are created. So the Fed is in the business of credit allocation. That is profoundly wrong and must be changed.

2015 Summary: It's also helpful to realize that over any given period of time, some investing styles will be in favor and some will be out of favor. The U.S. markets provided a good example of this last year. The S&P 500 Growth index gained 5.5%, whereas S&P 500 Value fell by 3.1%. (The two indexes separate the S&P 500 into growth and value buckets.) Similarly, the large-cap S&P 500 gained 1.4%, while the S&P SmallCap 600 lost 2.0% and the Russell 2000 fell by 4.4%. Even among large-cap stocks disparity existed, with shares of the largest companies as measured by market capitalization faring better than their comparatively smaller-sized large-cap brethren. In very simple terms, large-cap growth was in, while small-cap value was out. Depending on its objective and strategy, a fund either did better than average or worse than average—often through no fault of its manager.

Biotech: Jan 2016 Down 20%. Crude oil down 70% since June 2014

Stock buybacks have totaled more than $6.9 trillion since 2004. Over the past decade, the companies that make up the S&P 500 have spent 54% of profits on stock buybacks.

Last year, U.S. corporations spent about $700 billion, or roughly 4% of U.S. GDP, to prop up their share prices by repurchasing their own stock.

Year to year (Feb 15 - 16) 100% increase in MA foreclosures

Ups and Downs - The S&P 500 has gained 9.7 percent per year (total return) over the past 50 years (1966-2015) in spite of suffering through eight bear markets of at least a 20 percent decline each time (source: BTN Research).

In 2012, the U.S. shipped more oil fuels, including gasoline, diesel, kerosene and jet fuel, than any other single export for the second year in a row. The U.S. exported more than $117 billion of fuel and petroleum products in 2012, a 9 percent increase over 2011. In fact, in 2011 and 2012, the U.S. exported more fuels than we imported, and that hasn't happened since 1949.

U.S. mortgage debt as of December 2015 = $13.7T!

Baltic Dry Index 2008 = 11,793. On 18Jan2016 = 394.

14Jan16, The Hellenic Shipping News proclaimed "New low on Baltic-Dry Index could bring Indian Ocean trade to a halt." Note that it costs a ship operator about $50,000 a day to operate while underway. But given current record-low freight rates, they receive only about $15,000 a day to haul cargo. Unable to cover operating costs let alone debt service.

On 12Jan16: Saudi Oil = $26/BBL. Canadian heavy oil = $8.35/BBL. Low quality North Dakota sour crude sold for $1.50/BBL = a disposal problem,

The key feature of hedging assets is that their price at any given moment isn't based on the present value of future cash flows, as in stocks, but on supply and demand. That makes the markets for such assets quite different from stock markets, since without a cash flow, it's impossible to value them. They're only worth what the next buyer is willing to pay, and they may not be very liquid in the short term.

Feb 2016: According to the results of a global fund manager survey by Bank of America Merrill Lynch, average cash positions have reached 5.6%, the highest level since November 2001. BofA Merrill Lynch chief investment strategist Michael Hartnett described the findings as a contrarian indicator and therefore an "unambiguous buy signal."

Taxes - The top 10 percent of taxpayers in 2013 earned at least $127,695 in adjusted gross income (AGI), reported 45.87 percent of all AGI nationwide and paid 69.80 percent of all federal income tax (source: Internal Revenue Service, BTN Research).

World produces 97M barrels of oil daily. The U.S. uses 20MBBL daily. We now save an estimated $1.57B daily or $570B per year vs our annual budget deficit of $544B!

Feb 16: There are only 113 companies on the S&P 500—just 22% of them—that are trading above their 200-day MAs. This is the lowest number since 2011. The Dow Jones Industrial Average has shed 2,300 points (or 13%) since its May 2015 high. Almost 100% of the portfolios of institutional investors were invested in stocks. Now, that number is only 22%.

Woody Allen playing a stockbroker said, "I help other people with their investments until there's nothing left."

24Feb16 IBD: Nasdaq's oil shares = less than 1% vs S&P 500's 6.6%. The Russell 2000 remains more than 20% off its high - traditionally a bear market indicator

2016 - Warren Buffett "I never keep less than $20B in cash".

Gold & Silver tutorial: 2015 average production costs: Silver $17/oz & Gold $1,150/oz. Fully 55% of all silver produced is a byproduct of the mining of copper, lead and zinc with 13% from gold mining. In 2015 silver output fell in Chile by 4.6%, U.S.A. by 6.5% and Canada by 20%.

Canadian Silver Production: In 2001, U.S. and Canadian silver production totaled 96.6 M oz and that year Silver Eagle and Maple Leaf sales totaled 9.2 M oz. A surplus of 87.4M Oz. In 2015 Mine supply was 48.8 M oz vs US & Canadian coin sales 75 M oz = a deficit of 26.2 M oz!

IBD 50: From its July 2015 peak to its Feb 2016 low, it lost 26% = composition change

Withholding tax collections (FICA) have fallen between 7 and 8% from the previous year, and they've been going down more rapidly. As of 18Feb16, the annual rate of change was minus 5.6% in nominal terms, which is the corresponding period of a year before, and then it was down minus 3.7 % from the week before. In the month before, it was only 0.6 %. So, if you go back into last year, there was a period when the peak, which was February 2015, showed an increase in employment tax receipts. Actual money in the till paid by employers for their employee compensation was up to 8.7% over the 2014 number.

CapEx has changed from investment in actual physical production to investing in financial engineering. Therefore when companies have to cut back, there is no CapEx thus employees will have to be cut to save money. Example of how it is supposed to occur: IBD 29Feb16 - Shale Firms Stop Fracking, Whiting ceasing well completions and will cut its '16 capex by 80%. Apache sees capex down over 60% in '16.

IBD 20Feb16: To its February low, the IBD 50 declined more than 26% from a peak in July 2015 - the largest decline in the index since its inception in 2011. REITS arrive!

Auto Registrations down 7M since 2005

Per 21Mar15 Forbes: There are over 10 billion U.S. $100 bills in circulation worldwide.

U.S. Bull Markets: Oct '90 - Mar '00 = the longest @ 113 months
                     Oct '02 - Oct '07 = Shortest @ 60 months
Current   Mar '09 - Mar '16 = 84 months and the 3rd longest
                     so far.

Draghi's 10Mar16 Big Gun announcement (deposit rate to -0.4% and 20B more buy back = Immediate market reaction Euro down to $1.083, 3 hours later, Euro rebounds to $1.12. Bank shares close up less than 1% and Euro Stoxx index down 1.4%.

Day rates for Capesize vessels 180,000 tons capacity, in 2008 = $200,000 per day vs 2016's $3,000. China's imports of cement down 46% and iron ore down 38% since 2015. Valemax vessels 360,000 tons capacity were introduced in 2010, only 18 of the 60 planned were built and all are now Chinese owned controlling 30% of iron ore moved

Tracking Error: a 1-for-10 reverse split was announced this week for VelocityShares 3x Long Crude Oil ETN (UWTI). This exchange-traded note was designed to deliver three times the return of the S&P GSCI Crude Oil Index. Reverse splits (which replace cheaper-priced shares with fewer higher-priced shares) only occur when the share price has dropped too far and there isn't an expectation of a significant rebound in the near future. According to a Barron's blog post yesterday, the ETN is "down 32% so far this year, even though crude oil prices have rocketed nearly 40% from their lows last month." The disparity of returns is known as tracking error—ignore it and you won't like the impact it will have on your portfolio. Mar 2016.

14Mar16: the VIX's 1-year moving average pushed above its 5-year average. "The last time this happened back in 2007, a year later, the S&P 500 was down about 40%," he warned. "For the overall equity market this could be a bearish sign."

From March 2009 through January 2016, investors have yanked a net $189.7 billion from open-ended stock funds. Investors have sold a net $623 billion from U.S. stock funds since March 2009, according to the Investment Company Institute, the funds' trade group. Corporate earnings have risen 282% since the start of the bull market, even more than stock prices as a whole.

Mar16 - Peabody Energy, the largest coal producer in America, could go bankrupt in the next few months. Last year, it lost $2 billion. And this week, it filed a report to regulators and warned that it could go down.

22Mar16 IBD: The Biotech group has 414 names, only 19 (5%) have market caps over $1B. In the 21st Century you need to be over $3B in market cap to be even considered for small-cap status.

Mar16: David Stockman calls the S&P 500 to 1,300!

Japan's, China's and Taiwan's exports drop 15% in the 4th quarter.

Debt: USGovt = $3T, USPrivate = $40.2T, ECB = $3T. the result will not be inflation but deflation via de-leveraging the debt. Govts would prefer hyper inflation.

The S&P 500 index down 5.0% in January 16. Small-cap value stocks, usually strongest in January, down even more at –9.3% [as measured by the Guggenheim S&P SmallCap 600 Pure Value (RZV) All this coming off the worst pre-election year since the great depression.

Portfolio Rebalancing NOT recommended by AAII. Results from 1988 to 2015:

> Rebalance @5% thresholds, Annual Return 9.1%
> No rebalancing = 9.3
> Sell when S&P500 down 20% = 7.5

In 1900 the U.S A was 60% rural.

Per Harry Dent, the commodity cycle is 30 years. Gold hit its last peak in 1980 with best quarter in 1986!

The National Debt - The total debt of the U.S. government as of 15 March 2016 was $19.16 trillion, consisting of $13.84 trillion of debt held by the public and another $5.32 trillion of intergovernmental debt (source: Treasury Department, BTN Research).

Lay Down Rigs - The total oil and gas rig count in the United States (both offshore and on land) was 480 as of Friday, March 11 2016, down 31 percent YTD (from 698 as of Dec. 31, 2015). The 480 operating rigs is the lowest number recorded in the 21st century in the United States (i.e., since Jan. 1, 2001) (source: Baker Hughes, BTN Research).

In the just completed fourth quarter 2015, the blended earnings decline was -3.3%. This marks the first time the S&P 500 has reported three consecutive quarters of year-over-year declines in earnings since the three quarters beginning in 2009. (Source: "Earnings Insight," FactSet, February 26, 2016.)

Earnings in the first quarter of 2016 are expected to decline by 8.7% year-over-year. This will represent the fourth consecutive quarter of declines and the longest losing streak since the fourth quarter of 2008 through to the third quarter of 2009. (Source: "Earnings Insight," FactSet, March 18, 2016.)

From Preformed Line Products 2015 annual report: "Worse yet. are the misguided governmental decisions to destroy their manufacturing base and therefore demand for electricity and hence demand for new transmission lines."

Consumers are loading up on debt like it's 2008 all over again. The average household with credit card debt is at $7,800.

The PowerShares Buyback Achievers ETF (PKW), which tracks U.S. companies that have repurchased 5 percent or more of their outstanding shares over the past 12 months, is flat this year, underperforming the S&P 500. Meanwhile, the iShares Select Dividend ETF (DVY), which follows stocks with consistently high dividend yields, has risen 9 percent in 2016.

Student Loan debt = $ 1.2T. 43% are in default!

Bank of America's strongest earnings quarter is typically Q1.

It's all about the cyclical "El Niño — La Niña" ocean cooling and warming phenomenon in the Pacific. Weather forecasters and grain growers are abuzz about the expected shift over the next 12 months to the colder, drier weather that comes with the La Niña phase, and its impact on grain production in the U.S. and worldwide.

For instance, 2010 through 2012 saw growing seasons with consecutive La Niña conditions that resulted in drought across much of the Midwest. The result was a huge rally, as both corn and wheat doubled in price.

The big question is the timing of La Niña. If it starts this summer, the crop yields for U.S. and Canadian-grown wheat, as well as corn and soybeans, could take a big hit. If it starts in the fall or winter, then other global food exporters like Argentina and Brazil (in the middle of the southern hemisphere's growing seasons) would see a major impact.

According to the latest USDA estimates, China now stores 53%, or 111 million tons, of the entire global inventory of corn, and nearly 40%, or 94 million tons, of global wheat stocks!

Since 2008, there have been 606 global interest-rate cuts, alongside $12.4 trillion in "quantitative easing" — all designed to fix a global economy that Smith's "invisible hand" was perceived to be unable to correct? April 2016

Sector Performance: In the last 12 recessions since WWII: Utilities, Health Care and Consumer Staples were the best performers! In contrast, in up markets: Consumer Discretionary, Technology and Industrials outperformed.

The nine low-correlated primary sectors: basic materials, financials, real estate, Treasury bonds, technology, utilities, health care, gold and energy.

All other sectors are highly correlated to one of these nine.

U.S. economy growing: Hold DIA, QQQ and SPY

Low growth + high volatility: DVY

Americans will pay $3.3 trillion in federal taxes and $1.6 trillion in state and local taxes, for a total bill of almost $5.0 trillion, or 31 percent of the nation's income.

Americans will collectively spend more on taxes in 2016 than they will on food, clothing and housing combined.

In calendar year 2016, the deficit will grow significantly, from $592 billion to $698 billion. If we include this annual federal borrowing, which represents future taxes owed, Tax Freedom Day would occur 16 days later on May 10.

Time Flies - The S&P 500 bull market that began on March 9, 2009, is now in its 86th month. The average bull market for the stock index since 1950 (including the current bull) has lasted 60 months (source: BTN Research).

No Progress Made - After adjusting past numerical data for the impact of inflation, the median household income today ($53,657) is lower than the median household income ($54,443) from 1997 (source: Federal Reserve Bank of St. Louis, BTN Research).

The Last Bull-Market Pillar Collapses
Share buybacks are an integral part of the market, pumping more than $2.7 trillion into Wall Street since 2009. With buybacks fading amid an earnings recession, the bull market may be on its last legs.

College-education costs have risen 1,134% since 1978, when the Bureau of Labor Statistics started tracking it. That price has gone up 10 times faster than the cost of a new car. Right now, there is a total of $1.1 trillion in student loans. According to Bloomberg, only 37% of all student loan borrowers are up to date on their payments. Here's why: More than half of America's recent college graduates are either unemployed or working in a job that doesn't require a college degree.

Over the last month alone, foreign countries have dropped $56 billion in U.S. Treasuries. Japan, China, Belgium, Switzerland, the United Kingdom, Mexico, France, Germany and even Israel are bailing on us.

Minimum Volatility ETF's: USMV 1st Qtr 16: S&P500 down 10.3% vs USMV down 4.8% then on the up cycle 90% of S&P500.

Utilities in a heavy duty bear market: From Jan to Oct 2008 Dow Utilities down 47%.

April 21, 2016: FOMO is the "fear of missing out." TINA stands for the notion that "there is no alternative" to equities right now. There are legitimate reasons to dislike this kind of price action—earnings are terrible, the economy is slowing, and low oil prices may reflect lackluster demand in the world economy. Yet, FOMO and TINA are fueling investor appetite for stocks, some analysts argue. According to American Association of Individual Investors, market participants shifted cash into equities last month, raising their stock allocation to 64%, above its long-term average of 60%. Meanwhile, cash allocation fell to 18.5%, below the historical average of 24%.

22Apr16 IBD: Philadelphia Fed's first ever survey on regulatory costs said that manufacturers are now spending more money on regulatory compliance than they do on data and network security, or on equipment and workers!

This Year - The U.S. budget deficit for the first six months of fiscal year (FY) 2016 (i.e., the 12 months ending Sept. 30, 2016) was $461.04 billion (source: Treasury Department, BTN Research).

Tax Data - The top one-tenth of 1 percent of U.S. taxpayers (based upon adjusted gross income) paid more federal income tax ($228 billion) during tax year 2013 (the latest year tax information has been released) than the federal income tax ($169 billion) paid by the bottom 75 percent of taxpayers (source: Internal Revenue Service, BTN Research).

Hardly Robust - The Gross Domestic Product (GDP) of the United States grew by 2.4 percent in 2015. The GDP of the Eurozone, i.e., the 19 countries that use the Euro as their common currency, grew by 1.6 percent in 2015 (source: Commerce Department, BTN Research).

4May16: Mr. Buffett's advice for a mini-ETF portfolio — let's call it the "Buffett Special." Simply allocate 90% of your money to the Vanguard S&P 500 ETF (VOO) and 10% to the iShares 1-3 Year Treasury Bond ETF (SHY).

A roughly 10% increase in volatility correlated with a 3.3% increase in sales volume for the top 0.1% of earners, relative to less-affluent investors. When the VIX went up 25%, proportionate selling by the ultra-rich rose almost 8%.

Americans own almost $5 trillion in Treasury bonds, all told. That's more than twice as much as China, Japan and all the oil exporting countries put together.

"Commodities peaked in July 2008, collapsed to February 2009, rallied hard to April 2011 and then collapsed again to January 2016," he added. "This year they've been very strong, but it's been a punishing secular bear market that may have either ended this year or taken a long-term siesta."

Priced in gold, the U.S. stock market is not even close to where it was in the year 2000.

By 2020, Gen X and millennial's will control more than half of all investable assets — about $30 trillion, according to a recent survey by PricewaterhouseCoopers.

20% of hedge funds go out of business annually

The U.S. financial sector represented around 4% of the U.S. economy in 1980. It's now double that. Despite currently taking around 25% of all corporate profits, it creates a mere 4% of all jobs.

There are typically more than 100 new highs on the Dow between recessions. In 2013, 52, in 2014, 38 and 2015, 6 = 96!!!!!!!! In 2016, up to 11 May, investors had reduced their holdings of U.S. equity mutual funds and exchange-traded funds was $67.7Billion.

June 2016, S&P 500 has a trailing p/e ratio of 18.5, vs its 10-year average of 15.8.

Recently - Rounding to the nearest dollar, collective earnings of the companies in the S&P 500 index for the last five years have been $87 (2011), $87 (2012), $100 (2013), $102 (2014) and $87 (2015). Earnings results used are "as reported earnings per share" which includes nonrecurring revenues and expenses (source: S&P, BTN Research).

1988 - 2016: cost of living has doubled, annual dividend payout on a unit of the S&P has climbed not quite 5 fold, from $9 to $44. In 1988 you paid $29 to get a dollar of annual income from dividends. Now you pay $48. BUY 2/3rds into SCHB,50 and 1/3rd in VXUS,46.

The S&P500 since 1926 when measured against foreign based stocks has come out ahead 82% of the time (6.5%) in the second half election cycle. - BUY SCHB,50

Remember: Knowledge not experience, Cost not fees, commissions or charges, Financial security not financial freedom, works as advertised not "new", a financial strategy not a financial solution.

Skousen: In the midst of the collapse in oil prices and the sharp slowdown in China, the Federal Reserve under Chair Janet Yellen has turned on the spigots. The money supply (M2) is growing at a 9% clip, double the rate of a year ago. The Fed's decision to raise rates has impacted the bond market too, reducing the yields of longer-term Treasuries and mortgages. The situation indicates little inflation on the horizon. It appears the Fed is determined to reignite inflation and get the economy going again. That's bullish for stocks, gold, real estate, and our portfolio in 2016... precious metals have shown strength after analysts predicted the Fed won't be raising rates again this year due to the global slowdown. Gold is now around $1,250 an ounce. All of this adds up to the beginning of a new golden bull market.

Double Plus - Government outlays for Medicare have increased 9.8 percent annually over the past 40 fiscal years, rising from $13 billion (1975) to $546 billion (2015). Inflation, as measured by the Consumer Price Index, has increased 3.7 percent annually over the same 40-year period (source: OMB, Department of Labor, BTN Research).

A Decade Away - America's total public debt is projected to be 85.6 percent of GDP in 2026 or 10 years from now (source: Congressional Budget Office, BTN Research).

Sounds More Like Deflation - The annual inflation target for the 19-nation Eurozone is 2 percent. Actual year-over-year inflation, however, was negative 0.2 percent (i.e., deflation) as of April 30, 2016, and negative 0.1 percent as of May 31, 2016 (source: Eurostat, BTN Research).

Silver is the BEST natural biocide against some 400 viruses & bacteria. There is only about 1B Oz of silver above ground vs 4 to 5B Gold. Silver has gone down from 83 to 1Jul16 1344 vs 19.85 = 67 relation to gold and expected to get down to 50???

The S&P 500 has closed at its calendar year high in the second half of the year (i.e., from July-December) 73 percent of the time since 1950. In 14 of the last 25 years, the index's calendar year high has occurred during December.

Gold's preservation of purchasing power: The same quantity of gold that a Roman centurion earned annually under Emperor Augustus (27 B.C. to A.D. 14) would cover one years pay ($46,500 to $64,000) for a U.S. Army captain today.

Gold: In the first 6 months of 2016, the SPDR Gold Trust took in $12.2 B - more than all U.S. stock ETF's combined.

Is It Legal?

There's no legal obstacle to buying gold overseas. Ditto for buying it here and sending it abroad. And there's certainly nothing illegal about storing it privately. The fundamental reason for this is that gold bullion isn't money. That means it isn't subject to the sorts of reporting requirements of actual currency. If you bring into or send out of the U.S. "negotiable monetary instruments" (i.e., currency from any country, personal checks (endorsed), traveler's checks, non-collectible gold coins, securities or stocks in bearer form) valued at $10,000 or more, a "Report of International Transportation of Currency or Monetary Instruments" form FinCEN 105 must be submitted to U.S. Customs and Border Protection. If you don't and they find out about it, they will take it away from you — permanently. Bullion gold, on the other hand, is a "commodity" like any other. It isn't currency. When it comes to reporting to Uncle Sam, $10,000 worth of gold is no different from $10,000 worth of corn, car tires or paintings. That means you can ship it in and out of the U.S. without being obliged to tell anyone.

12 Jul 2016: DJIA has first record close since May 2015, its 109th in this bull run at 18,347.67!

Obama's 2012 Korean-U.S. Free Trade Agreement boosted our trade deficit by $16B and unemployment by 130,000.

According to the Bureau of Labor Statistics: Over the first 6 months of 2016 the economy created 1M new jobs while the working population increased by 1.5M.

Real median household income dropped from $57,601 in january to $56,853 in May.

WSJ 22Jul16: Fair Trade? - new U.S. government tariffs on steel reduced steel imports into the U.S. by 19.8% this year to 12.2M tons = benchmark hot-rolled coil index at $629 per ton in the U.S. up 36% from 12 months ago.

After all, stock securities— part of the shadow financial economy — are not real economic wealth. They are claims on future output. When you pay high prices for those financial claims, as many people have done in recent years, it all but guarantees low future returns. Likewise, another part of the shadow financial economy — pension funds — are doomed. To break even, the average public pension plan requires an annual return of 7.69%, repeatedly, year after year. Not Happening

ETF July 16: $617M out of Technology and $$1.2B into Real Estate.

SPHD in, SPY out.

The Great Depression and the Great Recession recoveries were frustrated by "Progressive" policies of overspending, overtaxing, and over regulation by government that suppressed freedom and economic growth disappeared. Note: Of the 30 economic contractions since 1870, only two failed to have strong rebounds after recessions. They are labeled "Great" because of the long period of suffering they caused.

Why Islam can win in America. Progressives have defined themselves out of existence. They reject traditional American culture and as such there is nothing for immigrants to adopt. They have no traditional habits or morals. Modern progressivism, based on the "unlimited sovereignty of the individual" will not allow the individual to be defined by anything external to him.

In order for silver to match its January 1980 peak ($49.50) in CPI-adjusted terms (which arguably understates real-world inflation), prices would have to climb to $144/oz.

While we are not there yet (15Aug16), those three — the Utilities Select Sector SPDR (NYSE Arca: XLU, buy below $48.50), the SPDR Dow Jones REIT ETF (NYSE Arca: RWR, buy below $95) and the iShares Core High Dividend ETF (NYSE Arca: HDV, buy below $79) — have declined 3.8%, 2.1% and 0.88% since then, respectively.

Aug 2016 - Neumeyer notes that silver is being mined at a rate globally of 9 ounces for every 1 ounce of gold. Yet it currently takes 68 ounces of silver to buy an ounce of gold in the spot market. First Majestic's CEO is betting that the gold:silver price ratio will over time move toward the 9:1 mined ounces ratio. That implies a HUGE outperformance in silver prices going forward.

Central banks have failed in their efforts to save Western economies. Proof of that rests in the fact that despite more than $12 trillion in quantitative easing measures by major central banks in recent years (that's a sum of money equal to 15% of the global economy), we still have lethargic growth all over the West, including in America, and we have negative interest rates covering roughly a third of the world. They are now buying some 80B euro's of private equity monthly!

CMS, the Centers for Medicare and Medicaid Services, the Federal agency that spends more than $1 trillion annually on health care for the poor, elderly and disabled. The worlds largest buyer of heart stents, hospital stays, arthritis pills, knee replacements etc.

Twenty years ago in 1996, there were 8,000 publicly traded stocks trading on the NYSE, Nasdaq and other exchanges. Today, that number has dropped to around 3,700 stocks.

At the end of 2015, the total value of the world's stock markets was about $67T vs the global bond market of $88T per the World Federation of Exchanges.

In 1996 China's debt was $500B vs the $30T in 2016.

2016 is the third-most overbought U.S. market in history after 2000 and 1929.

Modern Portfolio Theory came out in 1952 - 64 years ago / 10 Presidents

According to Ned Davis Research, the S&P 500 posts its weakest returns in the first year of the four-year election cycle. Since 1900, stocks have gained just 3.4% on average in the post-election year, compared with gains of 4.0% in the midterm year, 11.3% in the pre-election year and 9.5% in an election year.

Chile's pension fund's performance: Annual pension fund returns averaged 12.3% in the 1980s, 10.4% in the 1990s, 6.3% in the 2000s and just 4.3% since 2010. This is a problem that affects all pension fund and insurance companies throughout the developed and developing world.

30Aug16: The ongoing bull market for the S&P 500 (now in its 90th month) has achieved 118 all-time closing highs, the most recent occurring Monday, Aug. 15

Sept 16: As the second-quarter earnings season comes to an end, there's one thing that immediately jumps out: Stock prices are out of whack from their core value — earnings. According to FactSet, a financial research company that compiles financial data, earnings for stocks that make up the S&P 500 Index declined for the fifth straight consecutive quarter — the worst consecutive decline since the Great Recession.

But, as I have pointed out before, this is based on a company's reported bottom line, which ends up being distorted and manipulated extensively. When you step back and simply look at operating income, the second quarter actually marks the seventh straight decline in income for S&P 500 companies — i.e., the situation wasn't even this bad during the financial collapse of 2008. This gives you an idea of how dire most of the top corporate companies' income really is and sets the stage for the next financial collapse — which is where the out-of-whack part comes in.

Granted, United States now has a trade deficit with Mexico, but as the Wharton report states, "the U.S. runs a trade deficit with 90% of the countries in the world. So Mexico is not unique. In fact, the U.S. also runs a deficit with Canada, and that's mostly because of oil and gas." The auto sector has seen the most dramatic change. According to the Wharton report, Japan exported almost twice as many cars to the United States as did Mexico in 2008. Now, however, Mexico exports close to two million vehicles to the United States annually, surpassing Japan and Canada. By 2020, 25% of all North American vehicle production will take place in Mexico, compared to 10% in Canada and 65% in the United States.

Since 2008, Travelers' sales have grown by a spectacularly mediocre 1.5% a year. Yet earnings per share are up 93%. Incredible! Only it was sleight of hand. Travelers reduced its share count over the period by 48%. Reducing shares by half allowed the company to essentially double earnings on a business that didn't grow much at all. Travelers' P/E ratio would essentially double to 21 from 11, way too expensive for a company where net income has actually declined on sales that barely progressed. Sept 16 - Sovereign Investor

From the beginning of 2008 through today, the 30 companies inside the Dow have spent $1 trillion buying back their shares. That's nearly half of the $2.15 trillion in profits they earned. In the same period, they also paid out just shy of $775 billion in dividends.

Inclusive of dividends and buybacks, the Dow 30 companies have less than 18% of their profits remaining to reinvest in the business or employees. Recent numbers are even more egregious. The Manipulation Game So far this year, the Dow 30 companies have spent $337 billion on dividends and buybacks — 117% of their profits. They're paying/spending more than they're earning. Sept 16 - Sovereign investor

Gold's typical rhythm: August = low, Up the most = Sept followed by Jan then Oct.

There is $2.4T in the 1934 ETFs (41 closed in Aug'16, with 100 by end of year?)

Conclusion

Anyone that promises to double your money in 10 years may be using a back-of-the-napkin estimate instead of a rigorous analysis that accounts for fees and inflation. Will your money double in 10 years? Maybe, but it's far from a guarantee.

Instead of focusing on what you may or may not return over the next 10 years, it may be wise to focus on controlling what you can by minimizing costs, making efficient tax allocations, and diversifying your exposure. Save as much as you can and evaluate your situation only after the years have passed.

Professor Dani Rodrik of Harvard's Kennedy School of Economics argues that today's world faces a "political trilemma": Democracy, national sovereignty and global economic integration are mutually incompatible: We can combine any two of the three, but never have all three simultaneously ... If we want more globalization, we must either give up some democracy or some national sovereignty.

Silver/Gold ratio: Currently, this ratio is sitting at around 69, but in the past, peaks at 80 have proven to mark a bottom in the gold and silver market.

S&P 500:	George W. H Bush 89 - 93	Up 48%
	Wm. Jefferson Clinton 93 - 01	Up 210%
	George W. Bush 01 - 09	Down 40%
	Barak Obama 09 - 17	Up 160% - Sept 16

Unemployment: Official 4.9% "close to full employment" 7.8 Million
Aug16   Per Labor Dept. 20 Million = 12.6%
               Gallup 13.2%
               Bureau of Labor Statistics, U7 9.7%

As USA Today recently noted, REITs have "outpaced the S&P 500 for the past three-, five-, 10-, 15-, 20-, 25-, 30-, 35- and 40-year periods ending June 30 2016."

22Sept16: "We believe we are in the midst of the market correction we have been expecting," Mr. Citrone, founder of Discovery Capital Management, told investors in an e-mail obtained by Bloomberg. "It will likely persist over the next 3-4 months and be the largest correction since the 2008 crisis," he said. The firm managed about $12.4 billion at the start of 2016.

According to financial data company FactSet, the estimated earnings decline for companies in the S&P 500 is 2.1%. That would mark the sixth straight quarter of declining earnings from companies on the S&P 500.

Watch the VIX: If 10-13, not to worry. Above 20 - sell a little, Above 30 - Panic!

About 34% of all fund assets are now in index trackers. According to the latest data from S&P Global, fewer than 15% of active large cap stock funds beat the market index over the past 10 years. per Bloomberg Sept 2016

29Sep16: Commerzbank said it would lay off close to 10,000, or roughly 20% of its workforce, and scrap its dividend for this year as part of a wide-ranging overhaul.

Shares in Deutsche Bank dropped as much as 8% in early trading amid concerns some of its clients, including several big and influential hedge funds, have pulled billions of dollars from the bank.

Who knew: Only about one-third of the 19 million cars and trucks made in China last year were built with galvanized steel. It's much the same in India, where consumers bought a record 2 million vehicles last year; only about 20% were made with galvanized steel, according to India's Institute of Technology Bombay. Zinc is in BIG demand!

7Oct16 - "When gold is trading above its 200-day average, it advances at an annualized rate of 12.7%," said Jason Goepfert, president of Sundial Capital Research, in a research note. Gold prices on Thursday ($1,253) settled below a long-term trading average for the first time in six months, and that can spell a big dent in returns, especially if sentiment about the global economy isn't overly pessimistic.

The value of stock buybacks announced by U.S. companies is at its lowest level in nearly five years. Zero Hedge estimates that share buybacks in 3Q 2016 will be 15% lower than in 2Q 2016. This year, S&P 500 share repurchase authorizations equal $335 billion versus $454 billion at the same time in 2015.

The long-term cyclically adjusted price-to-earnings ratio (CAPE), which is quantified by the CAPE Shiller P/E ratio, stands near 27 -- far above its long-term average of 16.7.

The International Monetary Fund recently warned that global debt has hit an all-time high of $152 trillion. That's nearly twice the size of the global production of actual goods and services.

> 33% of market downturns recover within a month
> 50% of market downturns recover within 2 months
> 80% of market downturns recover within 1 year
> 95% of the time, those big "once or twice in a lifetime drops" return back to even in 3 to 4 years with an appropriate portfolio

Collectively, since 1871 the time it takes for the market to recover (top to trough to top again) is a mere 7.9 months

Oil revenue shortages, 2016: Okla. $1.3B, N. Dakota $1.3B, Louisiana $2B, Alaska $4B

Risk/Reward - Of individual stocks in the S&P 500, 106 gained at least 20 percent during the first nine months of 2016 (change of the stock price without factoring in the impact of dividends) including 25 stocks that were up at least 40 percent YTD through Sept. 30, 2016. Additionally, 161 stocks (32 percent of the stocks in the index) have dropped in value since the end of 2015 (source: BTN Research).

Presidents and stocks: Eisenhower and Reagan served 2 terms and the S&P 500 advanced 118% across both 2 terms. G.W.Bush's 2 terms = down more than 40%.

Johnson's 1st 2 year term up 24%. Nixon's 18 month 2nd term down 31%. Then Ford up 27% and up another 28% Carter. Summary: over the past 18 presidential terms, the S&P 500 has declined 3 times avg 25% and rose 15 terms avg gain 44%. IBD7Nov16.

Election Nasdaq results after several weeks: since 1980 down 5 (2000 -35%, 2008 -27% other 3, -4% to -7%) and up 4 (8 to 18%). IBD 7Nov16

Let's take a look at the Fed's largest financial stimulus in world history.

- Before the recession, the Fed held between $700-$800 billion of Treasury notes on its balance sheet. Today, the Fed has $4.5 trillion on its balance sheet.
- Last year, the Fed paid $8 billion in interest to big Wall Street banks.
- Banks reaped an estimated $13 billion of income by taking advantage of the Fed's below-market rates.

And what did we get for that insane amount of money?

"Too Big to Fail" banks are now 34% bigger than they were in 2007.
0.2% of U.S. banks control 70% of industry assets.
The top 1% of Americans have reaped 90% of the income gains since 2009.

In 2008 we were the number one confident economy, now we are 5th. The U.S. is 70% dependent on consumer spending. But now, the bulk of main street Americans have less wages and have basically maxed out their credit. All told, Americans are a measly 10% less indebted than they were before the crisis.

Labor rates, auto manufacturing: Mexico $8/hr (no med) vs US $49/hr includes med

Trump has control over both houses of Congress. That situation is historically rare for a Republican administration. In the years when that has occurred, stocks have gained an average of 14% per annum.

Cash overseas: Apple $216B, Microsoft $111B, Cisco $60B, Oracle $51B, Google $50B

The last bear was in 2007-2009, so you don't need to be a math wizard to figure out that means the next one could be starting any day now! If the market goes down 50%, it would take you 7.2 years to get back to break even – assuming the market will make 10% annually.

In late October, the world had taken a Hillary Clinton U.S. presidential victory for granted, and pretty much expected the U.S. economy and stock market to muddle along sideways as it has for the recent half decade.

It took a surprise win in the presidential race by Donald Trump to shift the market's mindset to full-on bullish mode.

Fast forward a month, and all of the most popular market indexes -- the Dow Jones, S&P 500 and NASDAQ -- each hit new all-time highs in the past week.

Women represent more than half of all Social Security beneficiaries age 62 and older and two-thirds of all beneficiaries over the age of 85.

Auto Worker's annual compensation: China $8,000 vs U.S. $ 52,000.

Horrors: Trump could place a 35% duty on incoming goods - 5Dec16 IBD In May 2016, "commerce boosted tariffs on Chinese cold-rolled steel to 522%".

Dec - For 2016 so far: Imports into the U.S. are down 3%, from China, down 6%!

After reaching another new all-time closing high on Friday, Nov. 25, the S&P 500 has set 122 record closes in the ongoing bull market that began on March 10, 2009, including 14 record highs in 2016 alone (source: BTN Research).

You can look for a prospective charity on the three major charity watchdog sites: charitynavigator.org, charitywatch.org and give.org. These sites reveal how organizations spend money, protect donor privacy and govern themselves. To provide a measuring stick, Charity Navigator's data shows nine out of 10 effective charities spend at least 65 percent of their budget on the programs and services they provide. You can also read a nonprofit's annual report, audited financial statement and IRS Form 990, which will show salaries of the highest paid employees. But bear in mind, $150,000 is a typical salary for a talented leader of a multi-million dollar organization.1

Harry Dents four key cycles, which are:

1. The 39-Year Generational Spending Wave.
2. The 36-Year Geopolitical Cycle.
3. The 45-Year Innovation Cycle (NEW).

The 8-13-Year Boom/Bust Cycle (average 10 years)

We Sell, They Buy - U.S. exports of goods and services to China have increased tenfold since 1999, rising from $17 billion in 1999 to $165 billion in 2015 (source: Commerce Department, BTN Research). Actual Goods: 2010 US 92B vs China 365B and in 2015 US 96B & China $490B.

Another Year, Another Trillion - Our nation's national debt was $18.922 trillion as of Dec. 31, 2015. It reached $19.898 trillion as of Wednesday, Nov. 23, 2016. (source: Treasury Department, BTN Research).

Losers Last Year - An equal investment at the end of 2015 into the 13 stocks in the S&P 500 that lost at least 50 percent last year was up a collective 60.4 percent YTD as of Nov. 30 (source: BTN Research).

Winners Last Year - An equal investment at the end of 2015 into the seven stocks in the S&P 500 that gained at least 50 percent last year was up a collective 25.0 percent YTD as of Wednesday, Nov. 30 (source: BTN Research).

The Russell 2000 has not seen a negative return in the first year of the last eight presidencies.

Guggenheim S&P 500 Equal Weight ETF (RSP) has beaten the S&P 500 Index with annualized returns of 7.84% in the past 10 years, versus its benchmark of 6.89% for the S&P 500.

RevenueShares Small Cap Index (RWJ) invests in the same stocks as the S&P Small Cap 600 but weights them according to top-line revenue instead of market capitalization. Even the most creative accountants find it tough to fudge revenues.

2017

4Jan: Today, the U.S. stock market trades at a Shiller-CAPE index price-to-earnings (P/E) ratio of 27.9. That's an eye-popping 67% above its historical average. In contrast, the Shiller-CAPE Index stands at a mere 14.4 for emerging markets.

Now America is saddled with nearly $20 TRILLION of debt. You could literally spend a million dollars a day, every single day, back to the day when Julius Caesar was born (12 July 100 BC) and still not even spend $1 trillion!

Extreme political polarization and income inequality is what gives! We're the highest on both. Today real incomes of the middle class are 5% lower than they were in 1970 and 12.4% lower than in 2000, when they peaked!

When we take the affluent 10% out of the picture, we see that the bottom 90% average only $32,352 in income per year. That top 10% skew the overall average dramatically, so the $55,132 you hear about isn't accurate. In the meantime, the top 0.1% have seen their share of wealth go up four times since 1975! And, since 1970, the "super elite" 0.01% has seen their incomes grow a whopping 628%!

Jan 17 - Treasury yields move higher for third straight year for the first time in 36 years as the Fed hikes rates.

An inflection point has been reached with the Fed and interest rates. The 10-year Treasury yield of 1.37% on July 8, 2016 marked the end of the 30-year bull market in bonds.

We've seen a recession every time someone was elected to replace a two - term presidency since Woodrow Wilson was elected in 1912. That's 100% correlation on a very small universe.

The two largest public for-profit prison companies in the U.S. The Geo Group, Inc. (NYSE:GEO) and Corecivic, Inc. (NYSE:CXW), formerly known as Corrections Corporation of America, have surged some 60% since Trump's election.

The Cost of Business - The break-even oil price for Saudi Arabian oil producers is $7 per barrel. The break-even oil price for Russian oil producers is $46 per barrel (source: Deutsche Bank, BTN Research).

More Than Two-Thirds - The total return of the S&P 500 over the last five calendar years (2011-2015) is 80.7 percent. The best 13 trading days during the five years (i.e., 13 days out of 1,258 total trading days) produced a 55.1 percent gain. Thus, 1 percent of the trading days over the last five years were responsible for 68 percent of the index's total return (source: BTN Research).

IBD 9Jan17 - Nasdaq goes above 5,500!!!! NEW HIGH except the old high of 5,132 was in March 2000. Adjusted for inflation it would now be 7,087.

Missing the Best - The total return for the S&P 500 was a gain of 12 percent (total return) in 2016. If you missed the three best percentage gain days last year, the 12 percent gain falls to a 4.4 percent gain (source: BTN Research).

Avoid the Worst - The total return for the S&P 500 was a gain of 12 percent in 2016. If you avoided the three worst percentage days last year, the 12 percent gain rises to 22.1 percent (source: BTN Research).

10Jan17 - The U.S. stock market has hit 17 new highs since Trump's election. It has added close to $1 trillion to its market capitalization. The Trump rally has made Trump critic and Hillary supporter Warren Buffett close to $5 billion richer. That's more than Donald Trump's entire net worth, according to Forbes magazine.

It is hard to say who despises Trump more -- the conservative columnist George Will or the left wing liberal economist Paul Krugman. No matter what Donald Trump says or does, it is dismissed as the ramblings of a racist, anti-democratic lunatic. The same also applies to anyone who does not board the anti-Trump bandwagon.

According to Open Secrets, the Pharmaceutical and Health Products industry spent $186,215,379 last year to buy favor with lawmakers. That's a whopping $75 million more than the insurance industry — which was the next biggest spender.

Every year, over 3.6 million baby boomers are retiring — 10,000 people every single day! By 2050, 81 million of them will reach retirement age. By 2060, 92 million Americans (20% of the population) will be 65 or older. Of course, they will all need the drugs peddled by the big pharmaceutical companies to extend their lifetimes. But just as importantly, they will also need a place to live. Retirement communities, senior apartments, assisted living, and all sorts of real estate associated with this demographic are sprouting all over the country. But supply of these properties is still extremely low. Demand will only rise as more Americans age. You see, the current growth rate of senior housing units is just 21,950 units per year. To keep up with demand, 60,000 units per year are needed. In other words, a 173% increase per year is required to even meet the demand, which is projected to peak in 2044.

111

20Jan17 - Harry Dent "At this point I would give the Trump rally through about July and then we could see one of those first, devastating bubble crashes that sees the markets down 30% to 40% in a few months."

There's been too wide a separation between the underlying reality and the happy talk that has justified the status quo. And in this, I think of the comment made by Gorbachev in the last years of the Soviet Union. He said, "Well, we said we were going to 3%, but I guess we weren't.

6Feb17 - Shiller P/E index is around 28 at this point. So that's 28 years of earnings to make up the price of a share of stock, essentially. That's what they're paying for. In 1929, it was 30. So it was certainly more expensive. But I would argue that 28 is extremely expensive.

VIX: Below 25 = Buy, Above 30 = SELL

The benchmark S&P 500 rose 1.8% in January, and is up nearly 4% so far this month. According to equity-research firm CFRA, this is an incredibly bullish sign...

The firm notes that since 1945, stocks have risen in both January and February just 27 times. And in every one of those years – 27 out of 27 times – the market has ended the year in green, for average total return of 24%. That's an impressive streak.

In the past two years, U.S. drivers with credit scores of less than 620 borrowed $244 billion to buy cars, a tally not matched since 2006 and 2007 when the same strata of buyers rolled off with $254 billion in auto loans. Car companies – and their captive finance units – make about half of all car loans these days, but they underwrite three-quarters of the ones going to subprime vehicle buyers.

Since the beginning of 2008, the S&P 500 has gained 63% while Europe's Stoxx 50 is still down 43%.

During the dot-com bubble, the S&P 500 rallied from January 1995 through September 2000 by more than 200%. In contrast, gold stumbled 27% during that same time period.

Or look at the market's rally from October 2012 through January 2016, when the S&P 500 gained 37%, while the yellow metal tumbled 35%.

In short, when times are good, gold is the forgotten child left in time-out until he can learn to play well with the other assets.

The California Public Employees' Retirement System (CalPERS) decided to pull out all the money it had invested in hedge funds ($4 billion). That was after they paid $135 million in fees during 2013 and received only 7.1% in returns from their hedge fund investments. As a point of comparison, the S&P 500 Index rose 29.6% that year!

In 2014, the Federal Government provided $18 billion in funding for the Housing Choice Voucher program, $12 billion for project-based rental assistance and $7 billion for public housing. Source: Congressional Budget Office.*

March 2017; Right now there is very exciting news in the silver market. The largest investment bank in the country today is JPMorgan Chase & Co. In 2012, they held 5 million ounces of silver in their corporate account. However, recent reports have revealed that JPMorgan Chase now holds a staggering 91.5 million ounces of silver! In just 5 years, they've increased their stockpile 17 times over. Just since the beginning of 2017, JPMorgan Chase has purchased 9.4 million ounces. That's a lot of silver for anyone to buy.

To summarize the Obama years — Eight Years of Gains - The ongoing bull market for the S&P 500 reached eight years in length as of the close of trading on Thursday, March 9. Over the eight years, the index has gained 314.4 percent (total return), an average annual return of 19.4 percent (source: BTN Research).

#1 item that needs correction to get the U.S. economy moving: Companies are allowed to expense the total amount they spend on interest. This is a huge incentive for them to use Wall Street's big investment banks to borrow as much money as possible. As of the second quarter of 2016, investment-grade corporations were spending $119 billion annually on interest expenses – the most since 2000, just before the big tech-debt bust of 2001. The difference today is that interest rates are much, much lower.

And that means the debt balances are vastly higher. In total, U.S. corporate debt has soared from less than $3 trillion to almost $7 trillion in just the last decade. Worse, a higher percentage of this debt is rated "junk" than ever before. Thus, American companies are now more exposed to either rising default rates or rising interest rates than they've ever been before. #2. capital investments are expensed...

Some items – like computers and software – can be fully expensed in the year they're purchased. They're treated like a routine cost of doing business. But longer-term corporate investments can only be expensed over many years. Inflation robs companies of the real value of these tax credits, providing a perverse incentive to not make big, long-term investments. #3. The only reason most U.S. companies are setting up manufacturing and research and development overseas is to avoid U.S. taxes and regulation.

More than $9.5 trillion in global corporate debt is coming due over the next five years. About $1.6 trillion of that debt is below investment grade, or "junk."

Do NOT trade near the market open! Volatility tends to be high as the markets price in the news. USE LIMIT ORDERS ON BUYS. DO NOT USE STOP LOSS ORDERS.

Per IBD's O'Neil: P-E ratio is useless regarding stocks to buy. Strong earnings growth, especially in the two most recent quarters is the key factor. High P-E ratios are the result of accelerating earnings growth, which itself is what attracts institutional investors to stocks and causes share prices to soar.

Rising but Not Roaring - The U.S. economy grew by 1.6 percent in 2016, the 11th consecutive year that our domestic economy failed to grow by at least 3 percent. In data tracked since 1930, the previous longest stretch of sub 3 percent annual growth was just four years (source: Commerce Department, BTN Research).

Time Flies - The S&P 500 bull market that began on March 9, 2009, is now in its 98th month. The average bull market for the stock index since 1950 (including the current bull) has lasted 61 months (source: BTN Research).

Stocks - The S&P 500 gained 6.1 percent (total return) in the first quarter of 2017, the fifth best opening quarter for the stock index over the last 25 years, i.e., 1993-2017 (source: BTN Research).

April 2017: Most silver comes as a byproduct of mining other metals. Only 30% of silver is from primary silver mines. In 2015, 34% of silver came from lead/zinc mining, and 22% came from copper. So, it's very hard to increase silver supply to meet demand. It's at the mercy of other metals. That tells me silver's price could be more explosive.

As of the second quarter of 2016, investment-grade corporations were spending $119 billion annually on interest expenses – the most since 2000, just before the big tech-debt bust of 2001. The difference today is that interest rates are much, much lower. And that means the debt balances are vastly higher. In total, U.S. corporate debt has soared from less than $3 trillion to almost $7 trillion in just the last decade. Worse, a higher percentage of this debt is rated "junk" than ever before.

According to a recent note from Michael Hartnett, chief investment strategist for Bank of America Merrill Lynch, central banks have bought an astounding $1 trillion of stocks and bonds so far this year. This has pushed central bank balance sheets to an all-time-high $14.6 trillion. More concerning, at this pace, they will buy up more than $3.6 trillion of assets for the full year. This would be the most on record at among the most expensive prices on record.

As Porter noted on Friday (21Apr17)... what could possibly go wrong?

Bears Follow Bulls - The average decline for the S&P 500 during the 11 bear markets since the end of World War II is 34 percent (source: BTN Research).

No Progress Made - After adjusting data for the impact of inflation, the median household income today ($56,516) is lower than the median household income ($57,909) from 1999 (source: Federal Reserve Bank of St. Louis, BTN Research).

Big Numbers - The U.S. bond market (including treasury, municipal, corporate, mortgage and asset-backed debt) was worth $39.4 trillion as of Dec. 31, 2016. The U.S. bond market was worth $4.8 trillion on Dec. 31, 1986 (source: Securities Industry and Financial Markets Association, BTN Research).

Up Early, Up Overall - The last time the S&P 500 was up on a total return basis for the first quarter yet finished down for the full calendar year was 2002 when the index gained 0.3 percent for the first three months of the year but was down 22.1 percent for the entire year (source: BTN Research).

Rainy Day Funds - Currently, 63 percent of American adults do not have $500 in a savings account to cover an emergency expense (source: CNN, BTN Research).

Using data from 1885 through 2015, Artemis discovered that stock and bond prices have historically moved in the same direction roughly 70% of the time. According to Artemis, it's only during the last two decades of falling interest rates and accommodative monetary policy that stocks and bonds have been negatively correlated. Otherwise, the firm reports, "Not only are stocks and bonds positively correlated most of the time, but also there is a precedent for multiyear periods whereby both have declined."

One Bad, One Dismal - The debt-to-economy ratio for Greece is 167 percent (i.e., $326 billion of debt stated as a percentage of the $195 billion Greek economy). The debt-to-economy ratio for the U.S. is 105 percent, i.e., $19.846 trillion of debt stated as a percentage of the $18.8694 trillion American economy (source: Commerce Department, BTN Research).

Where the Money Comes From - Property taxes represent 31.3 percent of the total tax revenue collected by states; greater than the 23.3 percent of tax revenue collected from sales taxes and the 22.9 percent of tax revenue that comes from individual state income taxes (source: Tax Foundation, BTN Research).

Goldman's options research group reports the strategy of buying at-the-money, one-month-out calls across the board has produced an average gain of +14% (excluding transaction costs) over the 19 years studied. (It was profitable every year, too.)

In contrast, the S&P 500 achieved a +7.4% annualized return over the same period (with four down years along the way: -9.1% (2000), -11.9% (2001), -22.1% (2002) and -37% (2008).

Can options trading really be this simple?

The data dictates that it can be.

Last week was busy with about 20% of the market reporting ...

Source: Earnings Whispers

Let's walk through an example ...

If you bought shares of Amazon stock the day before its earnings beat on April 27, you could have sold at a maximum profit of about +4% the following day. (Buy pre-earnings; sell post-earnings.)

But, if you bought at-the-money, one-month-out AMZN calls instead, you could have racked up a one-day gain of +38% using the options approach.

That's all looking through the rear-view mirror. Peak earnings are behind us right now ...

Going forward, FactSet thinks earnings will continue to have a strong 2017. The research firm predicts we will see the first year-over-year double-digit earnings increase since 2011 for S&P 500 companies this year.

Focus on the months of January, April, July and October if you're interested in employing this options strategy. The bulk of public companies report their quarterly earnings early- to mid-month in the months after standard quarters end.

And make sure you have access to a low-cost options broker!

13May17: Low-volatility stretches: In '92 to '93, we saw ultra-low volatility last for 179 days. In '95 to '96, low volatility lasted some 254 days. The current bout of low volatility has only lasted about 80 days. (The typical S&P 500 company is trading at about 25 times forward-looking earnings.

Historically, S&P 500 companies have traded at about 15 times earnings in more normal markets.)

According to the S&P Dow Jones SPIVA 2016 scorecard:

> 66% of large-cap managers ...
> 89% of mid-cap managers ...
> And 86% of small-cap managers ...

Underperformed the S&P 500, S&P MidCap 400 and S&P SmallCap 600, respectively.

88% of large-cap managers have underperformed the S&P 500 Index over the last five years.

Yet, it's even worse for smaller-sized stocks ...

Since 2011:

90% of mid-cap managers have underperformed the S&P MidCap 400 Index.

And 97% of small-cap managers have underperformed the S&P SmallCap 600 Index.

Over the last 10 years, underperformance checks in at 85% (large-cap managers), 96% (mid-cap managers) and 96% (small-cap managers). And going back 15 years, outperformance is still painfully high at 92%, 95% and 93%, respectively.

One thing's for sure ...

It's extremely difficult for professional investors to outperform their benchmarks over any period.

S&P 500 annualized returns during the stronger November-to-April span have been roughly 2X the weaker May-to-October stretch.

But, what few investors know is the "Sell in May" effect is even more pronounced in small caps. The same study for small caps shows a 10-to-1 performance variance over the last 91 years!

Plus, the combination of the Ibbotson SBBI and Russell 2000 (benchmarks for small caps) also easily outpaced the S&P 500 during the dominant November-to-April interval, +21.2% vs. +13.4%.

For the small-cap stock component (November-April), an investor could use an ETF such as the iShares Russell 2000 ETF (IWM).

And for the safe Treasury bill component (May-October), investors could sit in cash or cash equivalents, buy an actual T-bill or invest in an ETF like the SPDR Bloomberg Barclays 1-3 Month T-Bill ETF (BIL), the Goldman Sachs TreasuryAccess 0-1 Year ETF (GBIL), the iShares Short Treasury Bond ETF (SHV) or the PIMCO Enhanced Maturity Active ETF (MINT).

US$ Index: 8Nov16 = 97.86, 3Jan17 = 103.82 (14Yr high), 17May17 = 97.55

As the saying goes, "Some people are lucky enough to be smart. I'm smart enough to know I'm lucky."

The Fed has bought Treasuries, now totaling about $2.5 trillion, and mortgage-backed securities — loans packaged together as bonds now valued at around $1.8 trillion.

There are $10 trillion in negative yield bonds on the global level. Central banks are turning to corporate debt to pump cash into markets, and running out of stuff to buy.

The New York Fed noted delinquency rates for most consumer debt continued to tick higher. First quarter 2017, credit cards took the lead... The report showed 7.5% of credit-card debt is now "seriously delinquent" – at least 90 days late – up from 7.1% at the end of last year.

ETF Strategies that historically outperform. Dividend growth (NOBL and SDY), insider sentiment (KNOW), size factor: small beats large (IWC), spin-off stocks outperform (CSD) and equal-weight beats market-cap-weight (RSP).

- Discounted valuation. Regional banks (KRE) and airlines (JETS).
- Disruptive innovation themes. Cyber security (HACK), 3D printing (PRNT) and robotics & automation (ROBO).
- Undiscovered areas of the market with catalysts. Israel equities (ITEQ).
- Access to star managers at lower expense levels. Davis Advisors (DWLD).

With 1,832 ETFs (plus 196 ETNs) in existence and 1,300-plus ETFs in registration (as of 5/18/17), the U.S. exchange-traded product universe is — and will remain — a bountiful marketplace.

April 2017: S&P 500 @ 21.5 PE, Nasdaq 43, FTSE 100 @30, French CAC40 @19.5, Germany @19.8.

IBD 17Apr17 Best ETF's for 2017: RINF for rising inflation expectation, FNCL Fidelity MSCI financials & AMLP Alerian MLP.

Blackrock recommends: consumer discretionary, industrials, financials, technology & materials

Chinese Debt: Morgan Stanley puts at 279% of GDP as of the end of 2016!

U.S. fracking: In 2013 president Obama warned, "We can't drill our way out of the problem" ie $110.62 barrel of oil. We did!!! Oil now $50 a barrel. example: U.S. Geological Survey found the so-called Spraberry Formation in Texas holds 4.2 bilion barrels of recoverable oil at current prices, not the 510 million barrels estimated 10 years ago. Frackers produce half the U.S. oil.

In 2012 OPEC pulled in $1.13Trillion in revenue vs 2016's $433.4Billion

The "advance/decline" line is a simple indicator... You take the number of stocks that went up in a day, and you subtract the number that went down. If more went up, this line goes up. If more went down. In a strong bull market, more stocks should be going up than going down – right? Sounds basic. What if the overall market was going up... but more stocks were falling each day than rising? That's what was happening at the end of [the dot-com boom in] 1999. It's often not until the late "innings" of a rally when the two begin to diverge. This can be an early warning that a market is unhealthy

Lengthy- The current economic expansion (in its 95th month) is the third longest U.S. expansion based on data tracked since 1854, i.e., for 163 years (source: National Bureau of Economic Research, BTN Research).

2017, Feb $528.2B: S&P500 PE 24.5. Margin debt = new high. In 2000 and 2007 margin debt surged to record highs right before the bubbles burst ie 2000 down 50% and 2007-9 down 57%.

US Trade deficits 2016: China $347B, Japan $69B, Germany $65B

Break-even - The three summer months (June, July and August) have produced an average loss of 0.1 percent (total return) for the S&P 500 stock index over the last 25 years, i.e., 1992-2016 (source: BTN Research).

Too Pessimistic - An annual survey of Americans 65 or older gave the U.S. stock market at least a 50 percent chance of rising in the upcoming year only one time over 12 surveys conducted from 2002-2013. The U.S. stock market (as measured by the S&P 500) was actually up 10 of the 12 years (down in 2002 and 2008), gaining 105 percent (total return), an average of 6.2 percent per year (source: University of Michigan, BTN Research).

Decision making: Better to wait than to anticipate.

5Jun17: According to the latest data from oil-services company Baker Hughes, the U.S. oil rig count rose again last week for the 20th consecutive week. It now sits at 733 active oil rigs, the most since early 2015.

Reports of deep-sea drilling's demise in a world of sub-$100 oil may have been greatly exaggerated, much to OPEC's dismay. Pumping crude from seabeds thousands of feet below water is turning cheaper as producers streamline operations and prioritize drilling in core wells, according to Wood Mackenzie Ltd. That means oil at $50 a barrel could sustain some of these projects by next year, down from an average break-even price of about $62 in the first quarter and $75 in 2014.

June 2017: No Recession Here - The current economic expansion in the U.S. will reach eight years in length on June 30. No expansion in history has lasted longer than 10 years based on data tracked since 1854 (source: National Bureau of Economic Research, BTN Research).

OIL: Prices have fallen from above $100 just a few years ago to as low as $27 last year. Hundreds of thousands of folks in the industry are out of work. More than 200 exploration and production ("E&P") and oil-services companies have gone belly up. And nearly $100 billion of energy debt has been wiped out.

Sector rotation = Bulls can make money. Flight to safety = Bears love as it often heralds the beginning of a correction. Choppy, uncertain market (the worst) = bad enough to make it hard to hold stocks and just bad enough to make it hard to ride the sidelines.

Per IBD: Correction - the true market leaders tend to fall 1 1/2 to 2 1/2 times the decline of the major equity indexes. The minimum decline from high to low for a typical cup base is 12%, in many cases, the drop is in the 20%-30% range. Ditto for a double-bottom base. Even for a flat base, you would normally expect the stock to fall around 10% to 15% before bottoming out.

Oil: price above $50 = buy producers (Pioneer PXD, EOG and Continental CLR) vs below $50, buy (Phillips PSX, Valero VLO and Marathon MPC)

Oil production: US 9.3M per day and in 2018 10M vs 2016 Saudi 10.5M and Russia 11.2M.

Fracking: In the permian basin there may be from 4 to 13 horizontal zones. The U.S. to spend $10B in 2017 on shale projects. Each lateral drilling consumes some 100 train car loads of sand from U.S. Silica SCCA, Hi Crush HCLP, Emerge EMES, Fairmont FMSA. Every $10 decrease in oil prices translate to a 25 cent-per-gallon cut in gasoline prices.

Gold: The average grade of gold projects in North America is 1.3 grams per ton!

Commodities prices are down 5% this year so far. That means they've fallen in six of the past seven years.

Year	Return
2011	-13.3%
2012	-1.1%
2013	-9.5%
2014	-17.0%
2015	-24.7%
2016	11.8%

Some 41.5 million Americans collectively owe nearly $1.3 trillion on their federal student loans... About one in every four borrowers is either delinquent or in default. Total indebtedness has doubled since 2009.

The average new car price (about $35,000) is the highest price ever. Compared with average wages (about $50,000), cars are vastly more expensive than ever before. The value of auto loans that are at least 30 days in default currently totals $23 billion – up 14% in just the last year. And since 2014, the leading independent auto lender, Santander Consumer USA (SC), has seen its stock fall in half. An incredible 32% of all outstanding auto asset-backed securities (ABSs) issued in 2016 were "deep subprime" – up from just 5% in 2010.

Over the last few cycles, rate hikes alone didn't kill the bull market. What kills bull markets is when the Fed stops hiking rates. When rates hit a level the Fed thinks is appropriate, rates plateau. During the last cycle, rates bottomed at 1% in 2003. The Fed then spent 2004 and 2005 hiking rates, which eventually plateaued at 5.25% in 2006. That flat line in rates is what we have to worry about, based on history... not the actual hiking cycle.

Today, the Swiss central bank owns more than $60 billion worth of U.S. stocks, including a huge $1.7 billion position in iPhone maker Apple (AAPL) and $800 million in social-media titan Facebook (FB). The Swiss central bank continues to expand its balance sheet at almost $100 billion a year. Its total balance sheet has now grown to around $700 billion – almost $90,000 in securities per Swiss citizen. And it's growing every year... just by printing more Swiss francs.

Today, most people are investing through exchange-traded funds ("ETFs"). Most ETFs are structured according to various indexes. And several of the most popular indexes are "price-weighted," meaning that the capital is allocated according to nominal share price. Investors aren't buying these stocks because the business is undervalued... or because they pay a good dividend... or because they're growing fast. They're buying simply because the nominal share price (which conveys zero information about the relative attractiveness of the investment) is a large number and thus is more likely to attract subsequent capital.

Said another way, the "greater fool" is more likely to buy a big nominal share price stock over any other stock.

Thus, the same kinds of management teams that used to split their stock to gain the attention of investors are now not splitting their shares for the exact same reason. And in Japan, that kind of investment rationale has been taken to an extreme. In Japan, the central bank is the "greater fool."

Japan's central bank – the Bank of Japan ("BoJ") – has been buying around 3 trillion yen ($30 billion) worth of stocks via ETFs each year, radically warping the equity market. The BoJ focused its buying on ETFs that were structured according to the Nikkei 225, which, like the Dow Jones Industrial Average, is a price-weighted index.

Again... in a price-weighted index, the larger the nominal share price, the larger the allocation in the index. Fast Retailing, with its huge share price, makes up about 8% of the Nikkei, a huge position relative to the total size of its company.

For comparison, consider that Fast Retailing makes up only 0.3% of the larger TOPIX Index, where allocations are made according to firms' total market values, not merely the nominal price of their shares. It didn't take long for investors to figure out how to take advantage of the policy.

CLSA – one of Asia's biggest brokerage firms – recommended clients sell shares of Toyota, one of Japan's best global companies in 2016...

It replaced Toyota in its recommended portfolio with... you guessed it, Fast Retailing, purely because of its huge weighting in the Nikkei 225.

The broker also recommended Softbank (9984.T) for the same reason. It wasn't an endorsement of the company's reckless acquisition strategy, which involves a tremendous amount of leverage and a $100 billion "sidecar" fund that will surely cause all kinds of conflicts of interest. (Softbank is truly one of the scariest companies in the world... but that's a topic for another time.) It was an endorsement of its nominal share price. You see, after Fast Retailing, Softbank is the second-highest-weighted stock in the Nikkei. Sure enough, Softbank's shares have soared, thanks to the BoJ's investment scheme. Softbank's stock was "dead money" from the tech collapse until 2012. But once the BoJ ramped up its equity purchases, Softbank's stock has more than quadrupled, moving from around 2,000 yen to more than 9,000 yen...

According to bankruptcy-law firm Haynes and Boone, 114 exploration and production ("E&P") companies declared bankruptcy from January 2015 through last December. The combined debt for these companies totaled more than $74.2 billion. Over the same period, 110 oilfield-services companies went belly up... with total debt of more than $18.8 billion. That's 224 bankruptcies and $93 billion in debt.

But we're just getting started... We'll see another massive wave of bankruptcies before the oil and gas sector emerges from this ongoing bear market. The continued drilling and near-record production will keep driving oil prices lower. The companies with higher costs and big debt loads will become the next victims.

Two months ago, I attended the Oil & Gas Investment Symposium in New York. More than 70% of the companies presenting had debt levels that exceeded their market caps. Things won't end well for these companies.

Today, oil trades around $45 a barrel. But as long as oil stays below $50 a barrel, almost every oil play in the U.S. is uneconomic. Low oil prices are killing entire economies. The cost of getting a barrel of oil out of the ground in Russia is about $70. In Iran, it's in the mid-$60s. In the North Sea around Western Europe, it's $55.

With a few exceptions, the Saudis – whose production costs sit around $25 per barrel – are in the catbird seat.

Meanwhile, global oil production is about 98.5 million barrels per day, while demand is about 97 million barrels.

And yet... despite all of these headwinds, I'm bullish on oil prices. You see, in the next few years, oil demand is going to absolutely skyrocket.

Today, the U.S. is the largest consumer of oil on the planet. We use about 7.2 billion barrels per year, or nearly 20 million barrels per day...

the U.S. is the largest oil consumer on the planet. Japan uses a lot of oil, too. And again, given our high standards of living, that shouldn't come as a surprise. But zoom out and you realize that the total population of both countries is only around 450 million people – around 6% of the world's population. Meanwhile, China has a population of 1.4 billion. It uses 4 billion barrels of oil per year – about 11 million barrels per day.

In other words, the U.S. – with a population about one-fifth the size of China – consumes almost two times more oil. There are 1.3 billion people in India... around three times the combined population of the U.S. and Japan. India uses 1.5 billion barrels of oil per year, or about 4.1 million barrels per day. That's just a fraction of the oil used in China. But India is expected to add another 241 million "people of working age" by 2030. Today, the U.S. and Japan use about 19 barrels of oil per person per year. Even if China and India consume just five barrels of oil per person per year by 2030, that amounts to more than 13 billion barrels of oil... increasing world demand by more than 9 billion barrels per year.

Today, the U.S. remains the world's largest consumer of oil. We use nearly 20 million barrels of oil per day. This is nearly double the next largest consumer, and more than four times as much as any other nation on the planet.

The auto industry, like many industries, depends heavily on financing. More than 80% of the people who buy a new car borrow the money to do so, either via a loan or a lease. Lending standards had evaporated by 2014. There are dozens of stories in major publications about people who could clearly not afford to buy a car being given high-cost subprime loans. By 2014, subprime lending had grown to almost 30% of total new-car loans (a new high) and more than 60% of used-car loans.

Jobs - In July 2009, there were 14.6 million unemployed Americans and 2.2 million job openings. In April 2017, there were 7.1 million unemployed Americans and 6 million job openings (source: Department of Labor, BTN Research).

Factory Work-United States corporations account for 19 percent of global manufacturing, second only to Chinese manufacturers who represent 25 percent of worldwide manufacturing. However, manufacturing accounts for just 12 percent of the U.S. economy today, down from 26 percent of our economy 50 years ago (source: Bloomberg BusinessWeek, BTN Research).

Earlier this week - 16Jul17, the federal government announced that Medicare's Hospital Insurance Trust Fund will run out of money by 2029. This is one of two trust funds set up to pay the growing costs of Medicare, specifically Medicare Part A benefits and administration costs. That's only 12 years away. This isn't the first time we've heard threats of Medicare or Medicaid losing funding. But with budget cuts looming and an unprecedented number of Baby Boomers turning 65 each year, we could see major hits and increased premiums. If you're depending on Medicare, that means a lot more money out of your pocket. In fact, Medicare premiums rose in 2017. For about 70% of seniors, the premiums for Part B rose almost 4% despite a cost of living increase in Social Security of only 0.3%. But for the other 30%, the spike was much higher – 10%. These folks include those who are on Medicare but not yet collecting Social Security, those with higher incomes in retirement, and those who enrolled in Part B for the first time. Worse, deductibles for all Medicare participants increased by at least 2% as well. That includes deductibles on Part A, Part B, and coinsurance amounts for longer hospitalization or nursing care.

Since 1998, carbonated soft drink sales are down 25%. And last year, for the first time in history, sales of bottled water surpassed those of carbonated soft drinks.

Trump was in Iowa, talking about his plans for the border wall:

"The southern border – lots of sun, lots of heat. We are thinking about building a wall as a solar wall. So it creates energy. And pays for itself."

A solar wall? With thousands of miles of solar panels?

Every solar panel contains about 2/3 ounces of silver. If Trump built the 2,000-mile solar wall that he wants, it would require 11 MILLION ounces of silver. Can you imagine the drain this surge in demand would place on silver supply?!

24Jul17: Higher and Higher - Of the 11 S&P 500 bull markets since 1949, only the 1990-2000 bull market (308 record closing highs) and the 1982-1987 bull market (152 record closing highs) have achieved more daily all-time highs than the current bull market's 151 record closing highs (source: BTN Research).

Bull Market - Since bottoming on March 9, 2009, the S&P 500 has gained 334 percent (total return) and set 151 record closing highs through trading on Friday, July 14, equal to a 19.2 percent gain per year (source: BTN Research).

In the first quarter of 2017, earnings grew 17% year-over-year. That's the highest reading since 2010. A full 75% of companies announced earnings that matched or exceeded expectations, led by tech stocks, health care, and financials.

The most valuable insight from these earnings is the revenue. Over the past 12 months, revenue per share has risen 3.8%... what looks like the start of a strong up cycle in revenue growth.

International Travel to the U.S.: April 2017 up 6.6% and May 17 up 5.2% over 2016.

Immigrants best place to live: #1 Sweden, #2 Canada, #3 Switzerland with U.S. #7.

Worst: Tunisia, Guatemala and Kenya.

Stansberry Digest July 2017 Amazon (AMZN)...

Here was a company that had grown tremendously. Since 2013, the online-retail giant's revenues soared from $80 billion to $140 billion annually. Those are huge numbers.

And profits? There aren't any in its consumer businesses. Its corporate-services business (Amazon Web Services) makes about $1 billion a year currently.

So over the last three years, on revenues of $320 billion, Amazon made about $3 billion in profit – or less than 1% of sales. Nevertheless, it had invested an incredible $17 billion on acquisitions and capital improvements – before its $13 billion acquisition of Whole Foods Market (WFM). In total now the company has spent $30 billion on investments in it business... almost none of which are expected to make a profit.

But the biggest problems from Bizarro Capitalism will occur in the commodity markets. Virtually free capital has led to a huge increase in commodity production, from oil to corn.

Since July 2011, U.S. onshore crude-oil production has essentially doubled. The last time U.S. crude-oil production doubled, it took 25 years, from World War II until the mid-1960s. We've done it again in just six years. Corn has seen production grown by almost 50% since 2012, from 10.8 billion bushels to 15.1 billion bushels.

Deere & Co. (DE) as a primary beneficiary (in the short term) from Bizarro Capitalism...

The tractor manufacturer had lent farmers $38 billion to buy tractors and other items necessary for farming. (That explains the huge increase to corn production.) The Wall Street Journal noticed this, too. This week, it published a well-researched article, noting that John Deere had become the fifth-largest agricultural lender in the country...

[Deere] is providing more short-term credit for crop supplies such as seeds, chemicals and fertilizer, making it the No. 5 agricultural lender behind banks Wells Fargo, Rabobank, Bank of the West and Bank of America, according to the American Bankers Association.

Does that make any sense?

Should one of America's most important manufacturing companies be inflating the demand for its products by becoming one of the largest agricultural banks in the world? Isn't it obvious that these loans are going to lead to far too many tractors being sold, sharply lower corn prices, and, eventually, a new financial crisis in America's heartland?

Deere, like many manufacturers in this credit cycle, has used leasing, even more than lending, to sustain demand for its products. Since 2010, the value of Deere's outstanding leased equipment has soared, from less than $2 billion to almost $6 billion. The Wall Street Journal explained...

Deere accelerated its equipment leasing in 2014 when sales plummeted following almost a decade of rapid-fire purchases by farmers flush with cash. The leasing business has kept Deere from having to idle factories and has provided dealers with income from replacement parts and services for leased equipment.

[Leases] provided farmers with machines for one to three years for a fraction of their purchase price, alleviating the need for loans. A new tractor costing $250,000 can be leased for about $30,000 a year. That compares with the cost to buy with a loan, which would require a 20% down payment of $50,000 and more than $40,000 a year in payments for five years.

Trouble is, when you provide leases for equipment that make them much cheaper to own, you make it much harder to earn a profit selling the same equipment. Deere has seen its profit margins on its equipment sales fall from $5 billion to less than $2 billion. That's Bizarro Capitalism: plenty of revenue, but no profit.

Here's the real trouble...

Eventually, all of those leased tractors get returned. If they can't be sold quickly, Deere takes the loss. Over the last three years, the amount of equipment leased out by Deere is up 87%. But what have corn prices done? Nothing. So... what do you think will happen next, after three years of booming lease business and no profits from farming?

The stock market couldn't care less about these risks. Shares of Deere have moved from around $75 to more than $120 in roughly the last year alone. And right now, the bond market couldn't care less, either. Deere's long-dated bond (the 5.375% bonds due in 2029) is trading for $24 over par ($124) and yielding 3%.

How will all of this end?

Will Deere successfully use virtually free money (in the form of endless supplies of credit) to prop up demand for its tractors forever? Will U.S. oil producers be able to lower their operating costs forever? (Recently, the average break-even price for high-quality onshore production fell from around $50 to around $40, a change that has forestalled bankruptcy for a large number of U.S. oil producers.)

My bet is no. And like I told you in April... sooner or later, the gigantic credit bubble that lies at the heart of Bizarro Capitalism will burst.

Of course, I can't give you a date to put on your calendar. But keep your eye on the market for high-yield debt. The credit market will see these problems coming long before the stock market does.

Market Correction: History suggests we almost certainly will have one! Over the past 40 years, the S&P has experienced a peak-to-trough decline of 14% on average every single year. This year, the largest we've seen is 2.8%.

A correction would not be unexpected here.

In 2014, Switzerland's central bank began buying equities, too. But its domestic economy is so small that it decided to invest globally. Today, the Swiss central bank owns more than $60 billion worth of U.S. stocks, including a huge $1.7 billion position in iPhone maker Apple (AAPL) and $800 million in social-media titan Facebook (FB). The Swiss central bank continues to expand its balance sheet at almost $100 billion a year. Its total balance sheet has now grown to around $700 billion – almost $90,000 in securities per Swiss citizen. And it's growing every year... just by printing more Swiss francs.

The Nasdaq moved higher every single trading day from July 7 to July 20. The current market uptrend is strong. Specifically, buying after the Nasdaq jumps 10 days in a row has led to a 2.3% gain in one month and a staggering 14.6% gain in three months.

Did you know that years ending in "7" have had some of the biggest market sell-offs? Think 2007, '97, '87, and more. In fact, many of these big drops occur between August and October.

5Aug17 - If the dollar declines below critical support at 91.88 in the coming weeks, it is possible that we could see a rally of epic proportions in the raw materials sector.

Total Government And Personal Debt In The U.S. Has Hit 41 Trillion Dollars ($329,961.34 Per Household) | Zero Hedge.

Wallmart.com offers some 50 million things while Amazon offers 300 million!

American Enterprise Institute economist Mark J. Perry points out that since 1997, total real U.S. manufacturing output has soared 40% or $544 billion, while the number of factory jobs has shrunk 5.1 million or 29%. The reason = automation - robots and computers - not imports.

No Big Pullback - The S&P 500 has gone 324 calendar days without a 2 percent or greater one-day drop, the longest stretch without a tumble of 2 percent or more since Feb. 27, 2007, or nearly 10.5 years ago (source: BTN Research).

Credit Downgrade - Saturday, Aug. 5, was the six-year anniversary of the United States being downgraded by S&P from a top credit rating. Since the downgrade, the yield on the U.S. 10-year Treasury note has fallen from 2.57 percent to 2.29 percent, and the S&P 500 has gained 134 percent (total return), equal to 15.3 percent per year (source: BTN Research).

Social Security Status Report - Sixty-one million Americans received Social Security benefits (retirement or disability) in 2016. Social Security's total income (payroll taxes collected plus interest earnings) amounted to $957 billion last year, $35 billion more than the $922 billion of program expenditures and outlays. Social Security actuaries project the program will have just five more years (2017-2021) during which total income will exceed expenditures and outlays (source: 2017 Social Security Trustees Report, BTN Research).

The Month of August - The worst performing month for the S&P 500 since 1992 has been August. The stock index has suffered an average loss of 0.7 percent (total return) during August over the last 25 years (1992-2016). The best performing month since 1992 has been April, gaining an average of 1.9 percent (total return) (source: BTN Research).

Five Powerful Days - Over the five years of trading through June 30 (i.e., July 1, 2012, through June 30, 2017), the S&P 500 was up 14.6 percent per year on a total return basis, i.e., counting the impact of reinvested dividends. If you missed the five best performance days in those five years (i.e., five days in total, not five days each year), your average annual return was cut by 3 percent to 11.6 percent (source: BTN Research).

3 best ETF's Industrial Select SPDR ETF (XLI), iShares MedicalDevice ETF (MDT), The consumer staples select sector SPDR ETF (XLP) - by Bruderman Brothers 15May17 IBD

20Aug17 - Since November 2016 - The S&P 500 gained 15.9 percent (total return) in the 190 trading days since the Nov. 8, 2016, election of President Donald Trump (source: BTN Research).

Section 2

Precious Thoughts 2008

Department of Education: Although Ronald Reagan tried to eliminate it in 1996, today it has some 4,500 employees, none of which are teachers now. The Northwest Ordinance's 3rd article proclaims that "Religion, morality, and knowledge, being necessary to good government and the happiness of mankind, schools and the means of education shall forever be encouraged."

During W.W.II, the US Gov. set up 40+ internment camps for aliens. Over 10,000 Germans were put in camps and some did not get out until 1948 whereas the Italians and Japanese were released at the end of the war.

73% of Americans retire before age 65.

In the late 1950's, the federal government first offered taxpayer money to U.S. colleges and universities. There is NO constitutional basis for government involvement in education. One of the chief purposes of education is to train U.S. citizens to control the government. Today most colleges are highly regulated by the federal government via its subsidies.

U.S. Government's direct student loans started in 1994 at $ 400 million have grown to $ 11 billion. Indirect loans via banks etc. are $ 344 billion. New lending in 2008 is estimated to be $ 110 billion. The Government does not include estimated admin. costs of $ 708 million per year in FY 07 when comparing the cost of direct vs indirect loans.

As Britain stood alone against the Nazi's, some feel Israel is alone against the surrounding radical Islamists.

Tax Rebates: The 2001 rebates required Washington to borrow billions from the capital markets and then mailed it to families in the form of $600 checks. Predictably, consumer spending temporarily rose, and capital/investment spending temporarily fell by a corresponding amount. This simple transfer of existing wealth did not encourage productive behavior. The economy remained stagnant through 2001 and much of 2002. It was not until the 2003 tax cuts - which instead cut tax rates for workers and investors - that the economy finally and immediately recovered. In the previous 18 months business investment had plummeted, the stock market had dropped 18% and the economy had lost 616,000 jobs. In the 18 months after the 2003 tax rate reductions, business investment surged, the stock market leaped 32% and the economy created 5.3 million new jobs. Overall economic growth doubled. Both economic theory and practice show the superiority of tax rate reductions over tax rebates. - Brian Riedl, Heritage Foundation.

Washington Post - The percentage of households making more than $100,000 has doubled over the past 30 years from 12% to 24% while there has been no change in the percent of households making less than $ 30,000. The 'decline' in the middle class is due to its moving UP the income ladder, not down.

Cost-Of-Living: The U.S. CPI remained flat from 1801 to 1930. In 1978, Federal legislation first explicitly directed the Federal Reserve to conduct monetary policy with a goal that included "stable prices". Since then the CPI has tripled and the purchasing power of the dollar has decreased by 67%. (At a rate of inflation of 2.6% per year, in ten years the dollar losses 22% of its purchasing power)

Government's focused involvement on College costs and cigarettes have resulted in College tuition and fees up 229.6% and cigarettes up 225% in the period 1990 - 2007 vs the CPI increase of 66.6%.

From Mark Steyn: Liberal Governments are focused on secondary impulses - health care, day care, etc. The two most corrupt jurisdictions in North America are Louisiana and Quebec - both French derived. Of the 10 most free economies in the world, 8 are British derived (Switzerland & Estonia the exceptions). Canada: between 2001 and 2006, population up 1.6 million composed of 400,000 natives and 1.2 million immigrants. Unionized workforce: U.S. 13.9 % vs Canada's 32 %. The Quebec civil service is the same size as 5 times its population - California. In Canada, collective rights outweigh individual rights.

Policies that artificially limit price increases also tend to limit supply.

There are 200 million people in the middle-east with 100 million guns.

There are over 8 million companies in the U.S. with less than 100 employees.

Half of all U.S. draftees in WWII were unfit for combat service. Either 4F or non combat

The liberals love playing Robin-hood: "you will live better at the cost to others"

End of the World: 21Dec2012!!!.

Per Arthur C. Clarke, "Any sufficiently advanced technology is indistinguishable from magic."

From W.B. Crow's, "A History of Magic, Witchcraft & Occultism:

> Lotus, a water plant with large flowers and leaves above the water, the rhizome is in the mud below the water and the flower- and leaf-stalks pass through the water. The symbolic significance of the flower, is a mandala i.e. it represents the physical universe. The pistil in the middle represented Mount Meru, which was supposed to be the centre of the universe. The stamens surrounding it represent mountain. The petals were continents, four large ones at the four quarters, each accompanied by two smaller ones on each side, as in the map of the Brahminic and Buddhistic universe. The flower represented the spiritual order, emerging from Chaos, represented by the waters. Its counterpart in mythology was the great mother goddess. Gautama and other buddhas are usually shown seated on the lotus. Brahma was represented as born on the lotus. Osiris floated on the lotus after his birth. Curiously enough, the lotus no longer grows in Egypt.

The chief witch celebration called Walpurgis Nacht by the Germans. The Eve of St. Walburga's Day or Roodmass in England. St. Walgurga's Day is May 1st. The night before this was the witches' great festival, and the reason has nothing to do with the saint. April 30th was connected with

Hades or Pluto, God and King of the infernal regions, and his festival was celebrated on this day. In the church it is dedicated to St. Donat or Aidoneus who is a dragon-slaying Saint, signifying the casting down of the evil one to the lower regions. That no doubt is why the witches chose it.

Limited war favors belligerents of limited means. Only total war allows liberal democracies to exploit weapons of mass destruction!

J. M. Wronski 1778-1853, Polish mathematician: Messianism - According to Wronski, whilst Christ was the Messiah to save individuals, a second Messiah must be a nation, to save nations.

8 March 2008 - per Moqtada al-Sadr, Asharq Al Awsat: "I have failed to liberate Iraq and transform its society into an Islamic society." Background - A radical Shiite cleric and head of his Mahdi army. Had earlier taken control of Baghdad's Sadr City (named after his father, and home to two million Shiites on the east bank of the Tigris).

Per Daniel Henninger: Democrat Party's ethos is as it was in the 1930's - dark forces arrayed to thwart the delivery of benevolence to fragile masses.

Iraq's 5 years: The capture of Saddam persuaded Libya's Moammar Gadhafi to abandon his nuclear program and seek reconciliation with the US. This in tern led to the rolling up of Pakistani scientist A.Q.Khan's proliferation network, whose arms extended to Iran and North Korea. Iraq, one of our two principal enemies in the Middle East to one of our 2 principle allies. Has 425,000 in the Iraq security forces, producing 2.4 million barrels of oil a day and $ 100 million to the provinces

Per Frederick Hess, "When a leader tries to wrestle with these things (hard things) there are influential constituencies that he upsets. It's much easier to manage the status quo than to enforce change."

Murders: Per FBI statistics, between 2004 and 2006 the number of whites murdered dropped from 7,005 to 6,956 vs black homicides up from 6,680 to 7,421 or 11%. Blacks make up 13% of the population.

Girl Scouts: now 2.8 million, ages 5 to 17 (losing 1% to 2% membership a year for about 10 years) sell some 200 million boxes of Girl Scout cookies each year.

In 2006, the median income for working-age husband-wife couples (ages 25-59) was $ 73,765. Eighty percent of Americans over the age of 40 own a home.

40 years of AMT: 1967 155 filers with AGI's over $ 200,000 paid no income tax. In 2004 196 (of 240,000) with AGI's over $ 1 million paid no income tax.

Jihad: Per Ayesha Jalal; The literal meaning is "striving for a worthy and ennobling cause." The Arabic root of Jihad means, "to strive against an undesirable opponent-an external enemy, Satan, or the base inner self." It cannot "be interpreted as armed struggle, much less holy war, without twisting its Quranic meaning."

It is illegal to publish "Mein Kampf" in the Netherlands.

Quoting Afshin Ellian, The criticism and Islam Issue is "whether we are capable of defending our values against the intolerance of radical Muslims. A strand of Western society - a combination of European nihilism, self-loathing and timidity-favors appeasement. It is not the strength of our enemies but our weakness that might be our ruin. Any weakness in the resolve to defend our democratic legal order should be seen for what it is: Betrayal and cowardice."

The percentage of alimony recipients that are male = 3.6%. In 2005, 33% of wives out earned their spouses.

The lines a drawn per Grover Norquist - a world divided between taxpayers, small businessmen and women, 2nd amendment voters, home schoolers, property rights activists, communities of faith and parental rights, the growing investor class, the police and military vs the Taking Coalition (government employees, labor unions, non profit sector, universities, trial lawyers and coercive utopians) - and yes there is overlap.

2008's Tax Freedom Day is 23 April, day 113. Government @ 113 days, federal taxes 74 days, housing 60 days, food, clothing & housing 108 days.

Fuel can color coding: Yellow = diesel, Red = gasoline & Blue = kerosene.

Projected 2008 worldwide income: $ 53 trillion will be double 1995's. US income = $ 14T

Harvard undergrad tuition, room, board and student services fee 08-09 $ 47,215

Carnival Cruise 3 months fuel costs ending 29 Feb 08, up 78% over 07 to $ 392 million

Projected new car sales of 14.95M for 2008 are the lowest since 1994.

Language does not describe smells and tastes very well.

A silence, like none I'd heard before.

A wife's shopping for her husband's bathing suit, to the shop person. "He has a trim figure, and I would like to get something modern but not too youthful, and modest but not too conservative. As for length, it should be on the longer side but short enough that he can get a little color on his legs."

Liberal focus on material welfare leads to psychological, emotional and developmental damage.

Democracy where political divisions bargain for special advantages for the groups that elected them and the national interests are forgotten

Democrats appear to be pushing for a collapse of the system to assist in their acquisition of more power. All that serves to precipitate governmental crisis, every disturbance of the states power, every weakening of the system - is viewed as good, very good for democrats.

Barack Obama supports, "Common sense gun safety*" and not the 2nd amendment.

* "opposed allowing ordinary citizens to carry concealed weapons and that a federal law banning concealed carried weapons except for law enforcement is needed." "Common sense gun safety" funded ($18M) by

the anti gun Joyce Foundation and Obama was an activist member of its board of directors

Global Warming: to prevent or to adapt? Should we spend trillions today or let future generations with superior technology, greater scientific knowledge and greater wealth do the job??

WSJ 8Feb08 - "far more Americans say they'd never vote for a Mormon than those who admitted they wouldn't choose a woman or an African-American."

From Robert Harris's "The Ghost" - "a steel-and smoked-glass office block with all its pipes on the outside. It nestled among pebbledash housing estates like an abandoned spacecraft after a fruitless mission to find intelligent life." and "like the declarations of undying love is a stranger's bedroom at midnight, shouldn't necessarily be held against you the next morning." and "Most of my friends had long since entered the kingdom of family life, from whose distant shores, in my experience, no traveller e'er returned." and "The business of the night transacted, the visiting party retreats to their own quarters, as keen as a vampire to avoid the unforgiving rays of dawn." "I reclined on my back, my hands folded across my stomach, as motionless as the stone effigy of a crusader knight on his tomb." and "On the Richter scale of bad ideas, this registered a ten."

To support the war in the middle east and thus democracy and tolerance or do we to do nothing and support extremism and totalitarianism.

Some Arab intellectuals reject democracy as a foreign, particularly Western concept.

Per Hara Marano: In 1968, 17.6 % of high school students had A averages - vs 2004's 47.5%. Using the classic benchmarks of adulthood - leaving home, finishing school, getting a job, getting married and having children - 65% of males reached adulthood in 1960 vs only 31% in 2000.

An estimated 35,000 tons of space debris (mainly meteorites) hits our atmosphere daily and what survives lands mainly in the ocean.

If you accept the threat of Islamic fundamentalism, it means either acting against it or national suicide.

Institutionalized mentally ill: In 1955 - 559,000 vs 2005 - 47,000. The mentally ill in 2006 were one sixth of US suicides (5,000), some 10% of incarcerations (230,000) and 10% of all homicides (1,700) as well as 1/ 3 of the homeless. Per US Justice Department: 56% of state prisoners, 45% of federal prisoners and 64% of local jail inmates suffer from mental illness. The paramount civil right of someone who is severely mentally ill should be adequate treatment not freedom! Supreme Court Justice Anthony Kennedy wrote in 1999: "It must be remembered that for a person with severe mental illness who has no treatment, the most dreaded of confinements can be the imprisonment inflicted by his own mind, which shuts reality out and subjects him to the torment of voices and images beyond our powers to describe."

Involuntary Institutionalization's justification?

The nations out-of-wedlock births are 38%. (Whites 28%, Hispanics 50% & Blacks 71%)

40% of single mother families are in poverty.

The US Dept of Energy calculates that every 10,000 liters of water produces 5 liters of ethanol or 1 to 2 liters of biodiesel! In 2008, the US will consume 130 million tons of corn for biofuels. Biofuels are economic nonsense, ecologically useless and ethically indefensible.

Genuine freedom is anchored in objective truths that we ourselves do not invent. You need both reason and faith!

Per a Pew Research Center poll: To the question, "can you afford what you want" the 'yes' response in 1992 was 39% and in 2008, 52% of American's answered in the affirmative. Why then do 80% say the US is on the wrong course - unending pessimism in the news media - where major layoffs are becoming routine!

US children: 20 million now live in a household with NO father, some 28% vs 14% in 1970.

The areas in the US with the worst problems today are areas that have the most government interference - education, health care and energy!

Political institutions encourage people to earn income by being predatory, not productive.

Integrated oil companies control 3.8% of oil reserves while country run oil reserves = 83%

Obama's windfall tax on oil's criteria?: 2007 gross profit margins? Oil 8.3%, electronics 14.5%, computer equipment makers 13.7% and Microsoft 27.5%. Or 2007 total profit dollars?: Oil & gas companies = $ 86.5 B, Financial Services Industry $ 137.5B, Info Tech Companies $ 103.4B.

McCain's push to direct oil company investments in alternate energy: from 2000 to 2005, oil companies funded $ 12B of the $ 46B alternate energy research. Did we require the Railroads to fund aircraft research. Let the oil companies do what they do best - look for and develop oil / gas resources.

Highway Trust Fund forecast $ 3B shortfall in 2008 due to decreased vehicle miles traveled / gasoline taxes. April 2007 was the 6th consecutive month of decreased miles driven (1.8%) and down 1.7% during the period November and April.

In the US, natural blondes = 3%, while blondes make up 30% of our female population.

Health care: uninsured; 38% reportedly either went without or delayed health care during 2007 while 17% of insured reported the same

Can America afford to defend itself?

Per Roosevelt in 1933, "unsupported threats to foreign countries were not only useless but dangerous, undermining the authority of the individual country espousing them." He put more trust in military strength than in the State Department's ditherings and moral indignation.

In 2005 the US population increased by 2.9 million while marriages dropped to 2,230,000 (7.5 per 1,000) from 2004's 2,279,000. 2005 divorce rate @ 3.6 per 1,000 people was the lowest since 1970! Peak year was 1981 @ 5.3 per 1,000.

Only 63% of US children grow up with both biological parents - the lowest figure in the Western world!

One percent of coupled households consist of unmarried heterosexual partners.

Massachusetts has the 2nd lowest divorce rate @ 2.2 per 1,000 people.

Two-thirds of all Engineering Ph.D's granted in the U.S. go to non-citizens.

In 1932, 19,372 protestant clergymen who supported pacifism, refused to defend their country.

An American should prefer international cooperation between sovereign nations as opposed to the European preference for global governance by transnational institution

Over 60: China has 150 million (11% of the population) projecting 400 million in 2050

Alien Abductions: During the 1970's and 80's, some 2 million Americans reported their abductions.

As a result of the water saving efforts of the residents of Natick, MA - "Due to decreased usage, water rates for the Town of Natick are increasing in FY2009 - approximately 23%!

18 July 2008 - So far in 2008 the Mexican army says it has confiscated more than 500 tons of marijuana in the state of Baja California alone.

2nd Amendment: Justice Antonin Scalia, 26 June 2008, "We start therefore with a strong presumption that the Second Amendment right is exercised individually and belongs to all Americans."

Obama and guns: 1. Voted against "Protection of Lawful Commerce in Arms Act", 2. endorsed the total ban on the manufacture, sale and possession of handguns, 3. Totally opposed the Right-To-Carry, 4. Supported a ban on the sale and transfer of semi-automatic firearms. He supports, "common sense regulations" and the "rights" of cities and states to regulate guns and gun owners.

Pennsylvania has banned hunting on Sunday since 1873 and 4 of 10 Democrat primary voters were gun owners

Speaking the truth is dangerous.

Government responds to constituencies and takes great pains to preserve the existing institutions.

Per Larry Summers, "It is hard in this world to do well. It is hard to do good. When I hear a claim that an institution is going to do both, I reach for my wallet."

The U.S. spending $ 581B on SS, $ 387B on Medicare and 291B on Medicaid = $ 1.24T, equal to Canada's GDP

Platanium is a stainless-steel alloy.

Insurance Losses - Toilet failures: The average cost, after the insurance deductible was paid is $ 5,584 per incident..

There are 250,000 sweat glands in each of our feet.

The reality is that when it comes to dangerous jobs, firefighters don't even make the top 10, according to the federal Bureau of Labor Statistics. Who does? Loggers, fishermen (Are you taking note, Gloucester firefighters?), pilots and navigators, structural metal workers, drivers-sales workers, roofers, electric power installers, farm workers, construction laborers and truck drivers.

Per NAEP studies: pre-schooled children show NO improvement in fourth grade math, reading and science scores over 1970's no preschool students.

August 2008: In Sept 2007 - MoveOn.Org called General Petraeus - General Betray us. In April 2008, Harry Reid declared, "the war is lost". Hillary Clinton said the general's claims of progress were not credible.

Iran buys more than 1 million tons of US hard red winter wheat, first buy in 27 years!

The CIA's security contractor, SOC, pays its protective service employees $ 715 per day in Iraq.

Per Stephen Leacock: "Most people tire of a lecture in ten minutes; clever people can do it in five. Sensible people never go to lectures at all."

Chinese believe that Yan = good luck as do odd numbers = 1935!!!!

A gallon of corn ethanol contains 76,000 Btu of chemical energy and normally takes 60,000 Btu of fossil fuel to produce the crop and distill a single gallon.

The US spreads 16 million tons of salt (Rock) to our roads annually to melt ice.

Negative thinking is mental malpractice.

Cypress, a traditional symbol of eternity

Italy 'overthrows' fascism and declares war on Germany - 25 July 1943

2008 Obama:

Blacks	95%
Single Women	70%
Under 30	66%

Beaujolais Nouveau: a red wine made from Gamay grapes, is the first wine of the new season and by French law, is made available on the third Thursday of November. In 2001, 3.9 million bottles were shipped to the US vs 2.55 M in 2007

Per Seneca: Because they themselves could not prosper they want everyone else to be ruined. This dislike of others' success and despair of their own, causes their minds to become enraged against fortune.

What are the differences between: The Weggie, The Wet Willie and The Rear Admiral?

The Cypress is the traditional symbol of eternity

Heroin becomes morphine after metabolism in the liver

US Pandemics Fatalities:

	Worldwide	US	
1918-19	Spanish Flu	50 million	500,000
1957	Asian Flu	2 million	75,000
1968	Hong Kong Flu	1 million	36,000
2007	Bird Flu H5N1's mortality rate 61%!!!!!		199

FEMA has 125,000 empty trailers.

A cow produces 4 tons of methane per year, mostly burping. Agriculture produces 14% of pollution.

Precious Thoughts 2009

The key elements of being American: The English language, Christianity, religious commitment, English concepts of the rule of law, The responsibilities of rulers, and the rights of individuals - all derived from the "distinct Anglo-Protestant culture of the founding settlers of America in the 17th and 18th centuries". - Samuel Huntington

Percent of people over 15 who smoke daily: Greece 48.2%, Russia 43.4%, Austria 40.7%, Germany 26.7%, Switzerland 20.7% and US 18.7%

Belgium has Western Europe's highest rate of suicide

There are 31 million single women (divorced, separated, spouse died, never married) in the US. They make half the median household income at $ 22,592 vs $43,130. Net worth one-third of all households at $ 32,850 vs $ 93,001.

Many years of bottom-up activism later, I struggle to cling to what she called "our 'foolish illusion' that we can effect change (which) fosters in us the capacity to act." Her new paradigm requires voters who are really paying attention, and media feeding a voracious appetite for valid information.

Detroit, Michigan has not had a republican run for mayor in 40 years. Every election 2 democrats run! After 40 years of Democrat leadership, 49% of the adults are illiterate and only 21% of kindergarden students eventually graduate from high school

Philanthropy is the refuge of rich people who wish to annoy their fellow creatures - Oscar Wilde

The new 'energy efficient' light bulbs consumed 10 metric tons of mercury in the 2 billion sold in the US through 2007.

The use of gold in jewelry was 3,000 metric tons in 2001 down to 2,000 metric tons in 2008.

U.S. Army desertion rate in 2008 was less than 1 % or 3,500 world wide with 71 in Europe

The Governments rate calculation for poverty dates from 1965 and uses "a family's reported annual income. Per the Bureau of Labor Statistics Consumer Expenditure 2006 Survey: purchases by the poorest 20% of American households were more than twice as high as their reported incomes. Note: the 30 million blacks in the US have a higher standard of living than the 30 M Canadians.

Lotteries are voluntary taxes on the stupid.

For all those men who say, 'Why buy the cow when you can get the milk for free?', here's an up date for you. Nowadays 80% of women are against marriage Why? Because women realize it's not worth buying an entire pig just to get a little sausage.

Union College, Schenectady 2009 Tuition, room & board = $ 48,552

Deaths from prostate cancer: US 200 per million men each year vs Europe's 400

Medicare spends $ 8.7 B of its $ 500 B budget on medical equipment in 2009

Decision is a risk rooted in the courage of being free - Paul Tillich

Korean War: Started 25 June 1950, Armistice signed 27 July 1953. However, "The war period was extended to 31 January 1955 by the United States Congress to define a period of benefit eligibility in the wake of uneasy peace negotiations after 27 July 1953".

Medical valuations: statin study - 8,000 placebo had 60 deaths while 8,000 statin had 34 deaths = small absolute benefit (0.6%) vs large relative risk reduction 34 vs 60 = 43%.

"Beneficial" medical results = prevent one serious event for every 18 people treated over a 5 year period. Equivalent to daily aspirin regimen to reduce heart attack risk.

In 2009, there are some 800,000,000 people living in India who earn less than $2 daily

New York State loses 150,000 in population annually

What is the value of a degree with a "Recreation Event" major???

The Christian ideal of individual moral equality before the Creator.

Oaths by their nature are unconditional: They are made to ward off the possibility that the intensity of the relationship they govern will slacken and fall prey to moral weakness or negligence. - Tilman Allert's 'The Hitler Salute'.

African Aid: Runs at $ 50 B per year with some $ 1 T over the past 60 yrs. Results are lower per capita income than in the '70's with 50+% or 350 M receiving less than $1 per day. Twice the number of people 20 years ago.

No New Taxes per Obama: On 1 April 2009, US Govt taxes on cigarettes goes from 39 cents a pack to $1.01. 1 out of 5 in US smoke. One half of smokers are low income and 1 in 4 is poor!

500 years ago, Francis I of France was asked what misunderstandings had fueled his constant wars with the Habsburg Empire's Charles V. He replied, "None, we are in complete agreement. We both want control of Italy."

Previous predicted world catastrophes: #1 In 1898 the catastrophe facing the globe was the exhaustion of nitrogen based fertilizers which would, in 20 years, lead to starvation in the Western World. In Europe gangs exhumed cadavers for essential nutrients, in the US, the bleached buffalo bones were collected and shipped East for processing, some 20 million tons of Peruvian guano were exhausted between 1850 and 1870.

#2 In 1926, Calvin Coolidge's Federal Oil Conservation Board reported "Total present reserves in pumping and flowing wells...are estimated at about four and half billion barrels which is theoretically but six years supply." Sometime in 1932, the experts warned, the ground would yield its very last drops.

Women: 12% of adult women live in poverty vs 8% of adult men. From 1996 to 1998 women's share of US private wealth was 51% - 25% from marriage, 20% from inheritance, 2% from divorce. In 2005 51% of women ran there wealth without a husband's involvement. 25% never married, 11% are divorced and 9% are widowed and 5% are separated. Women now hold 57% of bachelor's degrees and 59% of master's degrees.

Per Talleyrand: Nations have everlasting interests rather than eternal friends or enemies.

International politics is about power and position, about preventing injury and protecting interests. Love and friendship move people, not nations.

The EPA was established under President Nixon

Rigorous hand-wringing

Per The Hadith, an Islamic scripture second in authority only to the Quran, remarks on Muhammad's practice of 'ghazu' or bounty raids in which camels and caravan drivers were held for ransom. Ghazu was a recognized part of 7th century Arabian economy The cover for modern day Muslim pirates.

What about the U.S. House members passing out $ 9.1 million in bonuses to their staff members on top of the $ 2.5 million in automatic pay raises that lawmakers gave themselves? I understand the average House aide got a 17% bonus. I took a 5% cut in my pay to save jobs with my employer. You haven't said anything about that. Who authorized that? I surely didn't!

Executives at Fannie Mae and Freddie Mac will be receiving $ 210 million in bonuses over an eighteen-month period, that's $ 45 million more than the AIG bonuses. In fact, Fannie and Freddie executives have already been awarded $ 51 million, not a bad take. Who authorized that and why hasn't anyone expressed outrage at this group who are largely responsible for the economic mess we have right now.

Although the liberal press disparaged the Bush 2005 inauguration cost of $ 43M as lavish, no such comments on Obama 2009 inaugural costing $ 150Million.

Regarding the Federal Government's right to tax and spend, in 1841, Congressman Thomas H. Benton opined, "The distribution of public property for the promotion of party or personal popularity is a vulgar artifice and requires not talent but impudence (lack of shame / offensively impertinent), to execute it.

Thomas Calhoun: "What could be more unjust than to distribute a common fund in a certain proportion among the states and to compel the people of the States to make up the deficit in a different proportion, so that some shall pay more and others less than what they respectively receive? What is it but cunningly devised scheme to take from one State and to give to another - - to replenish the treasury of some States from the pockets of the people of the others, in reality to make them support the Governments and pay the debts of the other States as well as their own?"

The debate as to the limitation of Federal Government funding of other than "general welfare" and its definition: ie only internal security, external security and the banking system which were deemed to be the only "general" ie national interests.

Mexico's Drug War: Mexico's severe gun laws generally prohibits civilian possession of firearms or ammunition in calibers commonly used by the Mexican military, such as 9mm or larger handguns, and .223 and .30-caliber rifles. Unauthorized possession has = up to 15 year imprisonment. Only 1/ 3rd of the 15 million firearms in Mexico are registered (as required by Mexican law). Current US law prohibits selling guns to non-US residents, to illegal aliens and to most legal non-immigrant aliens. There are heavy penalties for selling guns for use in a violent or drug trafficking crime, illegally exporting arms. Gun restrictions on Americans will not solve Mexico's drug crime, this is a scapegoat move.

Little more than half of graduating High School seniors go on the college, the remainder go to work.

A Bomb: 1st test 16 July 1945, Truman orders bombs use 25 July 1945, Bombs dropped 6 and 9 August.

India: Has 15 million blind and Mumbai's over crowded trains kill an average of 10 people a day.

Every day some 1,800 veterans die in America. Per US law, they are entitled to a funeral with 2 officers, a flag and bugle player for taps. There are 24 notes in taps. Buglesacrossamerica.org supplies most of the buglers.

48% of car crashes involve only one auto! This is where size can effect survivability.

US infant mortality dropped from 58 per 1,000 in the 1930's to 7 per 1,000 today.

Most aircraft bird strikes occur between July and October.

Per a Princeton University study: boys raised by single mothers are twice as likely to end up in prison by age 32, that girls who are born outside of marriage are three times as likely to have a teenage pregnancy and that teens born out side of marriage are about twice as likely to drop out of high school compared with their peers who are raised in intact, married families. Only 7% of college educated women are having children out of wedlock compared with more than 50% of women with a high school degree or less. per a recent Child Trends study.

Islamic law stipulates the ages of maturity as: Boys @ 15 and girls @ 9!

Marketing Grape Nuts: Red & white wheat and barley are ground (until 5 years ago the husks were removed for cattle feed) - now they stay so Grape Nuts can sell as "whole grain"! Vitamins and minerals are sprayed on to qualify it for food-stamp programs.

Although the politicians love to say the more money spent on prevention will reduce health costs - it is not the case. Prevention reduces illnesses but at a cost. Think of the cost of mammograms for millions of women every year - do they reduce health care costs? Or statins used by millions with only a absolute reduction in deaths of 0.6% but a relative reduction of 43%. Definitely not reducing health care costs.

90% of the lower actual costs of health care in Europe is due to lower incomes in Europe. The percentages are not that different.

Canada does not authorize cardiac procedures for people over 65. It appears that the government emphasis on managing health care costs is to restrict expenditures on the elderly.

Cohabiting couples and children: 50% of children of cohabiting adults saw their parents part company by age 5 vs 15% born to married couples. Children of cohabiting adults are significantly more likely to experience emotional problems, school failure and physical and sexual abuse.

Only 7% of college educated women are having children out of wedlock vs 50% of women with high school degrees or less.

Why cohabiting women do not get married: working class and poor men have seen their real wages fall since the 1970's which makes them less attractive as husbands to their girl friends and mothers of their children and may explain why non-marital childbearing is concentrated among blacks, latinos and working class and poor whites.

In South Africa: 1,000 die daily of AIDS, 1 in 6 adults (5 million are infected with AIDS including 30% of pregnant women).

June 2009 - my government at work: 1. Tobacco bill legislates less tar & nicotine = more cigarettes to get fix. Menthol is ok to satisfy the 75% of blacks that favor menthol. Reduce advertising to keep Philip Morris's market share stable. No tort protection for full compliance = Democrat cash cow for tax revenue and tort bar campaign contributions.

2. Cash for Clunkers = needlessly destroys old cars, misallocates scarce resources. Revive the housing industry by burning down old houses? Removes inexpensive cars and parts. New parts are more expensive. This is green gesture politics!!!!

We are close to putting collective fiscal good over individual health.

Kyrgyzstan will close its critical airbase at Manas to US supply flights to Afghanistan on 18Aug09. Obama's 'goodwill' comes up dry.

EU greenhouse gases: 9 to 10% from farm emissions - more than all industrial processes such as steel making and chemical manufacturing combined. Livestock produced gases from manure = methane and nitrous oxide.

Spending on health and welfare makes up 1/ 3rd of Calif

$ 100B budget. New York spends $ 2,283 per capita on medicaid, highest in US. Medicaid + public schooling = 60% of state budget.

The US registers some 2 million new drivers every year.

The penalty of a Leninist system is that the loss of freedoms is not proportional to the 'increase' in standard of living.

Democracies are often harsh and disappointing and test the patience. Democracy will fail a people without the patience, skill or will to fight for individual freedom. The moral value of representative capitalist democracy is questioned as to its materialism and greed.

Half the people in the US vote for a living while the other half work for a living.

People with less than a college education have seen almost no improvement in health over the last 30 years. White males aged 50 years old who have no schooling beyond high school have mortality rates more than twice as high as those with college degrees.

Do not restrict the inputs of economic growth, which are people and capital!

If age had been indexed for improvements in mortality rates since inception of Social Security, Americans would be waiting until age 73 to get their first check.

The 75+ crowd spend 16% on health annually vs the 6% national average ($ 7,400 in 2008). 33% of Medicare payments fund the last 2 years of life @ $ 46,412 avg.

Spending on student services and administration has outpaced spending on instruction by a multiple of 2 between 1995 and 2006. This is a resource reallocation from classroom instruction to paper pushing. This does not improve the educational outcomes.

It is the person and the behavior that are to blame for crime, not the tools.

The housing crises was caused by misguided and intrusive regulations and political pressures. Forcing banks to make home loans to people not financially able to bear the costs, the highest foreclosure rates for any segment of the population.

Obama's Tzars average salary is $ 172,000 plus a staff.

Instead of funding growth, we are funding entitlements

Obama lied, the economy died

25 July 2009, Peggy Noonan described the support for Obama Care as coming from:

"European Christian Democrat spirit of community, of "We are all in this together." This spirit potentially unites Democrats, leftists, some Republicans and GOP populists, the politically unaffiliated and those of whatever view with low incomes."

Per Obama - our health care system is the most expensive in the world. What is wrong with this picture: You are coming up the escalator on the metro in Washington DC and there are several people with cups looking/begging/intimidating you for your small change handout. They are smoking cigarets which at over $ 7 per pack are the most expensive cigarets in the world. Are we ready to pay for their medical and possibly, in Massachusetts their dental insurance?????

Obamacare: 9 out of 10 American's would get less care. 20% of those without health care are illegals, 60% make $ 50,000 or more a year and can afford insurance, 30% are eligible for Medicaid or other government programs but do not participate. That leaves some 2% of all American citizens for which Obama wants to dismantle the world's greatest health-care system.

"Quality-adjusted life years" - takes into account the patient's life expectancy!!!!!!!!!! Used by the UK's National Institute for Health and Clinical Effectiveness. And AARP does not care.

Oshkosh's $1.05 B June 2009 order for 2,244 M-ATV (5 soldier vehicle) to be delivered by end of year for Afghanistan!

A European style welfare-entitlement state requires European-style levels of taxation on the middle class and will result in European-style low growth and high unemployment rates.

The liberal dream: yoking the middle-class to cradle-to-grave government entitlements.

The VA's budget, set annually by Congress, has long been too small to cover all the benefits promised to veterans. So the VA has increasingly rationed care by introducing income restrictions on new enrollees, cutting coverage for brand-name prescription drugs and raising copayment.

Medicaid: when states freeze reimbursements to doctors - fewer doctors accept enrollees.

The U.S. deficit for 2009 = 13% of GDP, the highest since WWII. Per the Chinese, spending creates deficits!!

As the governments' role in providing health care expands, the risk is that rising costs will lead to increasingly politicized efforts to control quality and access. Americans who want to spend more of their own money for their own insurance and care will always have the option of doing so. The U.S. spends $ 2 T or 1 out of 6 Dollars of GDP on health care. Government programs account for 46% of health care expenses.

In July 2009; of the 75 coalition troops killed in Afghanistan, 40 were U.S. Obama has doubled the U.S. troops in country to 62,000 with another 39,000 NATO.

Sigmund Freud hated America. He believed Americans had channeled their sexuality into an unhealthy obsession with money. "Is it not sad," he wrote to a German friend after WWI, "that we are materially dependent on these savages, who are not a better class of human beings?"

Was Freud responsible for our culture of therapy and victimization which through over our stoic legacy of Puritan restraint? 10% of Americans are currently on antidepressants!!!!

"The problem with socialism is that eventually you run out of other people's money." - Margaret Thatcher

The waiting list to enter a hospital in Canada is 830,000 while in England it is 1.8 M. Canada's population is less than California's.

In the 1980's, academia became increasingly open to politically correct speculation in lieu of conventional standards of proof.

Bee stings kill 50 people in the U.S. annually.

"If you suffer for doing good and you endure it, this is commendable before God" - 1 Peter 2:20

Unions are monopolies and as such can charge monopoly rates for their labor. Fosters inefficient work rules.

Preventive medicine saves money? There are 90 million cats in the U.S. In 2007, there were 247 cats that contracted rabies. Rabies vaccine costs $ 22 and is good for 3 years. To vaccinate 90 M cats = $ 198 M and would save 741 cats over the 3 year period or $ 267,206 per cat.

Richard Wagner described the miss-placed efforts of liberals as "since we went for freedom of the Folk without knowledge of the Folk itself, nay, with a dislike of any genuine contact with it."

The FY 2008 interest payment on the national debt was $ 412 billion. (Only Defense and income redistribution (HUD & Food Stamps) were higher.) 49 % or $ 202B was paid to Foreign Governments! The Congressional Budget Office estimates 2019 interest payments at $ 806 B

Members of Congress ensure they have gerrymandered seats where they pick the voters rather than the voters picking them."

Debt held by foreign governments as of May 2009:

China $ 802B, Japan $ 677B, Caribbean (off-shore entities) $ 195B, Oil Exporters $ 193B, Brazil $127B, Russia $ 125B

Should bar congressmen from accepting contributions from outside their districts.

The elements of the population that want more government are more politically active.

Nuclear Power: The 104 US reactors produce 20% of our electricity and 70% of all carbon free electricity.

Oil provides 40% of the world's energy but only 2% of US electricity. Recent prices for a barrel of oil: $ 40 in 2004, $ 147.27 in July 2008, $ 32.40 in December 2008.

Medical 'best practices' are developed from clinical studies providing averages from populations that may or may not apply to the patient. They exclude patients with multiple conditions, the elderly or people on multiple medications. They vary: Statin prescriptions for high cholesterol patients: US 52%, UK 35% and Germany 26%.

Applying the Migratory Bird Treaty Act: 13 Aug 2009 ExxonMobil fined $600,000 for the death of 85 birds that got into contact with oil. In July, PacificCorp fined $ 1.4M for 232 eagles that were electrocuted on its power lines. In July 2008, a wind farm at Altamont Pass, CA was found to be killing an average of 80 golden eagles yearly with its turbines and it was estimated that some 10,000 birds were being killed by Altamont turbines annually. The American Bird Conservancy estimate wind turbines kill between 75,000 and 275,000 birds a year with NO Justice Department action to this politically correct industry. Each megawatt of power results in from 1 to 6 birds killed per year. We now have 25,000 MW.

US 15 year olds math performance: 24th out of 29 industrialized countries.

"Green Revolution" - In the 1940's, Norman Borlaug developed wheat and rice strains increasing yields by sixfold. Today, famines are politically induced events not true natural disasters. A genuine green movement does NOT pit man against the Earth, but rather applies human intelligence to exploit Earth's resources to improve life for everyone.

Life expectancy: varies with age, US is higher than UK & Germany. It reflects not only health care but diet and lifestyles. US highway fatalities are 15 per 100,000 vs Japan's 6.6. Homicide rate in US is 10 times UK. Obesity: US 32.2%, Japan 3%, France 9.5%, Germany13.6% Canada 18%, Australia 21.7%

US health care expenses due to obesity = 10%. Obese Americans spend 36% more on health services and 77% more on medications than people of normal weight. 20 X more likely to develop diabetes, 2.5 times heart disease, 2 X cancer, hypertension and asthma.

Is obesity a preexisting condition?

American's have a higher survival rate for 13 of the 16 most common forms of cancer vs OECD countries. Cancer mortality in the US 166 per 100,000 vs Canada 173, UK 175.6

Infant mortality: a function of the mother's choices (notably age, marital status and drug use) Teen pregnancy rates are higher and pregnant women in the US more likely to be living alone.

Health-care: Forced Unionization - Govs. Blagojevich on Illinois (2005) and Gray Davis of Cali. (1999) repaid debts to Andy Stern and his Service Employees International Union (SEIU) by reclassifying state-reimbursed in-home health care (and child-care) contractors as state employees - and forcing them to pay union dues.

Obamacare: Under regulation by HHS, "power under the public health insurance option" would allow regulation of all health care workers including doctors and nurses being forced into unions.

Obama received 53% of the popular vote: African Americans 95%, Jews 78%, Hispanics 67%, Catholics 54%, Protestant 45% and whites 43%.

Keynesians wrong again: Pump money into the economy and create jobs - wrong. The government has borrowed some 1 trillion dollars out of the private economy and increased government spending by $1T. Bush $ 152B funded $ 600 for everybody. Obama $ 787B in tax credits etc. - Neither increased incentives for investment and / or entrepreneurship. Results unemployment 9.7%, 14.9 million unemployed, 9.1 million stuck in part-time jobs, 2.3 M looking = 26.3M unemployed or underemployed = 16.8% with total income down $ 427B. Same period Germany and France used fiscal restraint and had economic growth return 2nd Qtr 2009.

Medicare, the model? Will be bankrupt in 2017, The average family with private health insurance pays $1,788 a year to compensate for medicare/ aid underpayments. Reported Admin costs of 3% fantasy - does not include personnel, admin expenses etc. and pays no taxes that private plans do. FBI estimates fraud between 3 and 10%. shortchanges seniors - covers only 50% of health costs, limits number of hospital days etc.

Sec of Interior, Salazar plans a 1,000 square mile solar collector in NE, AR, Ca, Co producing 35,000 megawatts of electricity the same as 30 nuclear plants using 30 square miles of land. The desert based collectors must be washed monthly and need cooling water? He wants to build 186,000 50 story wind turbines and 19,000 miles of high voltage transmission lines.

A structural driver of inflation are the trade unions, able to extort above average wages due to their monopolistic position.

Market based consumption triumphed over the Soviet vision of mass entitlement.

Nazi's wanted to eliminate class conflict and thus the appeal of Marxism.

Obama lost 12 of the last 14 primaries.

Who will control health care decisions????

Prof. Victor Fuchs explained that national health insurance movements rose alongside larger transfers of responsibility from the family to the state. " Every time the state assumes an additional function, child care or benefits for the aged, the need for close family ties becomes weaker." "One of the most effective ways of increasing allegiance to the state is through national health insurance."

Over 65: 1 in 5 Germans vs 1 in 8 US. German GP's $ 80,000 vs US $ 161,490

During the Spanish civil war, the communists murdered some 16,000 priests and nuns as well as 14 bishops.

The Kinder Morgan "Rex" gas pipeline from Meeker, Co to Clarington, Oh (1,679 miles) consumed 1.4 million tons of steel, primarily 42" pipe and cost $ 6.7B completed1Nov09

In 1764, France expelled all Jesuits

Financial Crisis: Commercial bank capital holdings are governed by the Basel regulations, which are set by the financial regulators of the G-20 nations! In 2001 U.S. regulators enacted the Recourse Rule requiring American banks to hold far more capital against individual mortgages and commercial loans than against mortgage backed securities rated AA or AAA. The effect of these regulations was to create immense profit opportunities for a bank that shifted its portfolio from mortgage and commercial loans to mortgage-backed securities. The 'Crisis' came about due to the G-20's own Basel rules. Now the G-20 has decided to blame the crisis on bank compensation systems.

Traduced = speak evil, to slander, to speak falsely

Stridulously = harsh sounding, strident

threnody = song of lamentation at a persons death

Due to the financial support from domestic unions, the American left opposes all efforts to replace dictatorships with democracies as democracies pose the threat of less costly labor.

Obama is not pushing free-trade agreements with our friends (Columbia and Panama) and supports our enemies such as Chavez, Morales and Castro.

Left wing trade unions, greedily demanding their public sector members be exempted from the pain they want others to share.

"Agreement in principle" - diplomacy's three slipperiest words!!!

Our politicians say the financial community is a bunch of greedy scoundrels, while the financial community says the government is a bunch of incompetent bureaucrats.

Social Security has the image of a large scale insurance where on the individual level there is a link between contributions and benefits, the accumulation of funds for future use ---a link between effort and reward. It is actually a system of taxation where today's contribution pays for today's benefits which replaces the principle of thrift with the practice of entitlement.

Government Employment: During economic contractions Up 1.8% annually and during expansions UP 2.4%. Employment: Fed Gov. 2.8M, State Gov. 5.2M and Local 6.6M for a total 14.6M - does not include military. Gov. employment now at its highest since 1993 @ 17.1%. The 1975 peak was 20%.

To prepare for a pandemic: www.pandemicflu.gov

The constitution enumerates the legitimate powers of the federal government in Article 1, Section 8. Congress is authorized to do 21 things - 3/4 ths of what Congress taxes us and spends money on is nowhere to be found on that list!

German workers pay 14.9% of gross pay for medical insurance.

Wearing leather (that noble material) shows man's superiority - as the stronger over animals.

Are you tired of waiting for sanctions to work?

Where Liberals rule: NY - between 2000 and 2008, 1.5 million left the state with NY City losing 1 M and some $ 4B in taxes not paid. Calif: same period 1.4M left. More would have gone in 2008 but they could not sell there homes. NJ: Supreme court allocates over 50% to 31 "special needs" school districts of 585. Asbury park spends $ 35,000 per pupil and gets $ 29,895 from 'special needs'. Has beautiful beaches, historic downtown and a train line to NYC but is a wasteland. Chicago: Democrats in power for 50 years = 73,000 homeless, 570,000+ (20.9%) in poverty, (256,000 50% below poverty @ $ 100 / wk), sales tax 14%, Parking meters $ 3 / hour, child deaths to violence highest in the US, all within a 2 sq. mile area! Sales tax 10.25%. Add 3% for soft drinks. 10% unemployment. Both our Governor and the President bringing their Chicago life style to the US?

In Chicago's Harold Ickes Project, you can get an apartment for $ 25 per month.

Obama majorities with under $50,000 and over $ 200,000 income groups

The 'Greens' practice a crude form of religion - pantheism, the worship of the earth and all its manifestations

Boys & College: Bachelors Degrees 42%, Community college 2 yr degrees 38%.

For every 167 females in 4 yr. colleges there are 100 males. At the same levels of education, women avoid risky business start-ups. Revenue of women-owned businesses is less than 5% of all revenue. Women earn only 20% of bachelor's degrees in physics, computer sciences and engineering termed 'economically important majors"! Colleges over accept men, not for national economic interests but for campus social interests as when the female-male ratio goes over 60/40 - the point at which men take advantage of their scarcity.

Humpback whales: In the 1960's, the population was less than 5,000 vs today 60,000!

Per a 2008 Pew study: substantial numbers of blacks believe there are two kinds of black people in America: Those with an education, jobs and stable families and those left behind.

There are three characteristics of all progressives: honesty, intelligence and liberal convictions. Luckily no progressive possess all three. He who is intelligent and honest was not a progressive. He who is honest and a progressive is not intelligent and he who is intelligent and a progressive is not honest.

Court Cases per year: State civil 17M, criminal 21.5M. Federal civil 265K, criminal 73K

Type 2 diabetes prevention: per Harvard Medical School, drinking coffee reduces risk up to 42% and drinking alcohol reduces risk up to 43%

European culture evolved over centuries to place the individual subordinate to the collective whole.

WWII German military philosophy misplaced 'Triumph of the Will' over reason and obedience over initiative.

A trial of the terrorists in the US demonstrates the principle of giving terrorists even more legal protections than the Geneva Convention provides uniformed soldiers fighting in a recognized war zone! Terrorists reject both the laws of war and the laws of American civil society.

Government run health care's decisions are based on the governments best interests, not the patients.

MA's 2009 25% sales tax increase should have been accompanied by a Government salary freeze

Gun Owners, US: Total 90M. 30M have either military or law enforcement experience.

2nd Amendment: Guns for both collective and personal defense.

Teachers can actually move students backward and continue to have a job, continue to get their step raises and continue to get their negotiated union increases!

Andy Stern, "American workers have not gotten a raise in a very long time. We've decoupled productivity from wages. And unions happen to be, despite what you think about them ideologically, a way to distribute wealth that doesn't cost the government a dime." WSJ 23Nov09

WSJ 23Nov09 - Kathleen Sebelius, Sec of Health and Human Services: "The most recent study I saw looked at 19 nations. We are 19th out of 19 countries in terms of our health results to everybody else. And we spend twice as much as any nation on earth on per capita costs on health care."

The day after Thanksgiving is Roto Rooter's busiest with some 6,200 jobs clearing bones etc. 50% higher than normal.

His comments weigh like a feather

Municipal busybodies that build a cause which is not complete until it has been imposed on all one's neighbors.

The Pilgrims gave America a theoretical concept of work and an attitude toward life that upsets the modern notion that a person's occupation equals his value.

In Oct 09 unemployment rate for men was 11.4% vs 8.8% for women. By the end of Oct 09, the US had lost 7.3M jobs with 5.3M men. The work force is now 50/50. The 'stimulus' package directed toward women, very little infrastructure work done.

Simpson's Paradox: aggregated data can appear to reverse important trends in the numbers being combined - a common but misleading statistical phenomenon rooted in the differing sizes of subgroups. Example:

Defense Spending: US 4%+ of GDP, Germany 1.3%, France and Poland 2%+. Problem is the modern welfare state where in Germany is consumes 52%. Germany, 49.3% vs US 30.2% in taxes on labor costs. There is no money for adequate defense in the Euro system. Belgium spends 74% on military personnel vs US 30%. They can not afford planes / helicopter etc. A welfare state will always triumph over the pentagon!

Intensive interrogation

Obama's EPA (Lisa Heinzerling) adopts "the precautionary principle". "When an activity raises threats of harm to the environment or human health, precautionary measures should be taken even if some cause and effect relationships are not fully established scientifically." This is 'close-enough" science = not scientific!!

Global Warming Beneficiaries: Phil Jones, director - U of East Anglia's Climate Research Unit. CRU was the recipient of $ 19 million of research grants between 2000 - and 2006! GW research: EU $3B (does not include individual EU country research) NASA $ 1.3B, NOAA $ 400M and Nat Science Foundation's $300M. California $600M

North American Jews immigrating to Israel in 2009 = 4,000 up 33% over 2008.

Obama wants a Franco-German welfare state, with mammoth public sector and still be able to compete with China, India, Brazil, Korea and the rest. This is a pipe-dream.

Obamacare propaganda: Peter Orszag, Budget Director's claim that it would "bend the cost curve down" is a complete fraud and mimics Al Gore's SS 'Lock Box".

14Dec09 - Obama attacks banks for not lending to small business as the cause for weak economy vs reality of the NFIB and Fed Reserve found only 10% of Small businesses report problems with obtaining financing!

Barney Frank and Chris Dodd - the two Members of Congress that did more to encourage the financial crisis are writing the NEW bank regulations!!!!!

Comment by Norman Baynes in "The Speeches of Adolf Hitler" - regarding AH's "Mein Kampf" - "Hitler from the first recognized the preponderant significance of the spoken word: the force which set in motion all the great historical avalanches, whether political or religious, was from the beginning of time the spell of the spoken word." - Hitler had in mind the oral teaching of Christ.

and a further comment

"It is not without interest to observe that the history of the Christian Church provided Hitler with models for his own Movement. The greatness of every mighty organization as representing the incorporation of an idea in this world lies in its religious fanaticism in which, fanatically convinced of its own right, it triumphs intolerantly over every other force. If an idea is essentially right and is in this way prepared for the struggle and thus enters into the battle on this earth, then it is unconquerable and every persecution will only lead to an increase of its inner strength. The greatness of Christianity did not lie in any attempts to come to terms with similar views of the ancient world but in the remorseless, fanatical proclamation and championship of its own teaching."

In the Anglican communion there are 70 million congregants world wide with the Archbishop of Canterbury, Rowan Williams at their head. The American Episcopal Church has 2 million.

Snow Fall: Water content (1") vs snow depth at various temperatures

@ 19 Degrees 1" water per 18" snow.

@ 28 Deg 1" water per 10" snow.

The draft was repealed under Nixon. This has led to over deployment of the National Guard.

Obamacare Doctors: The crack down is on specialists/surgeons and medical devices which are the costly end of medicine. Primary care doctors will face financial penalties for referrals to specialists. Incremental device improvements be penalized. Improvements will move to a 3 to 5 year cycle as in Europe to qualify as unique and therefor covered.

The Consumer Product Safety Improvement Act (CPSIA) decreed that children's products can not contain a component with more than three one-hundredths of 1% lead.

This include zippers, belts, hinge's on dressers, bicycles etc. subject to annual testing.

Cultures exhibit energy and will. When permanence is added it is a civilization. Treasures of the body

Culture and civilizations can become static

Americans have lost their sense of evidence

Communists accuse capitalists of practicing 'conspicuous waste'. Capitalists call it "Destructive Creation". the deliberate introduction of new, perhaps improved generations of durable goods that destroy, directly or indirectly, the usage value of units previously sold inducing consumers to repeat their purchase.

Each engine on a B-29 had 18 cylinders

Fertilizer markings: 10/10/10 = percentages of nitrogen/phosphorus/potassium

As 2009 closes - Greece and California have the same credit rating!!!!

Precious Thoughts 2010

Unions miss focus from improvements & efficiency to job security & benefits. Unions delay technology to maintain numbers of employees, Focus on work rules Flexibility is out the window thus less productive

Procedure based not results based. This is left hemisphere thought process focus on rule bound and control

Powers of the mind and spirit. Our sense of truth is under attack

Obamacare: Extending benefits to some Americans by cutting care of others is not reform - - it is unfair!

Obama bribes to Senators:

Florida's Bill Nelson $ 3.5B to keep Fl seniors Medicare Advantage. Other states to lose same.

No tax on Medigap insurance provider Mutual of Omaha.

Vermont $ 600M a year for Medicaid for 6 years

Massachusetts $ 500M a year for Medicaid for 3 years.

Nebraska & Michigan, NO tax on Blue Cross/Blue Shield Medigap insurance

Libby, Montana / superfund site everyone gets Medicare

Longshoreman's "Cadillac" healthcare plans exempted from 40% tax.

Harry Reid has exempted the 17 states with the highest health costs plus longshoremen, construction workers, some farmers and sundry other liberal allies.

Summary Unions: exempted from the 40% 'Cadillac   tax" = $ 60B payoff

The world's annual consumption of cheese is 20 million tons!!!

Portugal's Evora cloister - Praca do Giraldo, founded in 1559 by the Jesuits, was suppressed along with that order in 1759, was reopened as a university in 1975!

Obama Care: With the demise of OC, democrats now faced with Keeping their Word or Keeping their Jobs favor the latter.

An organizer demands solutions, a leader actually delivers solutions.

Poison Murders: Between 1998 and 2005 there were 523 confirmed, less than1% of all homicides. Infants #1 and the elderly #2.

Symphony Orchestras in danger: Most are outsized for their markets. Cleveland pays its conductor $1.3M with average player $140,200 + 10 weeks paid vacation, 26 weeks paid sick leave etc. Total players = 100 and can not be cut and remain a symphony!

California Public Sector: 235,000 employees (does not include higher Ed) with 85% in Unions. Over the past 10 years, pension costs for public employees up 2,000% while state revenues up 24%. Some 15,000 receive over $ 100,000 / yr.

Memorable Obama comments: Doctors prefer to cut off feet than treat diabetes. With the stimulus package heavily tilted toward jobless benefits and income transfers, job creation was impossible. His idea that adding 30M people to health care coverage and it would reduce costs was nonsensical.

In 1962, President John F. Kennedy signed executive order 10988 allowing the unionization of the federal work force.

Obama's cabinet members have zero private sector experience!

Budget deficits: Post WWII average 2.7%, Bush 3.2% and Obama 4.2%. Obama spending so far: Stimulus $787B, Child healthcare $30B, non defense increase $ 410B

Unions spent $ 100M on effort to get health care instead of organizing. Led to drop in Union participation in the private sector and no health care!

Organized labor lost 10% of its members or 834,000 in 2009 to a new low of 7.2% of the private sector work force. Union membership remained flat @ 12.3% due to increased public sector and overall drop in general employment. In 1980 it was 20%.

Public employee unions have a lucrative racket: they essentially leverage the tax dollars they receive in dues from the salaries and benefits of their members to lobby for more tax dollars to secure even fatter pensions and pay.

Obama wants change by government programs not opportunity.

Supreme court gives corporations 1st amendment rights! Why did NY Times object, under McCain-Feingold media corporations were exempt!!!!! Under this regime, free speech was not a constitutional right but a privilege granted by Congress.

Obama increasing Federal employment by 14.5% to 2.148 M in 2010.

Obama is against a perceived "concentration of power" in corporations that already exists in the Federal Government.

The U.S. post office lost $ 3.8 billion in fiscal year 2009.

The US funds half the world's AID's relief.

Foreign Born/U.S.: 1870 = 14.4%, 1910 = 14.7%, 1930 = 11.6%, 2000 = 11/1% (31.1M)

The U.S. is the graveyard of languages, within 3 generations, native language lost.

Medical payments: Private insurers pay 132% of actual costs vs 93% by Medicare and 88% by Medicaid.

Clinton's unwinding of the Cold War Defense of the U.S: Defense employed some 973,000 civilians in 1992 which declined to 671,000 in 2008. Obama raising it to 720,000 in 2010.

The epic battle of our time is between the private and public sectors for political primacy.

In 1871, "The Psychical Degeneration of the French People" was published, a paper that left the impression that simply being French constituted a mental illness.

Medical Doctors and psychiatrists are vulnerable to peer pressure as well as the goodwill of the state, which provides the credentials and certificates necessary for their practice.

A definition of Fascism: The blending of state and corporate power???

In 1880, Ohio with 3M inhabitants had 37 colleges vs England's 23M inhabitants with 4.

Per Dr. Thomas Roeder's 1995 book Psychiatrists-the Men Behind Hitler: Hitler's philosophy and his concept of man in general was shaped to a decisive degree by psychiatry. From Jim Marrs book, The Rise of the Fourth Reich: the five prominent European scientists of the 1800's that were the origins of psychiatry were: Thomas R. Malthus, the British economist who viewed war, disease and starvation as beneficial survival mechanisms against unchecked population growth: Charles Darwin, the naturalist whose 1859 book The Origin of the Species convinced whole generations that survival of the fittest is a law of nature; Friedrich Nietzsche, philosopher and close friend to Hitler's paragon, composer Richard Wagner, who declared "God is Dead" and advocated the superiority of the Ubermensh, or superman, over lesser races, virtues and values; Joseph Arthur, Comte de Gobineau, a French diplomat who championed the concept of an Aryan aristocracy and its preeminence over others; and Houston Stewart Chamberlain, the British-born philosopher who moved to Germany, married Richard Wagner's daughter and promoted an "Aryan world philosophy." Combining Malthus with Darwin = Social Darwinism

Charitable giving in the US: $ 300B a year with 100B to religions, $30B to higher education. (Hurricane Katrina = $6B)

The 2010 Canadian hockey - 'Dream Team' made a combined $128 M in the NHL.

The early Boy Scout handbooks (1915-1950) were attacked by labor unions and socialists for exhorting obedience to employers and the U.S. government.

Ancora Imparo = I am still learning. Said by Michelangelo when an old man

Joseph P. Kennedy II decides to remain Chairman and President of the non-profit Citizens Energy Corporation at a base salary of $596,988 (2010) rather than to enter politics.

Organized Labor admits to spending $ 500 million on the 2008 elections.

The Crusades made to rescue Christians: In 600, the Middle East (from Turkey to Iraq, Egypt and the southern Mediterranean coast) was Christian. The Crusades were a belated counter-offensive of Western Christians to come to the aid of Christians in the East in defending their lands against the further expansion of Islam.

Paul Ryan wants to "maintain promised health-care and retirement benefits for those who require them - the sick and the poor! Would index Social Security benefits to wage growth for a family earning $28,000 but limit increases to inflation for those above.

Peer Review: This process violates the fundamental principle of fairness. We do not allow judges to be parties to a controversy they are adjudicating Their interest in the outcome will bias their judgements and corrupt their integrity. Why should we expect scholars, especially operating under the cloak of anonymity, to fairly and honorably evaluate the work of allies and rivals?

Todays campuses are home to a toxic confluence of fashionable ideas that undermine the very notion of intellectual virtue and to flawed educational practices and procedures that give intellectual vice ample room to flourish.

Per Roman historian Tacitus: "Who would want to visit Germany with its unlovely scenery, its bitter climate, its general dreariness to sense and eye?"

Germany is a place without which European culture makes no sense." - Simon Winder

Progressives believe that the natural course of history is the emergence of secular rationality as the true way to think about problems and of state power as the effective way to organize society along rational lines.

The U.S. has some 23 million active and retired state and local public employees. Some 80% are in defined-benefit plans under which monthly pension payment are guaranteed!

Census 2010: Living in group quarters: College dormitories 2,064,128 and prisons 1,976,019.

Per Norman Podhoretz: "Judaism in not the religion of most American Jews, but liberalism is."

For a democratic culture, nothing is more unpalatable than the reality of human inequality. Diligence will not overcome a lack of genius.

Winter 2009/10: 49 of 50 states had snow storms in this, the coldest winter ever recorded!

In Turkey's eyes, the U.S. has become a late Ottoman sultan - pampered, decadent, lounging on its cushions puffing a hookah but unable to rouse itself to impose its will in the world.

Parties can cause presidents to express narrow views and thus thwart the popular will.

The sea otter with up to one million hairs per square inch has the densest fur of all mammals.

Jeffersonian Republicans and Hamiltonian Federalists advocated: funded debt, a central bank, excise tax on distilled spirits

Per Federal data, in 2000, only 27% of 4 year students in for profits finished in 4 years and 38% in 8 years. Median debt level $ 32,650. Soldier of Allah (SoA) self description by Fort Hood shooter Maj. Malik: The Pentagon's 86 page report made no mention of Islam but did state, "religious fundamentalism alone is not a risk factor."

Racial extortion!

"M" machine of movie 'Metropolis'

Applying the Migratory Bird Treaty Act: 13 Aug 2009 ExxonMobil fined $600,000 for the death of 85 birds that got into contact with oil. In July, PacificCorp fined $ 1.4M for 232 eagles that were electrocuted on its power lines. In July 2008, a wind farm at Altamont Pass, CA was found to be killing an average of 80 golden eagles yearly with its turbines and it was estimated that some 10,000 birds were being killed by Altamont turbines annually. The American Bird Conservancy estimate wind turbines kill between 75,000 and 275,000 birds a year with NO Justice Department action to this politically correct industry. Each megawatt of power results in from 1 to 6 birds killed per year. We now have 25,000 MW.

Per Edmond Burke: " ALL THAT IS NECESSARY FOR THE TRIUMPH OF EVIL IS THAT GOOD MEN DO NOTHING".

Syria bans the niqab (face covering Islamic veil) to protect its secular identity!

German has obligatory 6 months military service: In 2009 of the 226,000 men deemed fit to serve, 150,000 filed as conscientious objectors. Most do alternate service in hospitals.

The public sector is sheltering itself from the destruction of the American standard of living.

Only 5 of the 28 NATO countries have the draft. Since the mid 90's, Spain, Portugal, Italy, France, The Netherlands, Belgium and Sweden have scrapped conscription.

The draft was seen as a way to instill a sense of civic duty in young men from across society.

National Happiness: Of 155 countries surveyed: Denmark, Finland and Norway were on top with US #14, Germany #33, Italy #40 and France #44. Per OECD, 2008 GDP per capita: US $47,200, Germany $35,400, France $33,100, Italy $31,252. The avg American produces 43% more than the avg Frenchman. The avg American works 400 more hours per year than a German and 300 more than a Frenchman. Retirement: Only 38% of the French age 55 to 64 are working vs 62% of Americans.

Death Panel: With Dr. Donald Berwick in charge, an FDA panel drops the widely used cancer drug and another which may not be paid for. The 'new' cost effective philosophy drops Avastin used by 17,500 women for breast cancer. Per Berwick - "We can make a sensible social decision and say, 'Well, at this point, to have access to a particular additional benefit (new drug or medical intervention) is so expensive that our taxpayers have better use for those funds."

Chris Dodd got his "Livable Communities Act" passed by the Senate Banking Committee. The government will design "livable communities, cities and towns". This with cap-and-trade that will allow the government authority over industries and the Great Outdoors Initiative letting government acquire control over millions of acres of both public and private land = a socialist-economic system

We the People = rush legislation so no one knows what's in it. Financial reform taxes gold, has 'quotas' for women and minorities?

Unfunded Public Pensions: 50 States = $ 3T + municipal pensions. Example: Illinois has $80B in unfunded pensions and $40B in unfunded retiree health obligations. Go to defined contribution plans vs defined benefit plans. Retire same as private sector except 1st responders at 60.

Obama's / FDR's 10 job killers: 1. Executive orders and regulations promoting compulsory unionism = a bargaining monopoly with above market comp & benies. 2. Forced restructure of GM = destroyed bankruptcy law to give UAW the farm vs bondholders. 3. Obama Care = 50+ employees = $2,000 penalty per employee. 4. Unemployment of 99 weeks paid by employers. 5. $787B Recovery Act: spent mostly in sectors and states with low unemployment rates! with enormous debt. 6. Min Wage = up 3 times in 4 years = highest unemployment for teens. 7. Finance Bill of 2010 = tremendous uncertainty while 11 fed agencies create 243 regulations . 8. Offshore drilling moratorium = in 6 months, 12,000 out of work up to 400,000 if permanent. 9. Bush tax cut expiration = cash out of private sector to Gov. 10 Obama's runaway spending = higher taxes.

Self proclaimed 'progressives' = Woodrow Wilson, both Roosevelt s, Herbert Hoover, Lyndon Johnson, Jimmy Carter and Obama. Stress the importance of centralized government control over American's lives as paramount. Discredit limited Gov, individualism, natural rights, property right discredited. Patriotism a danger, religion a vice, constitutionalism a mere historical tic to be eradicated.

Obamacare not about health but expansion of unionization, entitlement & dependency.

Our national soul has its values fundamentally corrupted by bribing people with promises of getting medical and other benefits paid for by other people, the rich.

Not since the Norman conquerors of England published their laws in French has there been such contempt for the people's right to know what laws were being imposed on them.

Envy and resentment the progressives keys to success.!

France deports 'illegal' Roma (Gypsies from Romania).

3 civilizations in conflict: The West, The Muslim (Islam) and the Confucian (China) In Islam the conflict between the Arabs, the Turks and the Persians.. In the battle, the Saudi's have spent an estimated $ 2B per year for the past 30 years to spread Wahhabism. Are we losing the battle?

The 'partners' in Obamacare were: Center for American Progress (funded by Soros), AARP, AFL-CIO, SEIU and AFSCME

AFL-CIO & SEIU pledged $ 88M for 2010 Democrats election cycle.

SEIU has 1.8M members with 300,000 members, paying $7 monthly to the union political-action committee.

The director of the Immigration & Customs Enforcement, John Morton wrote a memo on 20 Aug 2010 stating that being in the U.S. illegally is no longer sufficient reason to send someone home. An illegal has to be a security threat or else commit a crime - and a violent one at that. Otherwise, ICE turns its $ 6B blind eye.

Obama has transformed the economy from one characterized by growth, wealth creation and personal responsibility to one of wealth-sharing, government control and slow growth.

The French language's rich vocabulary to describe an affront. Hurtful, deplorable, shameful, gravely injurious, profoundly shocking, outrageous.

Persistent unemployment from misbegotten government policies is why we have poverty which leads to more dependence on government. For 3 years, the private sector has been punished for the sins of the federal government with higher taxes and greater regulation. Money siphoned from the private economy destroys investment and consumer spending.

Value of US household's financial asserts is 2.5 times as large as their real-estate holdings.

Boston - where state government runs healthcare: insured up from 93.6% to 97.4% and average wait time to see a family doctor is 63 days vs Miami's 7 days even though Boston has 14 teaching hospitals and the state with the highest concentration of doctors.

Medicare: In 2010 - New enrollees = 3%. High income beneficiaries (couples with income above $ 170,000) = 5% of all beneficiaries. Low income individuals = 17% of medicare beneficiaries and have their premiums paid by Medicaid. Higher premiums applied to high-income Medicare beneficiaries. Why should people pay different amounts for the same government-financed program???

"University administrators are the equivalent of subprime mortgage brokers, selling you a story that you should go into debt massively, that it's not a consumption decision, its an investment decision. Actually, no it's a bad consumption decision. Most colleges are four-year parties." - Peter Thiel, WSJ 9Oct2010

Those in power institute the regulations and rules, then they either exempt themselves or hire people to protect them from the burdens and demands of their legislation.

Example: Insider-trading laws do NOT apply to Congress

Oct 2010 - German Chancellor Angela Merkel declared the multiculturalism in Germany had been a "total failure". Has actually resulted in "parallel communities". Germany wants "German Leitkultur" a term that evokes the country's Judeo-Christian traditions as well as the principles of the age of the enlightenment.

The German Historical Museum in Berlin runs the 1st German exhibition on Adolf Hitler.

Does the town budget exist to serve the citizens or the town employees?

Public sector unions have a vested interest in more state spending and they also enjoy a unique ability to elect their bosses - the politicians who set their salaries and benefits and that vote to create more government workers.

Question: How much of the salaries and benefits of town employees are governed by union contracts? Who has more control over the towns budget, the unions or the people?

September 2010: Highest job losses = CA - 63,500, NY - 37,500, NJ -20,200 and MA -20,900 vs Texas +4,000.

Car-Deer accidents of 1.1 million cost $4 billion in 2009.

The amount you pay is the same as it costs for a lawyer to sneeze.

Coming to a town near you? European style protests from "the usual mix of communists, union thugs, illegal immigrants, students and criminals.

The democrats are like the bride of Dracula, locked forever in an embrace with infusions of public union money (more than $ 170 million in 2010)

Per President Coolidge, the American people "are profoundly concerned with producing, buying, selling, investing and prospering in the world. The great majority of people will always find these are moving impulses of our life."

Is the Democrat party collapsing into mostly urban, public sector redoubts - Los Angeles, San Francisco, New York, Boston, Chicago?

Obama wants to distribute the golden eggs with no concern for the health of the goose.

A 40% tax rate is higher than that imposed on medieval serfs. Letting people keep what they earn is not giving them anything - it's their money.

Edward Gibbon remarked on the "intolerant zeal" of those who "preached the tenets of Atheism with the bigotry of dogmatists and damned all believers with ridicule and contempt." Voltaire (a deist) wished religion on his servants to inhibit their thieving fingers. Rousseau's view of "civic" religion lead directly to the Jacobin's Cult of Reason and to the state's systematic murder of those who rejected such secular cults, a prefigurement of the age of Hitler, Stalin and Mao.

A balance between government spending and private-sector growth must be achieved.

US anti-poverty programs $ 600B, unemployment insurance $ 60B, SS & Medicare $ 1.2T = our social safety net, a staggering amount.

"If Paul Revere were around, he'd be riding through the streets of lower Manhattan yelling, 'Inflation is coming! Inflation is coming!'". - Chris Mayer, Analyst

Germany's term for what they perceive as our total lack of a safety net is "American conditions".

European flat tax countries: Bulgaria, the Czech Republic, Estonia, Latvia, Lithuania, Romania and Slovakia. Thinking about it: Hungary, Poland & Greece.

Dropped 'pay as you go' pension systems: Bulgaria, Estonia, Hungary, Latvia, Lithuania, Slovakia and Sweden for private pension funds.

Sweden has gone to 'private for profit' but tax payer funded schools, raising education standards in both private and state-run schools.

Tax the wealthy or the successful? Is class warfare more important than more revenue?

Airport Security: Is sexual assault a condition of flying? Why the need to fondle and grope passengers without having to buy them dinner first? Per Benjamin Franklin, "those willing to sacrifice liberty for safety deserve neither."

"It is not an endlessly expanding list of rights - the 'right' to an education; the 'right' to health care; the 'right' to food and housing. That is not freedom. That is dependency. Those are not rights. Those are the rations of slavery - hay and a barn for human cattle." Alexis de Tocqueville.

Keynesian policies of colossal stimulus spending, zero interest rates, the purchase of over a trillion in toxic assets by the Fed and the loosest monetary policy in history have done absolutely nothing to revitalize the economy.

Regarding debt per C. V. Myers: "every penny of every debt must be paid - if not by the borrower, then by the lender."

Curling: US Clubs 2005 = 134, 2009 = 148 and currently 162!

America today and the Roman Empire: Rome, the only super power in the late 2nd century. 100 years later = terminally ill, internal corruption and unsustainable spending.

In the 3rd century of decline the percentage of silver in Roman coinage dropped from 75% to 4% leading to massive inflation and a 35 fold increase in imperial bureaucracy. Citizens demanded subsidized food, public entertainment and infrastructure projects while scaling back military spending. After the collapse, it was 1,000 years before the world recovered.

Unfunded pension liabilities: Municipalities $ 574B & States $ 3T

Obama's effort to Europeanize America leads to a bankrupt welfare state

Hausers's Law: Tax revenues as a share of GDP = 19% under either top tax rates of 92% (1952-53 or 28% (1988-90). Better to cut rates and get 19% of a larger pie.

Top 1% tax rates vs Avg individual reported Div & CG's taxable income

Dividends:	2002 - 20%	2004 - 15%	2007 - 15%
	30,673	52,814	83,072
Cap Gains	145,433		427,930
		vs	
Avg. Salary	551,873		504,402

In 1987 the CG tax rate was raised to 28% from 20%. CG gains as a percent of GDP fell to 3% in 1987 from 8% in 1986 and continued for several years to 2%. Conversely, The CG rate was cut in 1997 to 20% from 28% with lower revenues forecast. In fact revenues were $84B above forecast. CG down from 20% to 15% produced twice the investment, entrepreneurship and GDP forecast.

Obama's "Making Work Pay" tax credits (up to $800 per couple) that was in the stimulus bill. Relieves couples earning up to $150,000 from paying their own Social Security benefits. Since they are refundable, many who pay no income tax received this welfare check disguised as a tax credit. Called a "tax cut" by Obama.

Raising the top 2 tax rates for 2011 would possibly bring in $ 14.5B vs a 1,000B deficit! This group accounts for 25% of consumer spending and a much larger share of investment, entrepreneurship and GDP.

Obama to scrape employer-provided health insurance: The average exchange subsidies for a family of 4 in 2016 range from $13,600 for income of $24,000 to $0 at and above income of $108,000! In line with the European goal of a democratic welfare state designed to improve economic justice through various social safety nets.

Stocks to buy: entrepreneur driven innovators whose shares have been brought public in recent years! The relative "strengths" of 26 of the Dow 30 is 38 out of 100. Only CAT is above 80!

Current conditions mimic the 1970's (the Carter Years) when America had an incompetent administration facing serious foreign and domestic challenges = flat DOW.

George Soros as described in WSJ, "His hand seems to be in anything that weakens individual freedom and destabilizes currencies and free governments, and makes him money in the process." 2Dec10 - re Food Safety Bill and his recent purchase of 895,813 shares of Monsanto (a beneficiary) for $312.6M

MA is strapped with a $2 billion budget deficit, yet it's spending millions of dollars on chauffeur driven rides to methadone clinics. Day in and day out, chauffeur driven livery cars make the trek to local methadone clinics with recovering heroin addicts and other drug users on board....In the last two years, more than $71 million were spent driving MassHealth members to medical appointment. Last year, in four regions of Massachusetts, the state spent an estimated $1.4 million just on rides to and from methadone clinics...

MA court system has 441 assistant clerks and if you add up vacation, sick days, personal days and holidays, 223 of them get 76 days, or nearly four months off.

Most of the remaining clerks, 146, get 61 days, or slightly more that three months off.

Israel & Jews vs "replacement theology" which is the medieval view that the church has replaced Israel in God's plan and that biblical references to Israel refer to the "new Israel" that is, to Christians. This denies any connection between today's Jews and Moses, Jeremiah and Isaiah. - 2.3M member Presbyterian Church (USA)

Dec 2010 - Senate comment on ethanol: "Historically our government has helped a product compete in one of three ways: subsidize it (45 cents a gallon), protect it from competition or require its use ((EPA requires the use of 13.95 billion gallons in 2011). We understand that ethanol may be the only product receiving all three forms of support from the U.S. government at this time." Some republicans dislike ethanol's costly industrial policy while some democrats dislike the hefty carbon emissions from corn fuels. What's not to dislike about ethanol?

Death tax: the greedy political confiscation of more than half of the wealth built by someone who saved over a life time. In 2009 it accounted for 0.6% of federal revenue.

October 2010 had 5 Fridays, 5 Saturdays and 5 Sundays, all in 1 month. It happens once in 823 years.

Municipalities hold a record of $ 2.8T of outstanding debt, with another $ 2T in unfunded pensions and health-care liabilities.

Flu-shots: 2009 = 110M but 61M got H1N1 and 12,000 died.

In the 6 years since the Democrats took control of congress they have rung up $ 4.85T in deficits - more than the total deficits of $ 4.68T in the previous 75 years.

The U.S. gives about $1.7B a year in climate-related aid.

Per the Bureau of Labor Statistics: 15.3M in Unions with the majority 7.9M in public employee unions! Note: the AFL-CIO represents 80% of all unionized workers. But only 12% of the U.S. work force is unionized.

Cohabiting Couples (US Census)

	2010	2009	% Change
Opposite-sex couples	7,529,000	6,661,000	13%
Same-sex couples	620,000	476,000	30

Between 2000 and 2007, Congress created more than 450 new crimes! America's military-industrial complex developed in WWII as a way to save money, not waste it. Industrialists and military men learned that working together on plane and weapons designs made for better weapons at a faster pace as battlefield experience was incorporated into existing designs.

Responsible Americans are made to feel like fools for being responsible.

Between 2008 and November 2010, the U.S. money supply doubled. QE2 will bring it to a triple increase.

In 1937, FDR warned that collective bargaining "cannot be transplanted into the public service."

In December 2010, China's Dagong Global Credit Rating Co. lowered its credit rating for the U.S. to A+ from AA with a 'negative' outlook.

Individuals around the world are waking up to the tyrannical financial system that coerces them to use paper money and fixes the interest rates. This is driving individuals to invest in commodities ie something of real value!

Bernanke testified under oath on 3 June 2009 in front of Congress, "The Federal Reserve will not monetize the debt." In December 2010 Richard W. Fisher, President of the Federal Reserve Bank of Dallas stated, "For the next eight months, the nation's central bank will be monetizing the federal debt." Congress indicted Roger Clemens for lying! What per chance about Mr. Bernanke?

The Roman Gladiator shows from the January 2010 Smithsonian Magazine: "To spectators, the stadium was a microcosm of the empire, and its games re-enactment of their foundation myths. The wild animals that were killed symbolized how Rome had conquered wild, far flung lands and subjugated Nature itself. Executions dramatized the remorseless force of justice that annihilates enemies of state. The Gladiator embodied the cardinal Roman quality of virtus or manliness, whether as victor or as vanquished awaiting the deathblow with Stoic dignity.

In 2009, 764,448 titles were published by entrepreneurs and other nontraditional authors, two times 2008 and 6 times 2007. Each marked with a unique ISBN number.

Random Thoughts 2011

Government unions use their political clout to elect those who set their pay: the politicians. In exchange these unions are rewarded with contracts whose pensions and health-care provisions now threaten many municipalities and states with bankruptcy. Government unions in turn demand higher taxes.

The 111th Congress, with its veto-proof Democratic majority racked up $3.2Trillion in new debt in just 2 years. Add the 2 years of 110th congress under Democratic control and the debt jumps to $ 5.2T.

In 2007 the total public debt was $ 8.95T vs 2010's $ 13.9T.

AARP & Obamacare: WSJ 6Jan - The AARP provided a big chunk of the $121M spent on ads supporting the bill's passage, as well as $21M on lobbying in 2009.

Rewards: On Dec 21, 10 AARP's lucrative "Medigap" plans were exempted from rate review and other mandates. AARP can require waiting periods before seniors with pre-existing conditions have to be covered . Insurers can not. The AARP is exempt from the new $500,000 cap on executive compensation (AARP's exec paid $ 1.5M in 2009).

Does not have to pay any of the $14B of new taxes on insurance companies. AARP needs spend only 65% of premiums on health care vs 85% on insurance companies.

By Dec 10 HHS had granted 222 waivers to companies as well as 43 Unions covering 1.5M employees of which 1/3rd are Union members although only 7% of workers are unionized*.

*Per Obama's March 2010 speech at the U of Utah regarding health-care reform, "A new set of rules that treats everybody honestly and treats everybody fairly."

The UN Food and Agriculture Organization's monthly food price index rose to a PEAK of 214.7. At the previous peak of 213.5 in June 2008 there were violent food riots in several nations!

Loved beyond words, Missed beyond measure

The Nazis wanted to conquer the world, the Communists wanted to save the world

1/3 of foreign visitors to the U.S. visit NYCity.

5Feb2011 - Obama administration ok's unionization of 45,000 airport screeners

The ugly companions to shortages: hoarding, black markets and profiteering.

Government Cost-of Living Inflation Rates: CPI-W (Urban Wage Earners and Clerical Workers = 32% of population. Used to adjust Social Security payments). CPI-U (All Urban Consumers - 87% of population) & CPI-E (experimental index for the over 62 age group). Since 1983 CPI-W up 119.7% vs CPI-E up 136.1%. CPI-W weight for medical care = 5.3% vs CPI-E's 11.1%. Using CPI-E, average annual social security payment would be $ 820 higher.

Iran's theocratic regime bans valentines day as well as the Persian New Year - Nowrooz: Anything prior to the Muslim era is jahiliyya, the so called 'time of ignorance'.

The 5 pillars of the Muslim faith: Allah is our objective; the Prophet is our leader; the Quran is our law; Jihad is our way; dying in the way of Allah is our highest hope.

Bin Laden's guide - Sayyid Quib the Islamist philosopher was executed by Nasser in 1966. One of the results was the renouncement of violence by the Muslim Brotherhood.

Unions gave Democrats $ 400M in the 2008 election cycle. The biggest public employee union, The American Federation of State, County and Municipal Employees gave $ 90M itself.

The word "democracy" does not appear in either the Declaration of Independence and the U.S. Constitution. Pledge of Allegiance = "the republic for which it stands"

Laws do not represent reason, they represent force. Under a democracy or monarchy they restrain the individual, not the government.

70% of income tax filers have an AGI of less than $ 58,000.

Muslims to build economic systems based in 7th century Shariah principals which bans interest and credit (no mortgages, CDs, credit cards or bank stock). Adding all GDPs of all Muslim economies barely equal the GDP of Germany - despite all their oil wealth.

The Islamic world is typified by: denying education and technical skills, little enforcement of property or contract rights. More books are translated into Greek (population 11M) than Arabic (population 1B).

15% of Social Security recipients are disabled.

Obama Doctrine: Not to act until the Italians, or the Saudi's approve or without a U.N resolution. Domestically: higher taxes, less patriotism, a bigger role for state bureaucrats and a transfer of sovereignty to global institutions.

Obama's Europeanization policy: European health care, European welfare, European carbon taxes, European day care, European College education, European foreign policy based on the engagement with supranational technocracies, nuclear disarmament and a reluctance to deploy forces overseas.

Difference between American and European unions is the location of power!

One compact fluorescent lightbulb (CFL) contains enough mercury to contaminate up to 6,000 gallons of water beyond safe drinking levels. Due to high amount of hand labor in manufacturing, most are made in China (lower labor costs and less environmental regulation)

In 2011, 35% of wages and salaries will be in the form of a government payment. Primarily SS, Medicare benefits and unemployment insurance. 97% of federal income taxes come from 50% of income earners.

Households of people ages 70-74 have the highest average wealth of any age group, but less than half the income of those 35-44.

The top 20% of households receive 50% of total income vs bottom 20%'s 4%. The top group has 4 times as many workers as the bottom and nearly 6 times as many full-time, year around workers.

Our workers are not trapped in an economic cast system. Only 2.2% of the population lived in poverty during an entire 4 year period.

2000-2009 household income fell 4.5% but consumer spending went up 22.4%? Households got smaller, reducing the number of income earners in a house decreases household income.

Government household income is pre-tax and excludes non-cash benefits: food stamps, health benefits, rent-free housing and goods produced and consumed on the farm.

The 7 Sins: anger, greed, sloth, pride, lust, envy and gluttony

NASA pays Russia $63M for each astronaut transported to the space station.

Currently, some 400,000 birds are killed in America by electricity-generating wind turbines.

Time to build an American electric car

Published: Wednesday, December 22, 2010, 11:25 PM Updated: Wednesday, December 22, 2010, 11:25 PM

By The Post-Standard

"Plans by a start-up company to assemble an all-electric car in Onondaga County have fallen apart. Bannon Automotive LLC filed a lawsuit Monday accusing the developer of the car, the Reva Electric Car Co., of Bangalore, India, and its new owner, Mahindra & Mahindra Ltd., of breaking agreements to give Bannon an exclusive license to make and sell the car in the United States."

A user of syracuse.com, jade4953, said this should be a wake-up call for American automakers:

"It is time to scrap the plan, design and manufacture a purely American product, use none of their patents, develop a superior model and market it worldwide with no agreement with foreign interests."

The Good Samaritan parable instructs us to attend to the afflicted voluntarily, not through coercive government programs.

Male-Female Wage Gap? Unemployment rate is higher for men @ 9.3% vs women at 8.3%. Labor force participation: Men 70.4% vs women 58.3%. Men's fields like construction, manufacturing and trucking hit harder in recessions vs women's clustered in insulated occupations such as teaching, health care and service industries. Per Dept. of Labor: full time working women spend an average of 8.01 hours per day at work vs men at 8.75 hours = 9% more. Women gravitate to jobs with low risk, more comfort, regular hours, willing to trade higher pay for other desirable job characteristics vs men in jobs requiring physical labor, outdoor work, overnight shifts, and dangerous conditions. Women take 3 times the sick time as men. In 2008 men represented 93 percent of all workplace deaths, even though women were responsible for 43 percent of all hours worked in 2008. In 2010, a study by Reach Advisors found that women earned an average of 8% more than male counterparts (single, childless urban workers between the ages of 22 and 30) Education the key?

Public employees unions extort concessions from politicians in exchange for campaign support and tax payers foot the bill.

U S Dept of Education: 2009 budget $ 62.3 B for 4,200 employees + $ 100B over 2 years from the American Recovery and Reinvestment Act of 2009/Obama.

Obama in 2012: 2008 for Obama - African-Americans 95%, Hispanics 67%, Asians 62%, Unions 60%, Abortion supporters 73%, GLBT community 70% = 67% of the electoral vote with 53% of the popular vote. These are the "kiddie" campus voters, the anti-American left, hard core environmentalists, nice people that vote for America's first black president. Income redistribution works!!! Government distributing 40% of GDP in a discriminatory manner among an increasingly diverse and Balkanized population. One third of eligible voters pay nearly all the taxes.

19Feb2011 - Town of Lawrence, MA gets $ 6.6M to rehire 38 fire fighters @ $ 173,684 each

Western Civilization = Rule of Law

Obama's only fears: the constitution and the facts

Social justice = redistribution

Civilian Security Force = Thugocracy

Agitators: Acorn, Storm, Earth Liberation, First Liberation Front, SEIU

Massachusetts law allows out-of-state and in-state wineries to ship to consumers but only if the winery produced less than 30,000 gallons per year. This production cap covers 100% of Bay State wineries but only 2% of out-of-state wineries.

A great deal of what humans do is neither in self-interest or altruistic. It is disinterested, done because we want to do it - not for personal advantage or the world's benefit. Such as making academic inquiries ("the disinterested pursuit of truth")!

Under President Reagan: Defense was 40% and entitlements 20% of the Federal budget. Now it is Defense 20% and Entitlements 40%

Illegitimacy: U.S. = 41% (whites @ 29%). In 2010 = 1.7M out-of-wedlock births. Poverty rate single parent with children = 37% vs Married w children 6%. 70% of unmarried women vote democrat. Means-tested Federal welfare $700B + states $ 200B not including SS or medicare. Fed has 77 means-tested programs including Temporary Assistance to Needy Families (TANF), food stamps, housing subsidies, Medicaid, day care, WIC, EITC up to $5,657 a year to low-income families, school lunches, school breakfasts, summer food, SSI, Head start and S-CHIP. These benefits amount to $16,800 per person in poverty. In 2009, 47% paid no federal income tax with 40% receiving cash or benefits paid for by the 53% paying taxes. Since the federal government created the child support bureaucracy, the majority of divorces have been initiated by women. States receive federal bonuses for mandating higher child support payments from fathers!

HIV prevention: Circumcision reduces the acquisition rate of HIV in heterosexual men by 35% to 50%.

An optimist laughs to forget. A pessimist forgets to laugh.

Raise the minimum wage? Democrats raised the minimum wage by $ 2.10, a 41% increase. Workers ages 16 to 19 unemployment went from 15% to 26% an increase of 1.5 million. Black teens to 43% and after the final raise to $ 7.25 in mid 2009 to 50+%

Note: beneficiaries of a minimum wage hike: 85% live with parents or another relative, live alone or have a working spouse. Just 15% are sole earners in families with children.

On 22 & 23 June 2011 the Group of 20 nations will address the forecast food shortages. The FAO's food index hit a record in Feb 2011. Food prices projected to rise 30% higher this decade.

U.S. Department of Agriculture: Budget $130B! Pays out $70B in food stamps for 47M Americans = 1 in 6. African-American farmers getting $ 1B. $20B is "crop supports". $5B in ethanol subsidies.

Obama administration formalizes ties with the Muslim Brotherhood who's credo is "Jihad is our way, and dying in the cause of Allah is our highest hope." IBD 7Jul11

Federal Jobs: In 1960 management layers = 6, today = 18 between sec of Ag to forest ranger.

Currently the Fed Government has income of $ 44,000 - spends $ 74,000, borrows $ 30,000.

Obamacare taxes: from 2013 - 2.9% tax on investment income, dividends, interest, cap gains etc. Add .9% if over

$ 250K. 2.3% on medical devices. Allowable medical deductions 10% of AGI from 7.5%

In 2008 about 320,000 Americans reported income of more than $ 1M or 0.3% of all tax returns and paid $ 250B in taxes that year.

July 2011 - 30 months into Obama's presidency and 2 years into the "economic recovery" our deficit is $ 1.4T!

Democrats are after "loopholes, exclusions, deductions and tax preferences" as well as abusive tax shelters and tax havens".

Senate (Dem) obliged by law to produce an annual budget has not done so for two years.

Doctor Training: In 1997, Congress incorrectly believed that the country would face a surplus of doctors so it set a limit of 16,000 by capping how many resident positions Medicare would fund. Current projected need is for 22,000 to 24,000 a year. Current Congressional response is proposing to cut Medicare reimbursement for doctor training by about $4B or half the current funds from the federal budget.

Current fraction of population employed is 58.2% vs the 59.4% as of the end of the recession June 2009. now, unemployed for more than 6 months is 44.4% vs the normal 15%.

In May & June 2011: private sector hired 130,000 while public shed 87,000. Public down 522,000 over past two years (mostly temporary census takers).

Since Obama took office 20 Jan 09 - to 4 Jul 11: Unemployment from 7.6% to 9.1%, Private sector jobs down 2M, 46% of the 6.7M unemployed out longer than 6 months, single family home prices at lowest level since April

2009, Gasoline from $1.80 to $3.56, Dollar down 12%, Federal debt from 36% of GDP to 70%, Food stamps from 10.5% of population to 14.4% or up 36% in 2 years.

The U.S. Government distributes some 70M checks a month. Social Security pays out $ 20B a month.

Forced union dues are collected and union officials granted monopoly power to speak for all government workers whether they agree or not. Huge portions of the funds are then funneled to elected officials who are then afraid to anger the Union bosses.

Right to Work: from 1999 to 2009 - GDP up 24.2% in the 22 RTW states 40% more than the 28 other states. Personal income 2000 to 2010 up 24.3% for RTW double the 28 other and migration: in 2009 there were 20% more 25-34 year olds in RTW than in 1999 vs 3.3% in the other 28 states.

From IBD's 25Jul11 - Socialism has always come down to contempt for the will of the people, to a benevolent elite force-feeding its enlightened policies down the throats of the masses. Karl Marx himself once dismissed free elections as merely "deciding once in three or six year which member of the ruling class was to misrepresent the people in parliament."

Per the Bureau of Economic Analysis: Government spending was 27% of GDP in 1960 vs 37% today and forecast to be 50% in 2038. Between 1986 and 2008, the percent of federal income taxes paid by the top 5% rose from 43% to 59%. Between 1986 and 2009, the percent who pay zero or negative income taxes rose from 18.5% to 51%. National debt to GDP from 1980 to 2009 rose from 42% to 100%.

The fight over statism is a moral one. Income redistribution = social justice. Free enterprise seeks freedom and opportunity for every one. Responsibility for your own affairs. Self realization, meritocratic fairness and a better future.

The Organization for Economic Cooperation and Development says that European per-capita income is about 30% lower the the U.S.A. due to higher tax rates.

Obama, 11 July 2011 - "I do not want, and will not accept, a deal in which...I'm able to keep hundreds of thousands of dollars in additional income that I don't need."

Senate Democrats have not issued a budget for over 800 days. Obama's February 2011 budget was rejected by the Senate 97-0.

In 2006, concern about the accumulating debt was expressed by then-Senator Barack Obama, when he voted against raising the debt ceiling:

"The fact that we are here today to debate raising America's debt limit is a sign of leadership failure . . . a sign that the US government can't pay its own bills . . . that we now depend on ongoing financial assistance from foreign countries to finance our government's reckless fiscal policies. . . .

"Increasing America's debt weakens us domestically and internationally . . . Washington is shifting the burden of bad choices today onto the backs of our children and grandchildren. . . Americans deserve better. . . ."

In the world of hi-tech gadgetry, I've noticed that more and more people who send text messages and emails have long forgotten the art of capitalization. For those of you who fall into this category, please take note of the following statement...

> "Capitalization is the difference between helping your Uncle Jack off a horse and helping your uncle jack off a horse."

Median household net worth 2009: White's $113,149, Hispanics $6,325 and Blacks $5,677. $16 trillion has been spent on the War-on-Poverty in 1964. Today 44M are on food stamps. The U.S. has over 70 means-tested welfare programs and the poverty rate is higher than in the late 1960's.

Instead of preparing students for life, the schools (French) solely prepare them to occupy public functions, in which success can be attained without any necessity for self direction or the exhibition of the least glimmer of personal initiative. - LeBon

Michigan State is preparing to cancel their 'Food Assistance' program for 30,000 University students that costs the state $ 75,000,000 annually.

When you include the costs of federal deficit spending and the regulatory burden this year, you don't reach the Cost of Government Day until Aug. 12. Americans will work for 103 days to pay for federal spending, 44 days for state and local spending and 77 days to cover the cost of the regulatory burden

WSJ 15Aug11: interracial crimes - black on white victims 45% vs white on blacks 3%.

In 2009 20% of hate crimes by blacks vs being 13% of population.

In 2009, there were 8,274 tax returns with over $ 10M income = $ 240B The budget should be balanced, the Treasury should be refilled, public debt should be reduced, the arrogance of officialdom should be tempered and controlled, and the assistance to foreign lands should be curtailed lest Rome become bankrupt. People must again learn to work, instead of living on public assistance." Cicero - 55 BC

From Gustave Lebon's The Crowd, published 1895:

> AmongAnglo-Saxons and notably in America, "Democracy" signifies the intense development of the will of the individual and as complete subordination as possible of the State, which with the exception of the police, the army and diplomatic relations is not allowed the direction of anything, not even public instruction.

> There are 20,000 school masters and mistresseswithout employment, all disdain the fields or workshops, all look to the State for their livelihood.

> The reason that socialism is so powerful today is it constitutes the last illusion that is vital. In spite of all scientific demonstrations, it continues on the increase. Its principal strength lies in the fact that it is championed by minds sufficiently ignorant of things as they are in

reality to venture boldly to promise mankind happiness. The social illusion reigns today upon all the heaped-up ruins of the past, and to it belongs the future. Whoever can supply the masses with illusions is easily the master; whoever attempts to destroy their illusions with the truth is always their victim.

This year 2011 spending on means tested income security programs like food stamps, jobless benefits and the unearned income and child tax credits will cost more than $400B.

Both Reagan and Obama inherited economies in collapse. Reagan passed the largest tax cut in U.S. history with deregulation, monetary restraint and spending controls. . Obama a $1 trillion spending stimulus. One program worked, one did not.

Recessions and the Rich (WSJ - 19Aug11)

Tax Returns	2007	2008	% change
$200K and above	4,536,000	3,924,000	-13
$1M and above	390,000	237,000	-39
$10M and above	18,394	8,274	-55
Taxes Paid			
$200K and above	$610B	$434B	-29
$1M and above	309B	178B	-42
$10M and above	111B	54B	-51

The $1M income are 0.2% of tax payers and pay 20.4% of income taxes

The $200K group are under 3% of tax payers but pay 50.1% of income taxes.

In 2007 the over $200K reported 1/3rd of the $7.6T in total taxable income vs 2009's 1/4. Per Obama, the best way to produce income equality is to destroy trillions of dollars of wealth. Everyone loses, but the rich more than the poor.

Section 8 Housing: 2010 budget $ 19B vs 1994's $7B. HUD now pays the rent for more than 2 million households; tenants pay 30% of their income toward rent and utilities. Monthly rental subsidies up to: Stamford, Conn = $2,851, Honolulu $2,764, Columbia, Md $2,582. Crime in Section 8 housing is 10 times the national average.

Atheists make up 4% of the U.S. population

Organic foods may have Vitamin C, salt or sugar as opposed to artificial preservatives. Potatoes that have a green tinge below the skin contain solanine which can make you ill if eaten in large amounts. The toxin is produced when the potato is exposed to too much light.

In 2010, 34% of women and 25% of men attend church weekly.

Total National Debt = sum of all federal bills, notes and bonds issued by Treasury

Publicly held debt = Treasury securities held by individuals, financial institutions and foreign governments.

Intra-government debt = treasury bonds held by agencies of the federal Gov. mostly Social Security Trust Fund

Liabilities = future pensions, health care, SS payments etc.

Note: All Gov. liabilities only as the current law stays the same!

Intra Gov. debt will be turned into National debt.

Bush Tax Cuts; When tax cuts took effect in 2003 - in the next 4 years, federal revenues increased.

Charter Schools: They are public schools operated independently of their local school districts - without teacher union involvement. They are the least threatening form of school choice, because they remain public schools, meaning they cannot charge tuition and their admissions practices typically are controlled by lottery.

The Tea Party is organized based on philosophy rather than Party affiliation.

Pension Funds - stocks down & 30 year treasury notes interest down from 4.5% in 2010 to todays 2.8%. Can pension funds still generate projected 8% annual earnings?

Aug 2011 - the recession officially ended 2 years ago.

Income = wages less taxes and inflation. Example: In July 2011 real disposable income rose 2.5% vs a year earlier, pretax Commerce Department data show. But it's up just 1.2% after tax and negative after inflation!

U.S. Department of Agriculture predicts that in 2011, for the first time - more corn will go into ethanol than feed! In Europe, some 50% of rapeseed crop is going into biofuel production and world wide about 18% of sugar is used for biofuel. 50years ago wide spread starvations were predicted for the worlds 3.5B population. Todays 7 billion can burn food in their autos. Note: in the 3rd world people typically spend up to 80% of income on food.

Unemployment: In 2009 unemployment eligibility was raised to 99 weeks - the fraction of the unemployed who are long term (more than 26 weeks) jumped from 1982-83 recession rate or 26% to the current rate of 44% suggesting that dramatically longer unemployment insurance eligibility period adversely affected the labor market.

Keynesian stimulus using transfer payments is either a Devine miracle - where one gets back more than one puts in - or else it's the macroeconomic equivalent to bloodletting.

There has been NO meaningful theoretical or empirical support for the Keynesian position. Conventional economics says that greater provision of social insurance and redistribution of income reduces the overall GDP pie. Can a government improve the economy by borrowing money and giving it to people - if yes, no one needs to work!

Illegal Aliens: Back during the great depression, Herbert Hoover ordered the deportation of ALL illegal aliens in order to make jobs available to American citizens that desperately needed work.

Harry Truman deported over two million illegal aliens after WWII to create jobs for returning veterans.

In 1954 Dwight Eisenhower deported 13 million Mexicans. The program was called Operation Wetback. It was done so WWII and Korean War veterans would have a better chance at jobs. It took two years, but they deported them!

The best measure of physical attractiveness is facial symmetry ((how closely the two halves of a person's face match up). A 1994 study found that more attractive "symmetrical" people are paid about 5% more than the average person while more homely "asymmetrical" people earn up to 10% less.

Social Security's income = Employer pays 6.2% & Employee 6.2%, FICA payroll tax = 81.9% + Interest income 15% and Income taxes on benefits 3.1%. Current avg monthly retiree benefit = $1,180 and totals $ 727 billion. For 64% of Americans over 65, SS provides more than 50% of their income.

Global Warming: In 1991 a paper identified a close relationship between solar variations and the earth's surface temperatures since 1860. In 1970 a second scientist saw this as a link between cosmic rays and cloud cover which was been demonstrated in 2009 at the European Organization for Nuclear Research's particle accelerator. Assuming politicians will allow it, more work to determine the relative responsibility between nature and man.

From Brad Thor's 'Full Black': One hundred years ago there were only 18 American tax-exempt private foundations. Today there are more than 16,000. The U.S. not-for-profit sector is the world's 7th largest economy with over $ 500B untaxed and largely unregulated dollars. Some of the largest foundations give out more a year than most countries GDP.

E-Book vs Print Book economics

	E-Book	Print Book
Retail Price	12.99	26.00
To the Retailer	-3.90 typically 30% -13.00	
Author's royalty	-2.27 25% of net sales -3.90 15%	
Gross	6.82	9.10
Production/distribution	-0.90	-3.25
- incl returns/inventory		
Publisher's Profit	5.92	5.85

E-Book sales 2010 = $ 878M

5th time - World running out of oil: 1st 1880's Pennsylvania unable to meet future demand and no oil west of the Mississippi - bingo in Texas!. 2nd after WWI and 3rd after WWII. 4th in the 1970's. 5th today. But for every barrel of oil produced between 2007 and 2009 - 1.6 barrels were added to reserves. World use 2020 - 100M barrels a day.

Oil used since start = 1 T barrels. Current est of petroleum in ground 5Tb with 1.4Tb deemed recoverable. U.S. net imports down from 2005's 60% to 47% today.

By Sept 2011, central banks had bought 180 tons of gold (5.8M ounces) = 2X 2010

WSJ 20Sep11: Average tax rates paid by adjusted gross income (AGI) 2008 - IRS

$ 1,000,000 and up	25.3%
$ 500,000 - 1,000,000	24.1
$ 200,000 - 500,000	19.6
$ 100,000 - 200,000	12.7
$ 50,000 - 100,000	8.9
$ 30,000 - 50,000	7.2

So much for the Buffett Tax rationale

In the last 19 - 3rd year of a presidency, only one ended with the S&P 500 down. Will 2011 be the 2nd - due to leftist incompetence?

U.S. Govt Debt: In 2010 net interest = $ 196B and is projected to be 2.8% by 2016 ($ 500B). Today, 30% to foreigners which clearly will not improve productive capacity.

In the U.S. Since 1790, when Federal debt to GDP was below 90%, the economy grew on average more than 3%. When over 90%, the economy sank an average of 1.8% and we are already over 90%.

Why it is easier to rule as a dictator; You have only a small group to reward: army, judiciary, inner circle of advisors vs in a democracy 51% of fickle voters.

Why public sector unions: See above - By focusing the aspirations of fickle government employees into their Union Bosses - the government can more easily manage the workers. They only have to satisfy the union bosses who in tern will maintain order in the working class.

In the classical world "language skillfully wielded revealed the truth of character." Also, "a standard of ancient eloquence" was identified as an indication of nobility and even genius. Today, by clever use of others words, read skillfully from prompters, anyone can create such a misperception of their character and ability, at least for some time.

Public Schools: Staffing - between 1969 and 2008 students per teacher went from 22.6 to 15.3. In total, students per employee dropped from 13.6 to 7.8. Results = flat line. WSJ 26Sep11

There are no companies and no jobs without investment first, and policy of dollar weakness have made the U.S. a bad place to commit growth capital over the last 10 years.

U.S. Military: Enlisted 11% from the poorest one-fifth of neighborhoods vs 25% from the wealthiest quintile. The top 40% household income = 49.3% of recruits.

Blacks: While 58% of 18-29 year olds are white, they were 64% of Army enlisted personnel. Army officers: 74% of 25-34 year olds are white with bachelors degrees they are only 72% of officers vs the 8% of blacks with B.A,s are 13% of Army officers.

Hispanics are 21% of population with high school degrees but only 12% of enlisted.

Summary: The urban elite (withdrawn from military service) believes the military is composed of poor, uneducated victims of an unfair society. The myth of a ghetto Army is as nastily racist as it is false.

Capital Gains Taxes: Only 10% of Americans making less than $ 200,000 pay them.

Obama, the Muslim's choice: In January 2009, his approval was Blacks 92%, Hispanics 75%, whites 58%. Now Blacks 74%, Hispanics 48% and Whites 33%. Muslims, where 10% think he is a Muslim, 76% favorable.

Food Stamps: Single annual gross below $ 21,660 and couple below $ 29,148

CPI inflation rate: August 2010 - 11 = 3.8%.

Dementia: Starting in the early 60's, the chance of having dementia doubles every 5 years. In the 80's, the likelihood of having dementia is 20%. Add to this the 30% chance of having 'cognitive impairment not dementia' = 50/50 chance of having impaired decision capacity at age 80!!!!! Find an estate attorney. Get an up to date Will, durable power of attorney, living revocable trust, living will / health care implementation and a healthcare proxy.

In retirement: personal consumption vs bequest/legacy motives

The U.S. receives 100,000 shipping containers a day.

Peripheral vision is 25% faster than regular vision.

Chrysler dealerships' owned by Republicans closed by Car Tzar.

The Washington Examiner, Newsmax, Fox News and a host of other news agencies discovered that the list of Chrysler dealerships was put together by the "Automotive Task Force" headed by no one other than Mr. Steve Rattner. Amazingly, of the 789 dealerships closed by the federal government, 788 had donated money, exclusively to Republican political causes, while contributing nothing to Democratic political causes. The only "Democratic" dealership on the list was found to have donated $7,700 to Hillary's campaign, and a bit over $2,000 to John Edwards. This same dealership, reportedly, also gave $ 20,000 to Obama's campaign. Steve Rattner is the guy who put the list together. Well, he happens to be married to a Maureen White. Maureen happens to be the former national finance chairman of the Democratic National Committee. As such, she has access to campaign donation records from everyone in the nation- Republican or Democrat. But of course, this is just a wacky "coincidence," we're certain.

Obama has used the term 'a federal emergency' every 2 1/2 days of his administration.

Oil: Obama wants to raise $ 40B by excluding oil industry from credits that go to all domestic manufacturers. When Carter applied a windfall profit tax on the oil industry - the rig count on active wells went from 4,500 to less than 55 in a matter of months.

Euro Zone inflation surges from 2.5% to 3% well above the ECB's 2% target.

U.S. disposable income down 0.3% = savings rate down from 5.6% a year ago to 4.7%.

Public education spending on facilities and equipment has more than doubled since 1989 - no improvement in educational outcomes.

Government contrived low yields on bonds results in reducing returns and increasing deficits to pension funds, causing companies to have to make larger payments reducing profits.

Today's students are being taught to learn vs to think.

Europe is based on a hereditary philosophy vs the U.S. on personal achievement.

The average U.S. light vehicle weighs about 4,000 pounds of which 70% is steel. Raw material costs is $3,770 in 2011. vs $ 3,350 in 2010.

Oct 2011 - The democratic controlled U.S. Senate has gone 900 days without proposing the constitutionally required national budget.

The Bush recession officially ended 17 weeks after Obama was inaugurated. Obama subsequently produced the worst economic recovery since the Great Depression. Unemployment is up, poverty is up, inflation is up, the Misery Index is up, national debt is way up. Meanwhile family income is down, more than 1 million private sector jobs have disappeared and Obama blames Americans for being soft.

FY2011: Highest ever Federal spending $ 3.6 trillion up 4.2% over 2010. (Defense spending up 1.2%, Medicaid 0.9% and Medicare 3.9% and interest payments 16.7%.)

Fed receipts up 6.5% (includes 21.6% gain in individual income taxes) WSJ 10Oct11

Obama Deficit Blowout

	Receipts	Outlays	Deficit	Deficit as share of GDP
2007	$2,568	$2,729	$161	1.2%
2008	2,524	2,983	459	3.2
2009	2,104	3,520	1,416	10%
2010	2,162	3,456	1,294	8.9%
2011	2,303	3,600	1,298	8.6%

Source: Congressional Budget Office. Billions of Dollars. FY 07-11

Summary: 2007 deficit of $161 or 1.2% of budget = Bush Tax cuts. 4 years later income down $ 265B but spending up $900B!!!!!!!!

Oct 2011 - In the 29 months that the Democrat controlled Senate has not passed the legally obligated budget: Spent $8.5Trillion, monthly deficits total $ 2.6T and added $3.6T to the national debt - a 32% increase. The Obama debt deal of August lets the Senate off the hook for two more years.

Household vs Federal Debt (figures as % of GNP

Year	Household	Federal
1987	57.9%	41%
1992	62.3%	48.3%
1997	65.6%	45.5%
2002	79.3%	34%
2007	97.3%	36.1%
2008	95.2%	43.7%
2009	95.4%	54.7%
2010	90.2%	63.2%

Harry Reid's Jobs Math - WSJ 20Oct11

Mr. Reid on the Senate floor - 19Oct11 "It's very clear that the private sector jobs have been doing just fine; it's the public sector jobs where we've lost hugh numbers, and that's what this legislation is all about." (A proposed $35B bill to hire more public workers). Note: Fed Exec Branch employed 1.875M civilians in 2008. By 2010 up 253,000 or + 13.5%. State Gov cut 49,000 to 5.089M. Local Gov down 210,000 to 14.076M.

Mr. Reid says private sector is "doing just fine". Private sector employed 111.822M in 2008 vs 109.349 in Sep 2011 or down 2.5M = the problem is in the private sector!

More on Mr. Reid's comment - IBD 20Oct11

Government data shows 6.257 million private sector jobs lost since December 2007, a 5.4% decline vs Government down 392,000 or 1.75%. (Federal Gov actually up 63,000, a 2.29% gain. Private sector has lost 16 jobs for every government job lost since 2007. Typical household in Washington Metro area earned $ 84,523 or 69% higher than the national median of $50,046. Fed employees took home $126,000 - 2 1/2 times the U.S. Median.

Earners: Bottom 40% report earnings of less than $37,090 and the bottom 20% = $17,900. Under 9-9-9 the top 20% would pay 51% of Fed taxes down 17% while the bottom 20% would pay 3.4% vs current less than 1%. Note: If non-cash income and transfer payments were included, low-income total income would increase 50%.

Top income quintile total income would drop 7% if taxes paid to fund welfare were considered.

Income not static, we have no caste system: Per Treasury Department - from 1996 to 2007 58% of the lower income quintile moved up and in the top 1%, 57% dropped down to a lower income group.

The day the democrats took over was not January 22nd 2009 it was actually January 3rd, 2007 the day the Democrats took over the House of Representatives and the Senate, the start of the 110th Congress. The Democrat Party controlled a majority in both chambers for the first time since the end of the 103rd Congress in 1995.

For those who are listening to the liberals propagating the fallacy that everything is "Bush's Fault", think about this: January 3rd, 2007 was the day the Democrats took over the Senate and the Congress: At the time: The DOW Jones closed at 12,621.77 The GDP for the previous quarter rose 3.5% The Unemployment rate was 4.6%, George Bush's Economic policies SET A RECORD of 52 STRAIGHT MONTHS of JOB CREATION!

Remember the day...January 3rd, 2007 was the day that Barney Frank took over the House Financial Services Committee and Chris Dodd took over the Senate Banking Committee. The economic meltdown that happened 15 months later was in what part of the economy? BANKING AND FINANCIAL SERVICES! THANK YOU DEMOCRATS for taking us from 13,000 DOW, 3.5 GDP and 4.6% Unemployment... to this CRISIS by (among MANY other things) dumping 5-6 TRILLION Dollars of toxic loans on the economy from YOUR Fannie Mae and Freddie Mac FIASCOS! (BTW: Bush asked Congress 17 TIMES to stop Fannie & Freddie - starting in 2001 because it was financially risky for the US economy). And who took the THIRD highest pay-off from Fannie Mae and Freddie Mac? OBAMA

And who fought against reform of Fannie and Freddie?

OBAMA and the Democrat Congress

So when someone tries to blame Bush...REMEMBER JANUARY 3rd, 2007.... THE DAY THE DEMOCRATS TOOK OVER!" Bush may have been in the car but the Democrats were in charge of the gas pedal and steering wheel they were driving.

Budgets do not come from the White House. They come from Congress and the party that controlled Congress since January 2007 is the Democrat Party.

Furthermore, the Democrats controlled the budget process for 2008 & 2009 as well as 2010 & 2011. In that first year, they had to contend with George Bush, which caused them to compromise on spending, when Bush somewhat belatedly got tough on spending increases. For 2009 though, Nancy Pelosi and Harry Reid bypassed George Bush entirely, passing continuing resolutions to keep government running until Barack Obama could take office. At that time, they passed a massive omnibus spending bill to complete the 2009 budgets.

And where was Barack Obama during this time? He was a member of that very Congress that passed all of these massive spending bills, and he signed the omnibus bill as President to complete 2009. Let's remember what the deficits looked like during that period: (below)

If the Democrats inherited any deficit, it was the 2007 deficit, the last of the Republican budgets. That deficit was the lowest in five years, and the fourth straight decline in deficit spending. After that, Democrats in Congress took control of spending, and that includes Barack Obama, who voted for the budgets.

If Obama inherited anything, he inherited it from himself.

In a nutshell, what Obama is saying is I inherited a deficit that I voted for and then I voted to expand that deficit four-fold since January 20th.

Of the 27 million risky subprime and other non-prime mortgages outstanding in 2008 - the Government issued 19.2M (over 2/3 rds) vs Wall St. 7.8M.

From "What Social Classes Owe to Each Other" by William Graham Summer written in 1883: Capital is force, human energy stored or accumulated.

The modern system is based on liberty, on contract, and on private property.

Acquiring Capital requires energy, courage, perseverance and prudence.

Plutocrats want the power of the State for their advantage

Politicians surrender public to private interests and then cure their mischief by newspaper and platform declamation against capital and corporations.

They reverse the distribution of rewards and punishments between those who have done their duty and those who have not.

They say that the man who has done his duty is responsible for another who has not done his duty

The yearning after equality is the offspring of envy and covetousness. It can only be satisfied by robbing A to give to B. It nourishes the mean vices of human nature, wastes capital and overthrows civilization.

Rights do not pertain to results, but only to chances.

Social Security COLA's: 2007 3.3%, 08 2.3%, 09 5.8%, 10 0%, 11 0%, and 2012 3.6%

In mid 2011, the U.S. Preventive Services Task Force of the Department of Health & Human Service declared that men should not be routinely screened for prostate cancer.

No more PSA tests. They also said no to rectal exams and ultrasounds. Prostate cancer is #2 cancer in men with 32,000 killed in 2010.

11 million slaves (largely immune to malaria) were brought to The New world from Africa, as the native population had been devastated by diseases from Europe.

In the 3rd Quarter 2011, personal disposable income fell 1.7%. The only way to increase spending is to reduce savings! Savings rates were 1-2% from 2005 to 2007, 6% in 2008 and in Sept 2011 3.6% down from 5.8% in June 2010.

In 2011 the European Union ruled that children under age eight should always be supervised when blowing up a balloon.

Cement: in 2010, 3.6 billion tons were produced and responsible for 5% of the world's human produced carbon dioxide.

Global Warming: Temperatures have gone up since the "little ice age" of 1300 to 1900 - the period favored by global warming alarmists. But global temperatures have been warmer for most of the past 10,000 years. Warmer temperatures have been better for human civilization than colder ones. Warmer temperatures expand forests, reduce deserts, improve soil moisture for crops and reduce extreme weather events.

Regarding income disparity: Obama's policy goal is to divide up the existing income rather than to allow the private sector to create more for all. When growth is fast, the incomes of the poor go up as the incomes of the rich go up even more. When growth is slow or negative, the real incomes of the poor go down the most.

Inflation?? Last 365 Vegan Cane Sugar, 4 lbs = $ 4.39. 8 Jul 11 = $ 5.69 Up 30%

America's Welfare State unsustainable:
Government Spending of National Income

1870:	US 7.3%,	UK 9.4%	Germany 10%,	France 12.6%
2007:	36.6&	44.6%	43.9%	52.6%

US payments to Individuals: 1960 = 26% vs 2010 = 66%.

US economic growth: 50's & 60's = 4% vs 2000 - 07 = 2.4% US elderly population: 2010 = 13% vs 2050 = 20%

Only 4% of college grads are unemployed.

75% of Medicare beneficiaries paid at the minimum monthly rate.

WWII munitions (bombs, shells etc) discovered in Germany every year = 2,000 tons.

Labor as a % of total national income: 50's = 61.3, 80's = 66.1 and 2000's = 63.7%.

In the 50's Wages & Salary = 94% of compensation. Today 81%

When labor share goes up - capital share goes down

Two ways to increase production: Labor = more or better labor. Capital = technology, automation etc paid for by investors or owners.

Self Publish: In 2010 133,036 titles vs 2006's 51,237 titles.

In 2011, Florida had gone through 6 straight seasons without a hurricane landfall - longest without a major storm since 1851.

Federal Criminal Code: 4,500 criminal statutes plus over 300,000 other regulations that carry criminal penalties including prison. Federal crime fighters have expanded from the FBI to include: Environmental Protection Agency, The Labor Dept., The Education Dept., The National Park Service, The Bureau of Land Management, The National Oceanic and Atmospheric Administration, The Fish and Wildlife Service, The Dept of Interior & Commerce.

Cancer chances during lifetime: Prostate 1 in 6, Breast 1 in 8 (1 in 36 will die), Lung 1 in 14, Brain 1 in 160.

Birth Control: In 1899 Teddy Roosevelt stated, "The worst evil was the infertility of the old native American stock, especially in the North East." The Harvard class of 1900 spawned less than 2 children per grad. Many were childless. The rich had small families, the poor large families = eugenics which was enormously popular in the early 20th Century. Supported by presidents Wilson and Hoover, leading scientists and the Supreme Court which issued an 8-1 ruling in 1927 upholding the involuntary sterilization of institutionalized citizens - the "feeble-minded."

Christmas Trees: In 1991, 40% of U.S. households had a live Christmas tree (37M of the 94M), in 2010 down 23% to 27M of the 118M households.

The SEC now requires all companies to disclose whether raw materials essential to their products include Cassiterite, Columbite-Tantalite, Gold and Wolframite from the Congo (source of 20% of same).

Have a handgun for home protection: When seconds count, the police will arrive in minutes. Akhil Reed Amar wrote, "Between 1775 and 1866 the poster boy of arms morphed from the Concord minuteman to the Carolina freedman."

The Heller case held that the Second Amendment protects the right to possess a functional handgun in the home for personal and household defense.

The ATF has advised gun dealers that anyone legally licensed to use marijuana for medical purposes is an "unlawful user of a controlled substance" under federal law and therefore prohibited from purchasing or possessing firearms. To be licensed to use, without actually using qualifies as an "unlawful user"! With Obama care requiring all medical records be uploaded to online access, everyone's records will be available to government scrutiny. When will they get around to people suffering depression etc. Obama Defense Cuts: Reduce Army and Marine corps by 100,000. Shrink Navy to 238 vessels and lose of two carrier battle groups. Reduce strategic bombers from 153 to 101, AF fighters from 3,602 to 1,512 = cuts of 100,000 military positions, 200,000 civilian defense jobs and 500,000 defense industry positions. = "the smallest ground force since 1940 and the smallest Navy since 1915 and the smallest tactical fighter force in the history of the Air Force." Recall Clinton's reduction of active Army down 29%, Reserves down 20%, Navy down 32% and AF down 28%.

In the preamble of the Constitution, President Obama swore to uphold and defend is the mandate to "provide for the common defense." It says nothing about entitlements.

TSA has cost $ 57B over the past 10 years.

The top 10% earned 39.1% of income and paid 74.1% of taxes.

Why the USSR failed:

Leftist - The Soviets perverted the noble ideals of socialism

Modernist liberal: The parasitic, cynical, ruling class enriched itself at the common person's expense.

Dedicated market capitalists: Communism made entrepreneurship a crime

Civil Libertarians: Government denial of freedom

Per Eli Lehrer: centralization - ended human creativity. Efforts to enforce ideological conformity are inconsistent with the diversity that characterizes a free society.

Obama proclaims he's the 4th best president after Roosevelt, Johnson and Lincoln:

23Dec 2011 Highest black unemployment in 28 years

IBD Lowest consumer confidence in 30 years

America's credit rating downgraded - 1st time in history

34 months of unemployment over 8%

Federal spending, budget deficit & National Debt are all at the highest level, as a percentage of GDP since WWII.

46 million now living in poverty, the most since the start of tracking poverty in 1959.

Misery index at 28 year high

Worst housing crises since the Great Depression

Under Obama, poverty rate swells to 1 in 6.

Record number of American' on food stamps

Rate of economic growth only slightly above the 1930's

The recession officially ended during his 5th month in office and he has been to almost all 57 states.

Results: He is actually the most arrogant president ever.

Why do all the people who hate the rich buy lottery tickets?

Per Obama: a child born right after WWII had a slightly better than 50-50 chance of becoming middle class. By 1990 that chance had fallen to 40%. A child born today will only have a 1 in 3 chance of making it to the middle class. He argues that more taxes on the "rich" will correct the situation. He overlooks that in 1963 only 7% of children were born out of wedlock, while 40% today with 70% in the black community. In 2009, 44.3% of children living in a female headed household experienced poverty as did 26.5% in male-headed households vs only 11.1% in married couples households.

Obama stated: "Some billionaires have a tax rate as low as 1% - ONE PERCENT," - "That is the height of unfairness." - later "an administration official conceded the White House had no actual data to back up the president's assertion."

Taxes: Per the IRS: Families with incomes between $50K and $100K paid an average of 8.9% in income taxes. Between $100K and $200K = 12.7%. The top 1% = 24%.

U.S. Gross Domestic Product is about $15 Trillion and state, local and federal spending is about $ 6.7 Trillion - so we are $800B away from taking half the GDP out of the private sector - before Obama care! When we get there, Government will be larger than society.

3M's Chief Exec, "in preparation for a world where the West is no longer the dominant manufacturing power." and "Given the moribund interest in science in the U.S., this is strategically very important." In the 6 years through 2009, about 85% of the growth in R&D workers employed by U.S. based multinational companies has been abroad.

Engineering degrees awarded in 2008: Asia 56% vs U.S. 4%.

Green Revolution? In January 2012, Der Spiegel reported: "For weeks now, the 11 million solar power systems in Germany have generated almost no electricity." Having spent $ 129 billion - Government officials refer to it as "a massive money pit."

In Spain, the Government now reports that for every green job that the country created, it destroyed 2.2 in the real.

Wind Turbines: To produce the same amount of electricity as the two nuclear reactors at Indian Point, N.Y. (providing 30% of NY Cities electricity) would require some 770 square miles of land, an area slightly smaller than Rhode Island covered with wind turbines.

Democrats use the term 'contributions' when discussing the payment of income taxes with 'fairness' thrown in. By definition, a contribution is "the act of giving money" and the definition of giving is "handing over as a present."

Problem with taxing the rich: California's top 1% pay 40% of state taxes. Their CG's in 1994 = $28B, 2000 = $165B, 2002 = $68B, 2007 = $153B and 2009 = $56B causing a $9B decline in capital gains tax revenue over those two years. Focusing on the rich's CG's creates an uncertain revenue source.

2012

The six basic emotions: joy, surprise, anger, sadness, fear and the only learned one - disgust.

Unions: Excluding Government employees, Canadian's in unions has dropped from 1997's 21% to 18%. In the U.S.12% of employees are in unions vs Canada's 32%

Caterpillar pay: Ontario, Canada $ 35/hr vs Muncie, Indiana $ 18.50/hr

Obama reducing military vs government union employees = soldiers don't riot or strike!

U.S. Hunger: The U.S. Government spends close to $1T a year providing cash, food, housing, medical care and services to the poor (almost 50M) and near-poor. Of that, $111B is spent on food in federal and state programs. In 1970 1 in 4 children got a free lunch at school, today it is 2 out of 3 lunches served in schools are free or nearly free.

From an article by Jeanne Shaheen, Barbara Boxer and Patty Murray - 8Feb12 WSJ:

"It was a historic victory for women's health when the Obama administration changed the law to require private health plans to provide preventive services including breast exams, HIV screening and contraception for free. This new policy will help millions of women get the affordable care they need." Free is definitely affordable!

BOSTON, MA - Despite three federal laws that prohibit federal departments or agencies from directing, supervising or controlling elementary and secondary school curricula, programs of instruction and instructional materials, the U.S. Department of Education ("Department") has placed the nation on the road to a national curriculum, according to a new report written by a former general counsel and former deputy general counsel of the United States Department of Education.

If it wasn't free, it wouldn't be worth it.

U.S. Surgeons operate on the wrong person or body part as often as 40 times a week.

Per AARP: Social Security Benefits paid to Retirement Benefits 64%, Disabled Workers 15%, Children 8%, Widows, Widowers & Parents 9% and Spouses 5%.

1 in 7 Medicare patients died or were harmed by hospital care.

The number of patients who die each year from hospital errors is equal to 4 jumbo jets crashing each week.

MA PropertyTaxes

The initial 3% state sales tax was supposed to reduce the property tax when it was first adopted in 1966. It didn't.

When the state lottery was instituted in 1971, it was going to reduce the property tax. It didn't either.

When that sales tax was jacked up to 5% in 1975 this too was going to do the same. It hasn't.

Hiking the sales tax to 6.25% hasn't helped reduce the onerous property tax either, nor has hiking the 5% state income tax since 1989.

Even new local option meals taxes haven't helped lower the property tax.

Rep. Atkins now promises that if Bacon Hill adopts a municipal income tax, her bill this time will reduce the property tax. It sounds so familiar. In

2006. Then candidate for governor Deval Patick made a solemn pledge to reduce property taxes if elected. We're still waiting .

Achilles response to Hector's effort to reason when outside the walls of Troy, "There are no bargains between lions and men."

Living in Poverty: Married couples 7% vs single female parent 29%.

Zimbabwe has a Minister for Youth Development, Indigenization and Empowerment. Heading up further redistribution of wealth by requiring 51% ownership of all business by black Zimbabweans per a 2008 law. ala the farm seizures. Unemployment is 90%!

When observing Union officials - be sure to identify if they represent Public Sector Unions or Private Sector Unions as there is a significant difference in relevance/appreciation of economic conditions.

Careful with your organ donation: A brain dead? person is listed as BHC = beating heart cadaver! Really brain dead?? NOT SURE as body reacts to being cut!

14Mar12 - Oil/Gas production since 2009: State & Private lands oil +29% natural gas +22%while on Federal land oil -7.9% and gas -7.9%. and

Big Oil taxes 2009 = $35.7B or $86M a day. Exxon pays $1.45 taxes for every $1 profit.

Working Class white males ($ 37,000, ages 30 - 49): In 1960, 84% married vs 48% in 2010

Tosca : Vissi D'arte, vissi d'amore (I lived for art, I lived for love.)

U.S. and Oil: We import 8.4M barrels a crude a day. We export 0.3% of our crude and 3M barrels a day of refined product of which 20% is gasoline. The remaining 80% is various oil products and byproducts such as diesel, kerosene and heavy fuel oil - some of which is unusable here due to environmental laws or other reasons.

The various governments in the U.S. employ 30 million and consume 50% of GDP

The U.S. consumes 10,000 tons of aspirin a year

HIGHLIGHTS - SAUL D. ALINSKY'S "RULES FOR RADICALS"

Throughout history silence has been regarded as assent - in this case assent to the system'

People who profess the democratic faith but yearn for the dark security of dependency, where they can be spared the burden of decisions.

I will argue the the failure to use power for a more equitable distribution of the means of life for all people signals the end of the revolution.

In this world laws are written for the lofty aim of "the common good" and then acted out in life on the basis of the common greed.

It is a world not of angels but of angles where men speak of moral principles but act on power principles.

A world where we are always moral and our enemies always immoral

A world where "reconciliation" means that when one side gets the power and the other side gets reconciled to it.

A world of religious institutions that have, in the main, come to support and justify the status quo so that today organized religion is materially solvent and spiritually bankrupt.

Moral rationalization is indispensable at all times of action whether to justify the selection or the use of ends or means.

Conflict is the essential core of a free and open society.

This is the basic difference between the leader and the organizer. The leader goes on to build power to fulfill his desires, to hold and wield power for purposes both social and personal. He wants power himself. The organizer finds his goal in creation of power for others to use.

It is only when the other party is concerned or feels threatened that he will listen - in the arena of action, a threat or a crisis becomes almost a precondition to communication.

The organizer's job is to inseminate an invitation for himself, to agitate, introduce ideas, get people pregnant with hope and a desire for change and to identify you as the person most qualified for this purpose.

It is common for policy to be the product of power.

When those prominent in the status quo turn and label you an "agitator" they are completely correct, for that is, in one word, your function - to agitate to the point of conflict.

Process tells us how. Purpose tells us why.

From the April 2012 American Legion Magazine article by Alan W. Dowd: U.S. GDP = $ 15T (same as EU's 27 countries combined), 50% larger than China and 300% larger than India's. Per-capita income $47,200 vs China's $4,260. Debt vs GDP: 2008 @ 38%, 2010 @ 63% and 2012 @85% = danger zone for entitlements. Japan's debt to GDP 199%, Britain 413%, France 250% Germany 185% and Australia 138%.

We have 18 of the 50 largest companies on earth. 70% of coke drinkers live outside the U.S. as are half of McDonald's restaurants. Walmart has 2,700 stores outside the U.S.

In the 1950's U.S. Active duty = 3.4M or 2.1% of our 160M population. In the 60's 1M troops overseas. Cold War spending = 6 to 10% of GDP. Today 1.4M troops out of 313M, 30% overseas costing 4% of GDP.

People who work the overnight shift have a greater incidence of diabetes, obesity, hypertension, cardiovascular disease and cancer.

U.S. Addictions: Pain Pills = 7M (15K die annually) vs cocaine's 1.5M.

Top U.S. College degrees 2008-09: Business 347,985 (21.7%), Social sciences and history 168,500 (10.5%), Health professions and related clinical sciences 120,488 (7.5%), Education 101,708 (6.4%) Psychology 94,271 (5.9%), Visual and Performing Arts 89,140 (5.6%)

Lest we forget: Nixon repealed the draft in 1973.

The DOE estimates that 1/3rd of total U.S. delivered energy goes to manufacturing with 2/3rds of this into bulk chemicals, oil refining, paper products, iron & steel, aluminum, food, glass and cement.

Although total domestic oil production was higher in 2011 than any year since 2002 - production on Federal lands fell to a nine year low and crude oil down 14% year to year.

Domestic natural gas up 21% since 2005 but down 24% on federal land.

March 2012: The Federal government spent $369.37 B ($1 bills around the earth 1,435 times) = $1,190 per American vs collecting $ 550!

Once Government takes over, what was private risk management becomes regulatory compliance.

The Buffett tax will raise $3.2B per year. So it will take 514 years to pay off the 2011 federal budget deficit by 2526. Luckily it has an exception for the favorite tax shelter of the wealthy - municipal bond interest remains tax free!!

The toll from the Deep Water Horizon 2010 oil spill: Dead animals - 497 mammals, 613 turtles, 6,381 birds. Collected alive: 26 mammals, 536 turtles and 877 birds Cleanup involved at peak: 8,044 vessels, 47,848 workers and 1.8M gallons of oil dispersant.

Obama fairness: Subsidize a wealthy person to buy a hybrid luxury auto

Millions to politically connected solar energy companies that go bankrupt

No jobs on Keystone XL pipeline to please a few environmentalists

In 3 years - More people in poverty, on food stamps, lower home prices, higher gas prices, higher unemployment.

Borrows 43 cents of every dollar spent

Adds $40,000 debt onto every U.S. household

Per Bureau of Labor Statistics: March 2012 there were 5.5M fewer jobholders than there were three weeks before President Obama assumed office, a time when US. population increased by 7.5M.

BRICS (Brazil, Russia, India, China, S. Africa) countries agree to largely eliminate the use of the U.S. dollar in trade among themselves

Commodities such as gas, cigarettes, liquor and wine, guns, airline tickets and tires are the favorite products to which the political class normally attaches excise taxes . The appeal is that levies are hidden in higher prices, rather than listed separately like a sales tax.

Elizabeth Warren described as the 'liberal papoose' by the WSJ.

Government spending is capital consumption.

Fiscal crises have a remarkable tendency to erupt into catastrophes overnight as panic consumes lenders.

Economies can only produce more goods and services in three ways:

Using more resources
Accumulating more productive capital
Creating new technology

(the first two inherently limited)

U.S. economic output: 1950's & 60's growth per year = 4.4%

(A mature Economy)

1970's= 3.4%
1980's= 3.1%
Since 2000= 1.7%

Sierra Club opposes Natural gas in 2012: Originally supported NG when it was $8 per million BTU as the price was high enough to make wind, solar and biofuel competitive plus it reduced CO_2 by 50% over coal. With NG at $2.50 - the CO_2 benefits do not outweigh the threat to alternate energy sources. Note - NG industry supports 8 times the jobs as the wind industry - chemical, fertilizer, manufacturing industries.

Zeus's daughters were the Three Graces:

Thalia, Goddess of fruitfulness
Euphrosyne, Goddess of of joy
Aglaea, Goddess of beauty

Obama's gaff at the Presidential Medal award (30May12) ceremony regarding "Polish death camp" - offended key polish voting blocks in Pennsylvania, Illinois and Wisconsin.

From Tom Rob Smith's Agent 6: He could sense the hostility of people "with no jobs to go to, no skills to offer, just an inbred sense of injustice."

He had some "expensive items of furniture like museum pieces salvaged from the wreck of a sunken career."

Communism was about racial and gender equality, an end to economic hardship for the many and lavish luxury for the few."

The event would offer a stark contrast to the elitist that typified concerts in capitalist countries with tiered ticket prices resulting in a stratification of the audience, where the poor were so far away they could hardly see the show while the truly impoverished lingered backstage, in the service corridors waiting for the concert to finish so they could sweep the floor.

Tax Burden comment from the CBO: "to the extent that additional tax revenues were generated by boosting marginal tax rates, those higher rates would discourage people working and saving, further reducing output and income."

"Fuel Poverty" is when fuel bills take up more than 10% of household income. Germany has half the world's solar photovoltaic capacity. Spain's Green subsidies at 3.45% of household incomes has led to a loss of 110,500 jobs. Green energy subsidies increase the cost of energy to the point where steel, ceramics, paper, cement, aluminum, and basic inorganic chemicals face a 140% energy cost increase by 2020 = these jobs will all go overseas.

Teacher's Union popularity sinks due to a general disgust with the featherbedding, extravagant pensions & benefits, absurd union rules and the poor educational product.

Obama favors big government and big, unionized companies that work with government to the detriment of small business resulting in the lowest number of startups in our history. In the 1980's, 13% of all companies were startups. In 2006 = 11%, in 2008 = 9% and in 2011 = 7%.

The current business cycle recovery is the only one during which people have reduced rather than increased their total outstanding debt. Low interest rates only work when people borrow - which is not the current case. Ultra low interest rates starve the savers and finance the speculators. Only when mortgage debt halts its decline would we be able to say that people may be close to the desired, lower level of debt. As of March 31, 2012, the average American has total household debt equal to 109 percent of his or her annual after-tax income, down from 131 percent as of Dec. 31, 2007

Aristotle and the church condemned the acquisitive spirit while Voltaire and Adam Smith praised it.

Italy, with virtually no meritocracy and where competition is considered a sin.

"Police and firefighters are great, but they don't create wealth. They protect it. That's crucial. Teaching is a wonderful profession. Teachers help educate people to become good citizens so that citizens can then go create wealth. But they don't create the wealth themselves." -Rush Limbaugh

Per the New Yorker - Obama "the most important policy he could address in his second term is climate change." Left wing foundations: Doris Duke 2007 - $100M to fight global warming. 2010 Ford $85M. Ford, Heinz, Turner and MacArthur fund NRDC (National Resources Defense Council) now with annual revenues of $ 97M. The 553 left groups assets = $ 9.5B vs 32 free market assets $38.2M. Govt funnels $569M in grant money to 247 Progressive environmental groups.

Food Stamps: 2011 44.7M up from 28.2M in 2008! Costs doubled to $ 78B in 2011. Fed's pays states $500M bonus to add people

What Doc Ford said in the latest Randy Wayne White novel: "We gave up life in the trees, the ability to hang by our toes and scratch our own backs, for this?"

Belarus: Annual potato consumption per capital = 397#, highest in world.

The National Reconnaissance Office = Vigilance From Above.

U.S. Navy = Force for Good

The U.S. Government mails out 10 million checks a week with 52M in poverty

Natick. MA 2011 - issued checks to 1,873 recipients, 6% of population. 63 with incomes over $100,000. 802 under $15K.

Typical private company expenses = 10% energy, 63% labor.

The sun: 4.6 billion years old. Every second, five million metric tons of mass are converted into nuclear energy, equivalent to the detonation of 90 billion one-megaton hydrogen bombs. For the sun and cooler stars, the proton-proton reaction is the driving force building a helium nucleus from hydrogen.

The top 1% of earners get 17% of income and pay 37% of income taxes while the bottom half get 13% of income and pay 2% of income taxes.

Governments are instituted by Men, deriving their just powers from the consent of the governed.

Consumer spending on food: US = 14%, vs 28% in 1960. China 33% and India 50%.

GM: Bailed out in 2009 - US Gov $ 50B before it could go into a managed bankruptcy. In 2010 gets own financing organization - GM Financial. From Q410 to Q112 sub prime customers up 79%. to $2.3B. 8.2% of 2012 sales. GM still owes the U.S. $26.4B with 500M shares, the price has to go to $53 to break even. Price $19.67 - 30Jul12

GM's auto workers compensation = $75/hr vs $42 in South thanks to Obama.

General Motors bail out = state capitalism, crony capitalism or corporate capitalism.

Student Loans: $900B of the $1T are Federal loans. 90% of defaults are on Gov. loans with 20% forecast for loans issued in 2013.

Hormuz: Every day 2 million barrels of oil passes thru to the U.S.A.

U.S. welfare = $952B in 2012. The bottom quartile receives $ 3 for every $1 earned.

India: Power problems - private CLP holdings 660MW plant's January 2012 start up delayed months due to inability of state owned Coal India to deliver coal!. State owned Air India has lost money the past 5 years, surviving on government handouts.

Justice Dept. Homicides, 1976-2009: Blacks by Blacks = 94%, Blacks by whites = 6%, White by whites = 86%, Whites by blacks = 14%

Rule of Law: Governed by rules that are transparent and enacted through the legislative process - not by the whims of our leaders. If legislators exceed their authority, courts must prevent or remedy the potential harm.

New Orleans Levees = $ 15B / 138 miles = $108.7M per mile

There are 90,000 kernels of corn in a bushel

Middle class shrinking = 6% moved up and 4% moved down

Is government growing more rapidly than the private economy's ability to finance it?

The Congressional Research Service reported that from fiscal 2008 through 2012, the federal government spent $68.4 billion to fight the phantom known as anthropogenic global warming (AGW) or man-induced climate change. This war on fossil fuels has decimated our economy, stunted growth and increased joblessness.

Obama redistributed $26.5B to the UAW. This money came from the taxpayers to the UAW allowing average $70 per hour in wages and benefits. Subverted bankruptcy laws

Subprime started with The Community Reinvestment Act of 1977 instructing banks to lower their credit standards and begin loaning in lower-income communities. In 1994 under Clinton rules were drastically revised to expand lending mandates on banks and giving regulators more power to punish banks for non-compliance.

Obama's Energy Department awarded $16.4B of the $20.5B "green stimulus" programs to members of his campaign finance committee, his campaign bundlers and major Democratic donors!

Recovery started in June 2009: Since then real median family income has dropped 4.8%.Union membership down 500,000. with 800,000 more long-term unemployed, 8 million out of labor force.

Per Obama: global popularity generates global power.

> Failed in effort to bring 2016 Olympics to Chicago
> Failed on ending Iran's nuclear program
> Failed to renegotiate climate change deal inCopenhagen in 2009
> Failed with muslims in Egypt
> Failed with Russia
> Failed with Israel
> Failed to keep residual forces in Iraq
> Failed to cut deals with the Taliban and North Korea.
> Failed to get China and Russia to condemn Assad
> Failed in effort to intercede in Europe' economic crises ("Herr Obama should above all deal with the reduction of the American deficit" advised German finance minister Schauble

Florentine advice "men worry less about doing an injury to one who makes himself loved than to one who makes himself feared."

The Bin Laden success, forever diminished by the administrations tawdry efforts to publicize it for political gain.

15% of parking lot attendants have B.A. degrees.

Better Off Now? - Sept 2012

Median income down 7.3% or $ 4,000. Since 'recovery'
down $ 2,544 / 4.8%
Long term unemployed: 811,000
Poverty: 2010 = 15.1% up from 2009 14.3%. 2011 est. 15.7%
Food Stamps: up 11.8M. 2009 = 33M @ $50.4B.
Now 46.7M @ $ 71.8B
Disability: up 1M
Gas prices Start $ 1.89. Now $ 3.84
Misery Index: Start 7.83, now 9.71
Union Membership: Down 500,000
Debt up $ 5T to 16T

Per Environmental groups: Desert Solar projects can disturb Pleistocene-era caliche deposits releasing carbon into the atmosphere negating solar carbon gains along with threatening habitats of "endangered species".

K-12 education: Since 1970 the per-pupil cost of education has exploded from about $55,000 to about $150,000 in inflation adjusted terms. Yet math and reading scores have stagnated and science scores have actually declined The results of having hired 3M more teachers and spending

$ 210 billion more per year on public education.

Germany's persistent belief in the supremacy of the State.

Median U.S.household income 2011: Asian $64,995, White $55,412, All Races $50,054, Hispanic $38,624, Black $ 32,366.

In 2009 the Federal Government spent $ 90B on green stuff

Household incomes: Fall 2008 = $55,587 vs June 2012 =

$ 50,964 while real median net worth is down 40%.

Since 1971 median income of American households has gone from $ 9,000 to $ 50,000 but after the dollar's 82% loss of purchasing power - the median household income rose just 12% largely due to the growing prevalence of two-income households.

For the 2012 Christmas season - Toy's are Us will hire 45,000 part time employees

Front page headlines - Investor's Business Daily
25Sep12 - Health Premium up $ 3,065; Obama vowed $ 2,500 Cut
26Sep12 - Household Income Down 8.2% Under President Obama
1Oct12 - BenghaziGate: People Died and Obama Lied
3Oct12 - Income Inequality Soars Under Obama

State & Local public jobs (19.1 million) are at a 7 year low but compensation gap over private workers has widened to

$ 12.30 per hour pay.

In 2011, some $ 372 billion cash was transferred out of the U.S.

The Martin Luther monument in Washington cost $ 120 million. - WSJ 6Oct12

Per Spectrem Group: Divorced women head 7% of households with net worth of $ 1M to $5 million and 9% of households with $5M to $ 25 million. Average age = 63.

Muslims: 2010 = 1.6B. Est 2030 = 2.2B. Indonesia = 205M, Pakistan = 178M, India = 177M. Bangladesh = 149M,

Egypt = 80M. Nigeria 76M, Iran & Turkey = 75M

Lady GAGA cancelled Indonesia concert when labeled "devil's messenger". "We will guard the plant and crush the bug. That's our job."

Jobs under the 2009 - $821B stimulus: 166,000 private sector out of 682K saved or created = 24% vs the promised 90% by Romer.

Obama's counter terror strategy: Lie and Deny. Fort Hood massacre = a random act by one individual;l. Christmas Day bomber = "an isolated extremist". Times Square Bomber = "a one-off incident". All linked to al-Qaida!]

Last 10 years - tuition & fees at: Private universities like Harvard up 2.6% over inflation and for Public universities almost 6% per year faster than consumer price index.

= rising federal subsidies have allowed colleges to raise prices.

Only 40% of student's with Pell Grant awards (currently $ 5,550) complete a 4 year college degree within 6 years. 2011 = $ 36,000,000,000!

The Assembly of Muslim Jurists of America has ruled that sending food and other aid to U.S. troops is a "sin".

per the Koran, "jihad is our way and death for the glory of Allah is our greatest ambition." of the 56 muslim nations!

Homes In poverty - 2010: Married 8.8%, single male 24.2%, Single female 40.7%

Percent of births to unmarried women: 1970 = 10% vs 2011's 40%. With great improvements in avoidance of pregnancy - - more pregnancies!! Woman's poverty at a 17 year high!!

European central banks have more than 10,000 metric tons of gold. 1 MT = 32,151 oz. Germany 3,396T, Italy 2,452, France 2,435, Netherlands 613, ECB 502, Portugal 383,

U.K. 310, Spain 282, Austria 280, Belgium 228, Sweden 126, Greece 112

The Obama economy blends the worst features of First World crony capitalism and Third World socialism.

Cheap money and record low interest rates promote over investment in the longest-term alternatives, typically real estate.

The U.S.A. was originally conceived to focus on social, political and economic ends not the arts. The Declaration of Independence focus on "the pursuit of happiness" requires prosperity as a precondition.

Those nations which have put liberty ahead of equality have ended up doing better by equality than those with the reverse priority.

The democrat party has reduced America to a bunch of tribes.

Every day 17 M barrels of oil and petroleum products pass through the Strait of Hormuz

Unions spent $400M re electing Obama.

Calif Prop 30 to increase taxes had the Calif Teachers Assoc's $11.5M, SEIU's $10.7M representing 350,000 gov employees & American Federation of Techers $4.2M support. The Calif Democratic Party gave $5.1M.

Calif Prop 32 - banning automatic union dues deduction opposed by labor to the tune of $ 55M = Cal Teachers Assoc's $21M and $13M by the SEIU.

Twinkie's problem: 372 collective bargaining agreements,80 different health and benefit plans, 40 pension plans and mandated a $31M increase in wages and healthcare for 2012. The striking union pay as much as $22/hr, medical benefits, 9 weeks paid leave & company pension..

Since the election: Average annual wage down 2% since Obama took office
　　2011 poverty 712,000
　　Food stamps up 15 million to 47% of population
　　Jobless claims up 79,000 to 439,000
　　Annual Inflation rate up 2.2% in Oct
　　Coal plants to close 353
　　Small banks disappearing
　　Stocks down 5% in 1st week.

Global Warming? WSJ 19Nov12 - Orange-juice futures surged 8.6%, settling at a one month high Friday, on concerns about a frost damaging the U.S. orange crop over the next few months.

Country guidelines: Servicing Debt - over 30% of total government revenue is unsustainable. Interest payments over 15% of total revenue are unsustainable.

Ethanol: By 2015, mandated use is 15 billion gallons = 5.3 billion bushels of corn = to 40% of the 2011 corn crop.

Student Loans: 11% were 90 days or more behind in payments. There are no restrictions on borrowing now up to about $1Trillion.

Small Business in the US = 22M. 3% with profits over $250K

SSI pays $1,000/mo

58M households pay NO income taxes.

Favorite word = inerrancy = unable to make a mistake / incapable of being wrong

2nd favorite word = Deicide = the killing of a God

In the 2009 Recovery Act - the Obama's administration sent $250 billion to help state and local government keep payrolls near pre-recession levels. Note: since 2008, state and local governments have fallen by 562,000. Per the American Time Use Survey: Private sector employees work about 41.4 hours

There are only 4 million paying AMT, with taxable over $ 75K.

Top Tax Rate	Top 3% AGI	Top 3% Fed Taxes	Bottom 66% Paid
1958 91% @ 3M	14.7%	29.3%	29%
2010	35%	27.3% 51%	6.7%

By 1965, the rules oriented culture of the postwar era was rapidly giving way to the rights oriented culture we have lived in since. - WSJ 24Dec12

Wind Power: There have been subsidies for 20 years with 2013 @ $12B

> To generate a Million Watt hours of electricity costs: Wind $53, Nuc $3, NGas $ 0.63

There are 26 countries with 10,000 or more Jews

During the Clinton years, 10 year U.S. Government Bonds paid 7.5%.

Massachusetts licensed gun owners went from 1.5 million to 230,000 in the last 14 years while at the same time we have a 20% increase in gun crimes with homicides up 3% per year.

Keep irrational hope alive

There are currently 30,000,000 surveillance cameras in the U.S. of A

His new TV program will be in North Korea interviewing celebrity guests.

2013

WSJ 4Jan13 - Fairly or not, there is a sense that those who played by the rules and did well have done something wrong or at least are under suspicion - and it is time for their government to seek atonement from them.

Egypt currently needs our $ 1.5B / month aid just to feed the people.

Social Security has the authority (Government IOUs) but not the resources to pay full benefits until 2032. Actually the trust fund will run dry in 20 years.

Head Start: Started under LBJ, cost $ 8 billion so far with $100 million in Sandy Relief package. Every subsequent study has proven it is a waste of money!

Budgets that ignore the buildup of debt are oriented to rewarding the public-employees unions with pay and benefits increases - while shielding them from desperately needed pension reforms - and ignores deep problems within the state's economy.

U.S. Health: AIDS in America is nearly 9 times the OECD average. Pregnancy in 15 - 19 year old girls 3.5 times OECD. Americans visit doctors 3.9 times vs 6.5 in the OECD in 2009. Life expectancy US 78.2, OECD 79.5, Japan 83.

Per 23Jan13 IBD: Obama's Real Record - Income equality: In 2011 only the wealthiest 20% saw their incomes go up. During Obama's years in office average incomes of the poorest households fell 8% back to mid 1980's level, median household income is down 7%, people on food stamps up 46% and 2.7 M more people in poverty. Transfer payment to the poor dropped from 54% in 1979 to 36% in 2007 (The rest going to middle and upper income households. The 3 richest counties in the U.S. surround D.C. and are twice the national average.

Cultural anthropology's three sacred cows: Un-contacted tribal people were peaceful, Darwinism had nothing to say about human behavior and culture, and that material resources were the cause of conflict! Do Pre-state societies War over protein or women? Latest research indicates the chief motive for raiding or fighting to be the abduction of women, their recovery or to revenge the abduction of women. Mortality rates from violence is common in small scale societies today and in the past. Almost 1/3rd of such people die in raids and fights with men dying at twice the rate of women. WSJ 26Jan13

IBD 29Jan13: College Grads: 48% (13M) hold jobs that DO NOT require a bachelor's degree. 5M have jobs that do not require high school diploma. 1M sales clerks, 300,000 waiters 100,000 janitors with college degrees. In 1970 1% of taxi drivers had a degree vs now 15%.

Department of Homeland Security has purchased 1.6 billion bullets, purchasing 7,000 assault weapons (semi/full automatic) and 30 round magazines = Obama's "a civilian national security force that's just as powerful, just as strong, just as well funded" as the military"?

Feb 2013 - Germany to repatriate some of its gold to increase domestic level to 50% from current 31%. All 12M Oz (11%) from France and 10M of the 45% in the U.S. and none from London's 13%. The Fed Bank of NY has 7 years to return the gold.

WSL 21Feb13 - "The left is cozying up to holy men who want adulterous women to be stoned, homosexuals to be hanged, and 1,200 year old laws emanating from somewhere in the Arabian desert to replace our free constitutions.

Germany has adopted the term 'Cultural

Enhancement' (Kulturelle Breicherung) as the PC description for Turkish residents. Germany has also identified the Turk's IQ as 18% below native Germans.

Looking for copper deposits = look for the becium homblei flower as it grows best in copper rich soil.

Sequester Fear mongering: FAA handled 23% more traffic with fewer controllers in 2000 and has 3,400 excess controllers costing $300M.

The top 20% of earners account for 38% of all spending same as the bottom 60%.

The swan knight Lohengrin is the son of Parsifal.

Hitler saw Parsifal at the age of 13.

You can't beat city hall but you can burn it down.

Median household incomes were about 8% lower in real terms in 2011 than in 2007.

DHS - Department of Homeland Security has 1.6 billion bullets of all calibers, just ordered 7,000 5.56x45mm NATO assault weapons, 30 round magazines and 2,717 MRAP (Mine Resistant Armored Protection) vehicles via the U.S. Army.

Austerity is the inevitable result of socialist math. Redistribution from one sector to another to redress unequal wealth is an inherently unsustainable idea. Austerity or total collapse are the only logical outcomes. These bankruptcies happen mainly in one party states. Austerity is the bitter fruit of socialism, a result of frittering away a nation's wealth.

Google Earth has several midpoints for the US - for MAC users = Chanute, Kansas, the PC version = Meadowbrook Apartments, St. Lawrence Kansas. Any link to Brian McClendon, VP Engineering at Google having lived in the Meadowbrook Apartments as a boy? or Google's senior software engineer Dan Webb having grown up in Chanute, Kansas?

Firearms deaths 2011; Suicide 19,766, Assault 15,593, Accident 851, Unknown 222.

Horse meat; Consumption was forbidden by the Catholic Church in the 8th Century. Legalized in the second half of the 19th Century as a cheap source of protein from old horses no longer able to work. French consumption peaked in the 1950's and 60's. Today there are 700 horse butchers in France. The last horse butcher in Munich is Kaspar Woerle's down from 20 in the 50's. Try the salami!!! In Paris - Le Taxi Janne in the Marais district serves horse meat .

Cats in 36 million U.S. households!

Of the 17 industrialized countries, American men die first with the lowest life expectancy of 75.6 years. Our women are 16th at 80.7 years!

In 1924 the Progressive Party (Robert LaFollette) ran on a platform of government ownership of public power and a return to government ownership of the railroads. (The Government had nationalized the railroads during WWI)

WSJ 11Mar13 - Producing an electric car generates 30,000 pounds of CO_2 (primarily the production of the lithium battery) vs 14,000 for a conventional car. With production and fossil fuel electricity production for the electric car it produces more CO_2 over 50,000 miles than a conventional car = 50,000 sold in 2012 vs Obama's promise of 1,000,000 by 2015!

A 2013 Federal study recently found that the $167B spent on Head Start since 1965 has failed to deliver sustainable improvements in school readiness among children who go through it.

The average cost of public and private schools jumped 92% between 2001 and 2011 vs 27% in the consumer price index. High school graduates down from 3.41M in 2010-11 to 3.32M this year. Between 2006 and 2011, private school students dropped from 22% to 20% of HS graduates.

Progressives view different achievements by different racial and ethnic groups as 'unusual'. Yet some racial or ethnic minorities have directed more than half of whole industries in many nations including the Chinese in Malaysia, Lebanese in West Africa, Greeks in the Ottoman Empire, Brits in Argentina, Indians in Fiji, Jews in Poland and Spaniards in Chile - among others.

Iconoclasm: the deliberate targeting of ancient and sacred objects and sites for destruction. A central mission of intolerant transnational jihadist.

Let's look at the State's education spending. The average annual earnings for community college professors in 2011 was $77,826, with professors at Greenfield Community College making approximately the same amount ($66,768) as the average toll collector. When one moves the lens over to statewide college instructors, the numbers worsen as the average earnings plummet to $45,148 annually, a third less than the average toll collector. Really? For a state that lauds education as its cornerstone, this goes beyond an oversight. - March 2013

Jesuits take the standard vows of poverty, chastity and obedience, they also take a vow of obedience to the Pope.

Top Swiss salaries were 93 times those of the lowest paid workers in 2011. Now pushing 1:12 where executive salaries can not exceed 12 months total salary of lowest paid employee.

The largest federal government union = AFGE has 650,000 members who pay $ 19.75 per month dues = $ 12,837.500 per year. Postal workers have their own union.

Out-of Wedlock birthrates: National 1964 = 7% vs todays 40%. Whites 1960 = 2% vs 30% and Blacks 20% to 72%. Hispanics 1990 = 40% vs todays 50%.

Social Science: per Sen. Daniel Patrick Moynihan, "Social science is rarely dispassionate, and social scientists are frequently caught up in the politics which their work necessarily involves...the pronounced "liberal' orientation of sociology, psychology. political science and similar fields is well established."

Since 2009, Cyprus has offered permanent EU residency to anyone who buys property worth at least 300,000e - mostly Chinese!

There are an estimated 1.5 billion families without electricity. They typically spend at least 10% of their income on kerosene, as much as $36B a year per the World Bank.

There are some 6M children diagnosed with ADHD. Costs $ 4B/year.

Americans 65 years and older: 2010 = 40M vs 2030 = 73M. By 2020 direct care workers projected to be 5M up 48% from 2010.

Over 100,000 veterans in the VA system have lost their gun rights forever based on a ruling of mental deficiency by a board of bureaucrats.

2011 tax returns: Total 143,399,737 with 1,481,966 audited. The chance of audit grows disproportionately higher as adjusted gross rises. AGI 1 to 25K = 40% of returns with 1% audited. $ 200K - 500K = 2.41% of returns vs 1.96% audit and $ 1 to 5M = 0.18% of returns vs 8.9% audited.

Government is now the largest banker for home mortgages and consumer debt.

Obama: No one of importance sent to Thatcher's funeral.

During WWII the US 8th Airforce (Europe) lost 26,000 KIA - more than the USMC.

The U.S. had some 4,400 tons of VX gas. The amount equal to Lincoln's eye on the penny would kill one person.

JEAN JACQUES ROUSSEAU (1712-1778) a failed individual, believed individualism was wrong and that man could achieve virtue only by belonging to a collective. Unable to compete, he opposed competition in society and the economy. Creating no wealth himself, he viewed private property as evil. Belonging to a lower social class, he promoted class warfare. And coming from a shattered upbringing, he considered family, church and school less effective than social engineering by the state.

In 1979, 20% of U.S. households received more in transfer payments than they paid in taxes. In 2009, 60% of households received more in the value of transfer payments than they paid in taxes. = ONLY 40% of U.S. households were making a positive contribution to total federal expenditures per the Congressional Budget Office.

Marx: His propaganda was often more about monopolizing the public discussion than persuading with ideas. The main thing was to command huge, virtually unwitting masses." to do your revolutionary dirty work.

"Capitalism, that economic system based on the private ownership of the means of production and distribution, as land, factories, mines, railroads etc., and their operation for profit, under more or less competitive conditions."

—My childhood dictionary
    "Capitalism is a social system based on the recognition of individual rights, including property rights, in which all property is privately owned."

—Ayn Rand, "Capitalism: the Unknown Ideal"
    "Capitalism has always been a failure for the lower class. It is now beginning to fail for the middle classes."

—Howard Zinn, "A People's History of the United States"
        After 4 years of Obama: Household income down 4.4%, 2 million fewer jobs than in 2007, 7.4% of Americans unemployed and twice that rate for minorities, a record 47 million Americans on food stamps, a record 16% of the population in poverty. U.S. debt a record $ 17T or 109% of GDP, Government spending 3.5T/year = 23% of

GDP = $28,000 for every household in America. 4 years of $ trillion deficits, this year $642 B

One million barrels of oil is shipped every day by train in the U.S.A.

ARod has been paid $325 million by the NY Yankees over the past 19 years.

GD CEO paid $6.9M in 2012

There are 400 million Buddhists!

The U.S. has 144,000 convenience stores.

In 1910 the largest occupations were:

Farmers	6.1M
Farm Laborers	2.8M
Farm Laborers, unpaid	2.5M

2012

Retail Salespersons	4.3M
Cashiers	3.3M
Food Prep	2.9M
Office Clerks	2.8M
Registered Nurses	2.6M

Tacitus: "Germany with its forbidding landscapes and unpleasant climate - a country that is thankless to till and dismal to behold for anyone who was not born and bred there."

Would you sacrifice your life in a useless defiance of authority?

Our system of government is responsive to groups, not individuals.

Global Warming: NOT. Weather related deaths: 1920's = 485,000 annually, 1970's annually = 74,000. Now = 19,000. Sea levels now rising 1/8" per year is at a far slower rate than the average for the past 17,000 years - the seas have been rising since the last ice age.

"From Rosy Bow'ers" - Ah! tis all in vain, Death and despair must end the fatal pain, Cold despair, disguis'ed, like snow and rain, Falls on my breast!

Private grade schools: 11% of all parents (urban & rural) use private. Public school teachers sending their kids to private schools: Philadelphia, 44%, Cincinnati 41% and Chicago 39%, Rochester NY 38%, SFO 34%. In Congress 37% House and 45% Senate with school age children.

The Liberals control of the public media deprives the people of independent thought.

The conflict in American politics: Regulators bent on the dream of a world without risk vs those who resist such an agenda in the name of freedom and responsibility.

Americans are a self-governing people.

President Obama skipped the 150th anniversary of Lincoln's Gettysburg Address on 19 November.

Barbara Anderson, Nov 13: I saw Gov. Deval Patrick on "Meet the Press" last Sunday, talking about appearing with President Obama in Boston to compare Obamacare with Romneycare. Patrick assured the national audience that "now we have virtually universal coverage ... It has not broken the budget."

Easy to say, when in your first term you increased the sales tax rate from 5 percent to 6.25 percent. And yet ... a Monday RedMassGroup posting reminded us of a 2011 news item from the Boston Globe: "Gov. Deval Patrick approved a record $9.6 billion last July for the state's health insurance program for the poor — sufficient, he assumed, to last a year. But the program's costs quickly outpaced expectations, forcing the governor to approve an additional $329 million in October and then seek $258 million more, which lawmakers approved last week. And even that may not last, with six months remaining in the budget year ... With Massachusetts confronting an estimated $1.5 billion shortfall in the coming budget year, Patrick has said he is committed to financing the program, known as MassHealth ..."

So, the governor passed another tax package that increased the gas tax, tobacco tax, and created a new tax on computer sales (since repealed), not to mention further automatic inflation-adjusted gas tax hikes that are presently being protested with an initiative petition. These were sold as necessary new revenues to cover transportation spending that apparently has been pushed aside in favor of paying the highest health insurance costs in the nation and record Medicaid spending.

Aristotle's student Alexander the Great had a standing order for his troops to crate up any interesting plant and animals to ship back to Aristotle so he could study them and integrate them into his categorization of nature. Aristotle also argued that Plato's radical theory of creating a society that was NOT based on the family unit was unrealistic and unhealthy. He also recommended that the most durable political organization should rest with the middle class, since it has a vested property interest without an excess of greed (the wealthy) or poverty (the underclass) that would distort sensible decisions for the community.

The medically Uninsured: per the Congressional Budget Office - 71% regain coverage within a year and almost 50% within 4 months or less. Only 16% went over 2 years. The young and healthy, those between 19 and 34 = 27% are uninsured while those between 45 - 64 = 16%. 25% of the uninsured are in homes with household incomes in excess of

$50,000 and many are not eligible for ObamaCare's tax subsidies. The 30M? uninsured: some 6 million who claim to lack coverage are actually enrolled in Medicaid and another 4 M are eligible for Medicaid but have not enrolled. 9.5M are not citizens! By 2023 despite spending $1.8T in subsidies, 30M will remain uninsured.

Per Charles Darwin: "ignorance more frequently begets confidence than does knowledge." and per Hayek "The curious task of economics is to illustrate to men how little they really know about what they imagine they can design."

Personal Income: Includes the nearly $ 2.5T of government transfer payments. Social Security and Medicaid were less than 43% of government benefits in the 3rd Qtr 2013.

In 2013 vs 2007: employee compensation up 11.5%, Proprietor's income up 3.7%, income from transfer payments up 41.5%, investment income up less than 1% (entirely due to rental income as interest income is actually down).

Ethanol: 5M acres of land set aside for conservation (more than Yellowstone, Everglades and Yosemite combined) have been put into corn production on Obama's watch. As early as June 2010, there existed in the Gulf of Mexico "8,500 sq.mile "dead zone' below the mississippi Delta due to bottom-water hypoxia caused by increased agricultural runoff caused by increased corn production for making ethanol. Per U of Minnesota - converting grass lands to corn releases excess CO2 emissions of 134 metric tons per 2.47 acres. It takes 4,000 gallons of water per acre per day to replace evaporation fom a cornfield and each acre requires 130 pounds of nitrogen and 55 pounds of phosphorous. This destroys habitat and pollutes water supplies.

ObamaCare: Sec. 1311c(1)C exchange plans must cover care at "essential community providers ...that serve predominantly low-income, medically underserved individuals." This means clinics, public hospitals and hospitals largely serving the Medicaid community. Note: a review of 900,000 patients undergoing 8 different surgical procedures found that Medicaid patients were 50% more likely to die in the hospital after surgery than patients with private coverage.

If you enroll in an exchange plan - - your care will be standardized by the federal government with an eye to reducing what you consume and how much it costs.

Common Care State Standards (CCSS)'s Common Core contains statements in its lessons such as "The commands of government officials must be obeyed by all" and "The wants of the individual are less important than the well-being of the nation." In the middle school, Common Core calls upon students to read only the First Amendment.

This is set by ideologically driven teachers unions and education statists.

Progressives have replaced the term "Achievement" with "Privileged" to engender resentment as opposed to emulation.

Tornados: Records kept only since 1950. 2013 is the 4th highest year. More in 1992, 2001 and 2002. From 1953 - 1982 = 38 F5/EF5's vs 1983 - 2013 = 20

Low income whites in England and ghetto blacks in the U.S.A. have generations long indoctrination in victimhood by the political left. In the U.S. the left uses race and in the U.K. class.

Incomes broken into 5 equal groups by the CBO: the poorest paid 0.4% of all federal taxes vs the top paying 70%. This does not include transfer programs like food stamps, disability, welfare, Medicaid, Medicare and social security. While the lowest income group reported an average income of $8,100, they received an average of $ 22,700 through Fed Xfer programs. The next group netted $12,000, a 41% boost to income. Mid 20% = plus $2,600. 4th 20% = -$8,800 and top 20% = -$ 52,500.

Misc: A 747 burns 5 gal of fuel per mile. We spend 2 years of our lives on the telephone. We are 4" taller than our great grand parents. The USA raises enough food for the US and 300M people around the world. There are 100M newspapers published daily in the world.

GDP vs GO: GDP is composed of 70% consumer spending and by 20% Government spending vs GO /Gross Output composed of 40% consumer spending, 50% business spending. Gross output is the natural measure of the productive sector, while net output (GDP) is appropriate as a measure of welfare. Consumer spending is largely the effect, not the cause, of prosperity.

QE: Between November 2008, when QE 1 began, and October 2013 the U.S. stock market provided a total inflation-adjusted return of 14.51% per year. Over the same 5 year period the one-year U.S. Treasury bill returned -0.75% per year after accounting for inflation.

Per Irving Berlin: "My ambition is to reach the heart of the average American. Not the highbrow nor the lowbrow, but that vast intermediate crew which is the real soul of the country. The highbrow is likely to be superficial, overtrained, supersensitive. the lowbrow is warped, subnormal. My public is the real people."

2014

Nearly One-Eighth - According to 2012 Census data, 13.7 percent of the United States population is 65 years old or older (source: U.S. Census Bureau).

The federal offense of committing violent acts against people because of their gender, ethnicity, religion, disability or sexual orientation is a blatant violation of the 14th Amendment's equal protection clause. You punish criminals for their crimes not their motives. Is there a difference between being assaulted for my religion or my money?

Relying On Social Security? - The number of people receiving Social Security benefits as of November 2013 is 57,917,000. This translates to a total monthly payout of $67,425,813,060, or an average monthly benefit of $1,164.18 (source: Social Security Administration).

The U.S. personal savings rate grew to 4.9 percent in September 2013, from 2.9 percent in September 2007.

Snow:	Temperature F	Inches of snow per 1 inch of water
	32	10 to 1
	20	15 to 1
	10	20 to 1
	0	30 to 1

Non-punitive justice = restorative justice, reparative justice, distributive justice. There are no offenders, only victims and demands the abolition of prisons.

War on Poverty: Start date 1964. From 1950 to 1960 the number of people living below the poverty line went down over 50%. Likewise, the proportion of people whose earnings put them below the poverty line - without counting government benefits - declined by about 1/3rd from 1950 t0 1965.

With "sex education" starting in the 60's: although teen age pregnancy and venereal disease had been going down since the 50's, both trends reversed and skyrocketed after "sex education" became pervasive. The murder rate had been going down for decades, in 1960 it was 1/2 the 1934 rate. With the liberal changes in criminal laws during the 60's, by 1974 the murder rate had more than doubled the 1961 rate.

War on Poverty became the Federal War on Work.

1. Extended unemployment benefits - in 2013, 4 years after the recession ended - benefits were extended for 73 months. 2. Food Stamps - in 2000, 17.1 M in food stamps vs 47.6M in Oct 2013.

3. Higher taxes on workers - In 2004 top marginal rate = 35% vs todays 43%.

4. Social Security Disability: in 1990 about 4M on disability vs 11M today.

5. Increased Pell Grants - in 2000 less than 4M ($83B)received grants vs 9M ($170B) in 2012 many of which never graduate. No nation can achieve greatness when vast portions of its productive workforce is idle.

The traditional Catholic bias in favor of state authority.

The impact of high taxes, regulations that hamper enterprise and gum up the flexibility of labor markets, and bloated public sectors, which absorb and waste resources that could be productively put to work for everyone's benefit by businesspeople and investors, are played down or ignored.

Walmart: 20% of customers use 18% of all Food Stamps =

$ 14B in 2013.

Comment by Ahmed Sharaf, Chief of museums at Egypt's Antiquities Ministry regarding the 24Jan14 truck bomb that severely damaged Cairo's Museum of Islamic Art, "They know the museum is right here. Something like 500 kilograms of TNT. They don't care what they destroy. They hate culture and heritage, even their own."

The Washington area is now the wealthiest in the nation. The presidents popularity is 81% in the District of Columbia.

If guns kill people,

Then pencils misspell words,

Cars make people drive drunk,

And forks make people fat.

The top 20% of earners = 60% of consumption.

US expatriations hit new high in 2013 of 2,999. (in 2009, UBS turned over info on 4,400 US account holders with $ 1.2B).

US rail tank cars: 68,200 built before 2011 and 12,000 after. In 2009 hauled corn syrup, caustic soda or bulk materials and averaged 18,000 miles per year. With shale-oil, now run up to 140,000 miles per year. In 2006, oil carloads 4,700 vs 2013's 400,000.

Population control programs in India, China etc. since 1970's have caused the abortion of some 163 million female babies - book 'Unnatural selection'.

The U.S.has 2,000,000 miles of natural gas pipelines and 175,000 miles of hazardous liquid pipelines. Is the 1,179 mile Keystone XL pipeline a hazard?

Obama achievements: Eliminate al-Assad and his chemical weapons 4.1% of his 1,300 tons promised 30 month ago. Unemployment would never exceed 8%. "High Quality" pre school will save 7$ for every $ spent, Keystone pipeline to produce 42,100 jobs per State Department vs Obama's "might create maybe 2,000 jobs", workforce participation at a 36 month low, in the 2nd half of the 5th year of recovery, a smaller fraction of the population is employed or looking for work than when the recovery began, promised to close Guantanamo Bay January 2009, will punish the Benghazi murders, affordable health care = guaranteed retention of of existing health plans and doctors, create 4 million new jobs and save families $2,500 a year in premiums, all while extending expanded coverage to more people at a lower cost, IRS confirmed delay of Tea Party related requests - after the people in charge quit, retired or invoked the 5th to the "outrageous" - Obama said did not entail "even a smidgen of corruption."

Of the individual income tax returns filed in the U.S. for tax year 2011, 47.8 percent reported less than $30,000 of adjusted gross income (source: Internal Revenue Service, BTN Research)

Across populations, men are roughly 10% taller and 20% heavier than women, need 20% more calories and live 6% shorter.

Luftwaffe dropped 57,000 tons of high explosives and incendiaries on Britain. Bomber Command and the U.S. 8th Air Force alone dropped over 1.6 million tons on Germany killing some 350,000 German civilians, 60,000 Italians, 53,000 French and 8,000 Dutch.

Are teaching the Humanities (art, literature, history, music, classics, philosophy and so on) a useless undertaking. Does undergraduate or graduate training in medieval literature or the history of religion enhance your chances of finding a job? The humanities equate capitalism with crass acquisitiveness and soulless materialism.

Diversity: In 2010 West Virginia foreign born 1.2% vs California's 27%. TANF (Temporary Aid for Needy Families) for a family of 3 in Calif $694/mo vs Texas $260 while both have 39% Hispanic populations.

Question: Is shareholder capitalism sustained not by law but by an institutional edifice of greed (there is no legal requirement for for-profit companies to maximize returns to shareholders?) vs the German capitalism model that adheres to the stakeholder model.

Illegal adult immigrants: Here at least 15 years = 35%, 10 to 14 years = 28%, less than 5 years = 15%. Home owners = 35%.

Per the Tax Foundation study, "The Distribution of Tax and Spending Policies in the United States" 2012 data on 150 m U.S. Families. Market incomes include wages, business and cap gains income and health and retirement benefits, but excludes transfers:

Transfers To achieve income equality

Average	$ 81,600		
Bottom 20%	9,560	21,158	50,885
Med 20%	56,882	7,376	17,339
4th 20%	100,240	- 4,089	-14,551
Top 20%	311,400	- 65,573	- 164,227

To get everyone to average income - need to take an additional $2.4T from the top 40% raising the total mount of redistribution to nearly $ 4T. Top 20% pay 21% of income now, need 74% to achieve redistribution needed. Currently take $1.5T from top 40% to bottom 60%. $ 4T needed to close gap.

From Barbara Anderson's Feb14 column: "A few months later, I received a notice that my Medicare Advantage program had been canceled. I found another policy for my small business but last week received a notice that this policy isn't allowed by ObamaCare because it doesn't cover pediatric dental care or childbirth classes for our three employees, all over 60 without dependents."

In 2012, the UAW contributed $11.8M to liberal groups and

$1.8M to Federal candidates all but $1,000 to Democrats.

The 2007 recession began in December with 146,273,000 Americans employed vs Jan. 2014's 145,244,000. SS disability up 21%, extended unemployment to 2 years, eliminated work requirements. Food stamps up 50% to close to 50M receptors. Fed & State pay $ 1T to the lowest 20% - not to work.

After 3 years of war in Syria, Obama has asked his staff for 'options'.

The Norwegian national government spends $500,000 annually on research projects to deepen ski-wax knowledge.

"Income inequality" - In 2010, 119M household tax returns / 1.1M in top 1% received 15% of national household income (before taxes) and $307,000 got you in. Salaried executives = 30%, doctors 14%, people working in finance 13%, lawyers 8%.

Super rich top 0.1% / 110,000 executives 41% and finance 18%. From 1980 to 2010, top 1% before-tax income share from 9% to 15% and Fed income tax from17% to 39%.

Individual taxes collected = $900B, Top 1% paid 39% / $350B. The remainder of the $2.2T collected came from corporate, estate and excise taxes.

Modern technological achievement is overwhelmingly a Western achievement, a source of great sadness for politically correct exponents of multiculturalism.

Major Welfare Programs - 2012:

Medicaid	$ 296B
Unemployment Insurance	126B
Disability	124B
Food Stamps	75B - 1 in 7, 3X
cost over 10 years	
Supplemental Security Income	60B
Earned Income Tax c\Credit	56B
Pell Grants	41B
Section 8 Assistance	28B
Drug Benefits	23B
Education for Disadvantaged	14B
School Lunches	10B
S-Chip	9B
Head Start	8B
TANF Cash Aid	7B

In 2011 Fed outlays on all means tested welfare programs for the poor = $746B

Does not include cash subsidies: Unemployment Insurance & Disability = $250B

State spending = $ 257B. Total aid = $ 44,000 per every poor family of four.

Valentine's Day 2014 for the First Family will be spent at separate locations. National debt up $6.6T so far. Median household income down 4.4% or $ 2,500 since Obama's "recovery" began. Average health insurance premium up $2,500 since ObamaCare became law. Underemployment level 17.7%. Payroll-to-population rate dropped to 42% from 63.5% in January 2010. 46.5M Americans living in poverty.

Feb 2014: 43,000 U.S. taxpayers have remitted $6B in back taxes and penalties as a result of tax scrutiny of Swiss banks

Christians living under fundamental Islam have three options: Convert to Islam, "face the Sword" or remain Christian but pledge submission to Islam. The last called dhimmitude, commits the Muslims to do no physical harm or religious targeting of Christians. In turn, Christians agree to abstain from renovating churches or monasteries, not to display crosses or religious symbols in public or use loudspeakers in prayer; not to read scripture indoors loud enough for Muslims standing outside to hear; not to undertake subversive actions against Muslims; not to carry out any religious ceremonies outside the church; not to prevent any Christian wishing to convert to Islam from doing so; to respect Islam and Muslims and say nothing offensive about them; to pay the jizya tax worth four golden dinars for the rich, two for the average and one for the poor, twice annually, for each adult Christian; to refrain from drinking alcohol in public; and to dress modestly. (as decreed in Syrian City of Raqqa in 2014).

Obama helps the "Little Guy": Costs originating from Government policies hit the little guy hardest - electricity bills up from KW-H 2003 = 8.72 cents to Nov 2013's 12.09 up 39%. Interest rates at 0% = for the elderly little guy his bank account earns less than inflation while the Government finances its deficit for free. Low interest rates allow companies to borrow money for free to buy capital equipment as a substitute for labor. Obama care rates and copays - UP.

Report to the NSA anyone you see at a library computer that has the technical specifications for portable nuclear weapons on the screen or plans to blow up the Louvre. Also, anyone discussing a conspiracy between the Federal Reserve and the archbishop of Canterbury to seize control of duck blinds.

Information serves the people in power.

WWII, the Ford Factory and philosophy came together to produce 8,665 B-24 bombers each with 1.3M parts, one every 55 minutes!

One should never underestimate the emotional and physical benefits of donuts.

Per William Gilkerson; "All these new weapons enabled the peoples who owned them to take other less fortunate peoples under their protection."

WSJ 6Mar - Week of 23 Feb 2014: Putin captures Crimea. Israel intercepts Iranian shipment of Syrian-made surface-to-surface rockets to Gaza, North Korea test fires four short-range missiles and four long range missiles able to hit U.S. bases, Moscow announces plans to use military bases in Cuba, Venezuela and Nicaragua (3 months ago, Sec. Kerry announced, "The era of the Monroe Doctrine is over.", Russian spy ship SSV-175 arrives in Havana Harbor, China announced a 12.2% increase in military budget within 24 hours of Obama's proposed decline in U.S. Defense spending. Mr. Obama campaigns in Connecticut for increasing the federal minimum wage, then to Boston for fund raiser - what me worry????

To quote Sue Banducci, "Old age comes at a bad time."

WSJ 6Mar14: Per Credit Suisse Global Wealth Databook - Median net worth of American adults is less than $45,000 vs Australia $220,000, France $142,000 and Greece $54,000. Almost 1/3rd of American adults have a net worth of less than $10,000. Household owned homes in 1980 = 65.6%, in 2013 = 65%. Per Robert Schiller: U.S. Stocks since 1890 have averaged +6% annually vs inflation adjusted 0.18% from houses. Buying houses as an investment has meant no money for retirement.

Per economist Steven Landsburg: for 99,800 of the past 100,000 years humans lived at the subsistence level. Today about 1B people live on $1 a day and another billion on $2 a day = 1/3 of the people live no better than our ancestors over the millennia. Over the past 50 years U.S. real incomes have grown at 2.3%, doubling every 31 years.

GROWTH does it!!!! Culture has a lot to do with it. Also taxes negatively effect growth. States do not invest effectively and regulations harm the economy. Almost every Obama policy has been anti-investment, anti-work, anti-production and therefore anti-growth.

Plato focused on the distinction between persuasion and influence. Persuasion engages the reason of a person while influence brings only psychological pressure and prejudice to bear and is mere propaganda.

To set things right - sudden and extreme violence or better still, the effective threat of it.

In 2013 there were 9.6M households with $1M investable assets. not including house.

The Massachusetts Constitution of 1780 described freedom as respect for man's inalienable rights "among which may be reckoned the right of enjoying and defending their lives and liberties; that acquiring, possessing, and protecting property (and) that of seeking and obtaining their safety and happiness." Just the opposite of Obama's kind of government - an all powerful central government delivering everyday needs.

Politics in Government contracts: On average, government dependent companies that had a Senator ascend to the chairmanship of a powerful committee saw a more than 30% increase in revenue from the government. WSJ 15Mar14.

While 7% of Public companies got 10% or more of sales from government

College Costs - The cost of tuition, fees, room and board at an average in-state public college has increased 5.8 percent per year over the past 30 years, reaching $18,391 for the 2013-2014 school year. If college costs had instead risen only by the rate of inflation (using the Consumer Price

Index) over the past 30 years (2.9 percent per year), then a year of college would cost $7,982 during the current school year (source: College Board, Department of Labor).

The unemployment rate for individuals that have a bachelor's degree or higher was 3.4 percent as of Feb. 28, 2014, approximately half the national unemployment rate of 6.7 percent (source: Department of Labor, BTN Research).

14 Years Later - The NASDAQ Composite closed at an all-time high of 5,049 on March 10, 2000. The index closed at 4,336 on Friday, March 7, 2014, down 14 percent after 14 years. However the index is up 289 percent from its bear market closing low of 1,114 that the index had fallen to on Oct. 9, 2002, or 11 and a half years ago. All the returns referenced are based upon the change in the value of the raw index and do not include the impact of reinvested dividends. The NASDAQ Composite is an unmanaged index of securities traded on the NASDAQ system (source: BTN Research).

Federal Contractors with 50 or more employees or more than $50,000 in government work must have a minimum of 7% disabled workers. There are 40,000 contractors.

Ordinary people, attached to reality as they must be to survive, view same sex marriage as an absurdity.

Pre-school teachers racist? Per Education Secretary Arne Duncan, "The fact that the school-to-prison pipeline appears to start as early as four years old, before kindergarden, should horrify us." and Attorney General Eric Holder vowed to "aggressively disrupt the school-to-prison pipeline" by cracking down on racist nursery school? Facts - Blacks are 18% of preschoolers with almost half suspended more than once. 82% of preschoolers suspended are male. White boys are suspended at double the rate of Asian boys. The problem is different parenting styles and cultures (no fathers) leading to bad parenting especially within the black community.

Achievement is no longer required to increase self esteem

Legislative Risk: In 2012, wealthy people were afraid that Congress would reduce the estate-tax exemption and so many planned to give away securities, real estate, art and other valuables that advisors could NOT find enough qualified appraisers to help clients make those gifts. Exemption was raised to 4.534M or $10.68M for couples - now the recommendation is to "hoard assets"!

World's population 50 or older = 23%, in 2050 = 40%. World's most performed operation = Cataract.

Per the Heritage Foundation: "only 22% of minimum wage workers live at or below the poverty line, while 68% enjoy family incomes over 150% of the poverty line." 60% of minimum wage earners are female.

Since 2006, the trial lawyer's lobby, the American Association for Justice, has given $14.2M to Democrat according to OpenSecrets.org. It spent another $37M lobbying Congress over those years. 22 of their state affiliates gave 100% of their money to Democrats.

U.S. average annual wage 2012: Oil & Gas industry $107,200, waiters & waitresses $ 16,200, retail trade $ 27,700.

Per EPA; U.S. houses heated with wood: 11.5M

Steel Production, worldwide: 1870 = 500,000 tons. Enter the Bessemer converter and the open hearth process! In 1900 = 28,000,000 tons

In 2013, federal revenues increased $324 billion due to tax increases. Fed Rev increase (of 13%) equal to 1.5% of GDP vs the real economies growth of 1.9%.

The U.S. Navy uses 30 M barrels of oil per annum.

George Soros' Open Society Foundation gave $58M to leftist groups in 2011. The 269 millionaires in congress are predominantly democrats. From 1989 to 2014 rich donors gave Democrats $1.15B vs Republicans $736M. When union, university, superPACS, nonprofit, left wing interest groups are added, the Dems get $7 for every $ to Repubs.

Massachusetts Hunger: 545,000 people fed by the Boston food bank annually.

A U.S. 1$ bill printed on cotton-linen blend, lasts 21 months. The Fed will spend $826.7M in 2014 to make 7.8B bank notes with a total face value of $297.1B

From IBD, March2014: Obama's civilian national security force??? 70 federal agencies including those not associated with national security or crime fighting employ about 120,000 full time officers authorized to carry guns and make arrests

per the June 2012 Justice Department report. Recent ammo buys: Agriculture Dept. 320,000 rounds, Social Security Admin 174,000 rounds of ".357 Sig 125 grain bonded jacketed hollow-point", National Oceanic and Atmospheric Admin 46,000 rounds for their enforcement division of 96 special agents and 28 enforcement officers who carry weapons to forecast weather and monitor the atmosphere for $64M.

The Salvation Army's "Doing The Most Good" vs the Navy's "A Force For Good"

A viable state requires the allegiance as well as the obedience of its citizens.

In 1982 there were over 3,000 criminal offenses listed by the U.S. Justice Dept.

Gold: Nevada produces 75% of all U.S. gold down 33% since 1998. The cost of mining an ounce of gold up to $745 in 2012 from $280 in 2005.

Organic farming yields 20% to 50% less than conventional agriculture.

Volcanoes emit an estimated 10 million tons of Sulfur Dioxide annually.

WSJ 29May2014: Changes in price indexes since 2000

All items 35%, Food 41%, Medical Care 63%, College Tuition & Fees 121%

Per AIER 2000 - 1May14 cost of living from $100 to $136.63

For-profit school serve 13% of students in higher education but former students account for nearly half the defaults on student loans.

Gifted youth (1 in 10,000) go on to get Doctoral degrees (44% vs general population 2%) with median income twice U.S. average. Most child prodigies are highly successful - but most highly successful people were not child prodigies.

He would rather beg for forgiveness than ask for permission.

The Public Sector and Trade-Union culture that believes growth depends on putting more money in people's pockets and so favor Keynesian demand-side policies vs the Private Sector.

An age of the triumph of symbol over substance and narrative over fact.

Rockefeller U. estimated that a wind farm equivalent to a 1,000 megawatt nuclear power plant would require 298 sq. miles and that a solar equivalent 58 sq. miles. with intermittency, noise, and bird kills.

Man is tempted to blame others of his misfortunes that are the natural and predictable consequences of his own choices.

The U.S. is state subsidizing idleness while importing foreigners to do unskilled work.

The murder rate would be 5 times higher if we were using the medical techniques of 1960.

Heroin addiction typically involves intermittent use for 18 months before becoming an addiction. Addiction is something they do, not something that happens.

Metropolitan Opera TV multicast = 75% of the audience is over 65 and 30% over 75! Met house seats 3,800 with an average ticket price of $156.

Since 1965, 50 million legal & illegal immigrants have entered the U.S.A.

WSJ 7Aug14 - Renewable energies are 24% of Germany's power generation. One kilowatt hour cost: Offshore wind 18 euro cents, solar power 11ec, onshore wind 8 ec and coal & gas 4 ec.

WWI: Rule of thumb - For every three soldiers, one horse. Each horse required 10 times as much food as each soldier.

Berlin: In past 150 years, the capital of 5 different Germanys - Bismarck's Reich, The Weimar Republic, the 3rd Reich, DDR, and since 1990 the Federal Republic of Germany.

64% of China's rich (assets over $1.6M) are either immigrating or planning too. Problems: Pollution, food safety, broken education system. More than 100M Chinese traveled outside of China in 2013.

U.S. Colleges: there are 1.4 women to every Man

According to the latest US Department of Justice survey of crime victims, more than 6.6 million violent crimes (murder, rape, assault and robbery) are committed in the US each year, of which about 20 per cent, or 1.3 million, are inter-racial crimes.

Most victims of race crime—about 90 per cent—are white, according to the survey "Highlights from 20 Years of Surveying Crime Victims", published in 1993.

Almost 1 million white Americans were murdered, robbed, assaulted or raped by black Americans in 1992, compared with about 132,000 blacks who were murdered, robbed, assaulted or raped by whites, according to the same survey.

Blacks thus committed 7.5 times more violent inter-racial crimes than whites even though the black population is only one-seventh the size of the white population. When these figures are adjusted on a per capita basis, they reveal an extraordinary disparity: blacks are committing more than 50 times the number of violent racial crimes of whites.

According to the latest annual report on murder by the Federal Bureau of Investigation, most inter-racial murders involve black assailants and white victims, with blacks murdering whites at 18 times the rate that whites murder blacks. Over 35,000 White Women are Raped by Blacks annually in the U.S.! while blacks by whites = none recorded.

The two greatest achievements of people in power: Rome under Caesar Augustus and the other, America's Revolutionary period. Augustus's boyhood tutor: "He will become what he will become, out of the force of his person and the accident of his fate." Month of August named after him.

The unity of the group vs the worth of the individual

40% of food stamp recipients have been receiving for 10 years or more!

Average hours worked per annum: US 1,790, Mexico 2,226.

Burger King is owned by Brazilian Company 3G Capital and only owns 1% of its 14,000 restaurants. 3G also owns H.J.Heinz.

While Rolex sells 700,000 watches a year, Patek sells 50,000.

In 1800, the U.S. had 1 million slaves and by 1865 - 4M. 2M slaves = $1B investment

Health & Human Services = 76,341 employees / $ 30B+ budget.

In 2012, 60,000 buffalo/bison were slaughtered in the U.S. vs 90,000 cattle a day.

Excesses were recognized and alternates were created.

Ancient latin: pecunia non olet = Money has no smell

Science confronting religion seems to William James shallow. Science establishes no new beliefs; it merely destroys old ones - - what about Global Warming?

3 of every 4 Americans killed in Afghanistan happened under Obama.

In 1945, the yield on 10-year T-notes embarked on a long, steady climb from 1.7% to 15.8%, the highest ever in U.S. history, in 1981.

More Americans own a cat than stocks!

Oct 2014: 46M on food programs. Labor participation was at a 36 year low.

Spending on Defense: JFK 9% of GDP, Reagan 6%, Clinton 3%, Bush 4% and Obama 2.3%. Democrats want to syphon money from defense and into domestic programs.

Life Expectancy for 65 year old: Men 86.6 years, women 88.8 years.

Of the 3.5M Jews in Poland in 1939, only one-tenth survived the Holocaust. 4 in 5 American Jews have their roots in Poland.

Napoleon: His casualty rates skyrocket, Fleurus 6%, Austerlitz 15%, Eylau 26%, Borodino 31% and Waterloo 45%. "It seems extraordinary that the French people continue to revere a man who presided over bloodbaths unprecedented in European history and who brought their nation to ultimate ruin. He financed his empire by brigandage, looting the entire continent's treasuries and palaces."

Executive Compensation: In 1980, Average US CEO pay was 42 times typical worker vs 2013's 331 times.

Government Social Spending: OECD ranks the U.S. 23rd with social spending at 19% of GDP but this is only the U.S. direct spending. When the cost of tax free health insurance and tax favored retirement savings accounts are added in, the percentage goes to 30, making the U.S. 2nd only to France at 32%.

Tax Returns 2012: 51.8M paid NO tax. 86% of those reported less than $30,000 AGI.

Life expectancy at age 65:

	Men	Women
In year 2000	19.6 years	21.4 years

In year 2014   21.6 years   23.8 years

The outcome that is most widely expected is the one that is least likely to be realized.

After 6 years of Obama, per Victor Davis Hanson: Friendship with America brings few rewards while hostility toward the U.S. has even fewer consequences.

Medical care: When economic activity was organized according to the principle of property, contract and liability, a society could tolerate peaceably a variety of life-styles because those who conducted more costly patterns of life would pay for them. But once the market principle of personal responsibility is abridged for some principle of collective responsibility, interest groups are automatically established that will bring personal life-styles on to the political agenda.

In 2014 there are 30 nations flying MIG-29's.

The U.S. exports 4 1/2 M barrels of petroleum products daily.

"Competitiveness" is not found in the leftist lexicon, but the concept of living wage is. This notion says that employees should be paid based on their lifestyles. Street protests and the lobbying of pandering policymakers have replaced a good education and an improved skill set. Companies are neither charities nor pipelines for income redistribution. Increased labor costs either force them to move to friendlier business climes, hire fewer workers, cut workers pay, pass costs on to customer, replace employees with technology, or all the above.

Last year the Federal Government applied a Harbor Maintenance tax on containers of $25 to $ 500 = Northwest U.S. ports see 11% drop in cargo from Asia in last year. All to Canadian ports then by rail to the U.S.

WSJ 13Dec14 - Nearly 1 in 3 adult Americans have a criminal record, nearly 80 million.

Populist = advocating government control. Per William Galston: "Populism identifies villains such as - corrupt officials, unresponsive bureaucracies, arrogant elites, large corporations, giant banks, immigrants, even the Jews. It legitimizes outrage. It flatters the people, whose virtue and common sense, it claims, could set the country right if only rich and powerful forces did not stand in their way. "

Killed by Cops: 2012 = Blacks 140 (2.74 per million) & Whites 386 (1.28 per million). From 1999 to 2011 = 1,130 B vs 2,151 W. 95% of police have never discharged their weapons.

By turning the question "What did we do wrong?" into "Who did this to us?", it restores some measure of self-respect and provides a course of action. In psychiatry, the clinical terms for this process are splitting and projection; it allows people to define themselves as victims. WSJ 1Feb15 - Jonathan Sacks

Free Community College: New job openings requiring associate degrees in 2022 = 17% while number projected from free college at 28%. It is the services that consumers want that drives the demand for workers, not the educational attainment the workers have.

2015

Skin in the Game - Twenty percent of American workers today have health insurance that has an annual deductible of at least $2,000 (source: Kaiser Family Foundation, BTN Research).

Lowest Ever - Economic turmoil throughout Europe has driven global debt investors to the U.S. Treasury market. Increased demand for 30-year U.S. paper has pushed prices up and yields down. The closing yield on Jan. 23, 2015, for the 30-year bond was 2.37 percent, its lowest closing yield ever. The 30-year Treasury bond has been traded globally since 1977 (source: Treasury Department, BTN Research).

They Like Our Stuff - Of the $6.1 trillion of U.S. Treasury securities held by foreigners, $2.5 trillion are owned by residents of China and Japan, i.e., 41 percent of the total (source: Treasury Department, BTN Research).

US Embassies closed since the Arab Spring of 2011: Libya, Syria & Yemen.

Executions during the 345 years of the Spanish inquisition were less than half of the 6,832 Clergy executed in 1936 by the Spanish Republican Red Terror.

IBD 17Feb15 - Waste Management recycles almost 14 million tons of material a year. "Lower commodity prices are making recycling unprofitable"!!!!

France's left changes its approach to Islamic Terror from a policy based on multiculturalism and political correctness back to its longstanding principles of secularism and liberalism. They now reject the politically correct, value neutral approach that has failed. Now the principles of the Enlightenment and tolerance will oppose reactionary fanaticism.

China's cement production: Over 2013 & 14, 4.2 billion metric tons of cement was produced! More than the United States produced in the 20th century.

Muslims: The Mecca Muslims - not inclined to practice violence, where Muhammad started with his Religion of Peace, after 10 years of little progress, Spread the word with the sword = the Medina Muslims - see the forcible imposition of Shari'ah as a religious duty.

Iran (Shiite) vs (Sunni) Saudi Arabia, Egypt, Qatar, The United Arab Emirates, Bahrain, Kuwait, Morocco, Jordan, Pakistan, Sudan and Turkey.

The U. S. dollar is the official currency in El Salvador and Ecuador. Some 11 billion one-dollar bills are in circulation. Their average life is 5.9 years and cost about 4.9 cents to produce. The $1 coin costs 20 cents to produce and lasts 25 years.

Brewster Buffalo B-239 aircraft: In 1939, the U.S. diverted 55 to Finland. Finnish pilot Lt. Hans Wind scored 75 victories against Russia in a B-239 (2nd highest Ace). Eino Juutilainen scored 94 with 33 in a B-239.

Under Obama, 80,000 soldiers have been slashed from active forces, including 13 combat brigades and three aviation brigades. He wants to cut a further $1 trillion in planed spending by the Pentagon over the next 10 years. - 7Apr15 IBD

Capra rejected social and economic theories based on progressivism or historicism - theories in which the idea of natural right is replaced with struggles for power based on categories of race (Nazi - a natural fight of races) or class (communism - an economic struggle of classes)

50 years of liberalism: Between 1950 and 1965 government spending outside of defense was 7.8% of GDP. After 5 decades of "great society" non defense spending is now 16.8% of GDP. Core prosperity-sharing government spending has more than doubled, while military spending has fallen from 9.5% of GDP to less than 3.5%.

In 1979 the top 1% paid 14.2% of all federal taxes. In 2011 that share had risen to 24%. The lowest quartile paid just 0.6% of all federal taxes in 2011, down from 2.1% in 1979.

Regarding income inequality: per CBO 2014 - The lowest quintile of income earners saw their market income grow just 16% between 1979 and 2011 while the highest quintile experienced 77% increase. After adjusting for taxes and transfers, the CBJO found the lowest quintile, which receives about a third of its income from transfers, saw an increase in income of 72% while the top quintile had a gain of 87%. - WSJ 23Apr15

Lifeline Program: Program subsidizes phone bills for low-income Americans. In 2014 cost $1.6B to provide discounts for 12.4 million phone lines. Phone companies receive

$ 9.25 a month per phone line.

Innocence walks hand in hand with ignorance.

"We're leaving behind a sovereign, stable and self-reliant Iraq." President Obama 14Dec2011.

From Jo Nesbo's "The Son" - "We don't punish people because they are evil, but because they make bad choices, choices that are bad for the herd. Morality isn't heaven-sent or eternal, just a set of rules that benefit the herd. And those who are incapable of following the rules the accepted pattern of behavior, will never be able to conform because they have no free will; it's an illusion. Like the rest of us, lawbreakers just do what they do. That is why they must be eliminated to ensure they don't procreate and so infect the herd with their negative behavior genes."

The key to the rise of Classical Greece: The citizens controlled their own destiny: no autocrat or foreign ruler imposed burdensome taxes or loaded the economic dice in his own favor.

IQ tests measure the kind of intelligence that makes you do well at school.

White privilege: Asian-American median household income = $ 68,636. White household income = $ 57,000. Did they win the Lottery? - "win" by chance???

Lack of academic integrity

The West = right of free expression, human rights, religious tolerance, constitutional government, independent judiciary, separation of church and state, free market economy, protection of private property.

Personal achievement does not equal "privilege".

A legacy of economic freedom forges long term incentives to build physical capital in the first place. It directly shapes the incentives that push countries to use existing capital effectively and productively. A large capital stock guided by market forces leads to high living standards; cronyism and central planning waste capital, eventually sapping consumption per capita.

California's problem??? the long term campaign by radical environmentalists using political pressure and profuse lawsuits in their quest to remove from production 1.3 million acres of farmland. Not solving the "water crisis"

Obama Care WSJ 24Jun15: Eight million enrollees, 74% satisfied, annual subsidy per enrollee $3,312 or $268 per month vs out of pocket $69. There are 12 million eligible who decline.

From John P. Marquand's "The Late George Apley":

> A dislike of external show is shared by others accustomed to money

> From the time of the Roman Empire down, indulgence in the externals of wealth has never benefited a community.

> All things that are worth while demand vigilance and sacrifice.

> Hyphenated Americans upset me

> Personal finances: 1/2 of annual income to be reinvested. The remaining 1/2 income to be applied to frugal living expenses and the remainder to charity.

The Greeks & Taxes: There was a tax put on private swimming pools in response to the European Banking system's "austerity" program. In the North of Athens some 300 pools were registered for taxes. An aerial survey identified some 16,000 in the area. Thomas Sowell: Fropools

There are 59 million Social Security beneficiaries today, 2015. That number is projected to grow to 78 million in 2025 and almost 100 million in 2040 (source: Congressional Budget Office, BTN Research).

Roughly 2 million registered girls play soccer in the U.S.A.

Ratios of 2014 GDP and 2013 debt: Puerto Rico 66.4% and 2nd Massachusetts @ 17.9%. 3rd NY 10.6%, 4th Maryland 8.1% and Avg. U.S. state 7.2%.

WSJ 30June15: Obama's foreign policy: lofty in its pronouncements and rich in self-regard, but incompetent in its execution and dismal in its results.

Artifacts bring history to life.

MA 6.25% State Sales Tax only applies to the first $1,000 regarding collectible coins.

Black Economic Catastrophe (IBD 2Jul15): The sub-prime mortgage crises wiped out roughly half the net worth of black families. Clinton's Community Reinvestment Act of 1977 = a strict quota system for lending in low-income minority communities. From 1977 to 1991, subprime loans cumulatively totaled under $ 9B. In 1992 they jumped to $34B. Over the ensuing 16 years - HUD pressured Fannie Mae and Freddie Mac to lower standards and accept subprime loans while the Justice Dept sued banks to open lending offices in high-risk urban areas and actually "target" minorities for sub prime loans - right to the moment of the housing crash - they expanded to $6Trillion!

IBD 6Jul15 - Largest reduction in workforce participation = 16-24 age group: 1990's = 66%, 2005 = 60.8% and 2015 = 55.1%. Minimum wage increases are pricing the youth out of the workforce and the myriad of welfare programs are effectively paying the youth not to work.

IBD 7Jul15: Per Obama - "We created 223,000 jobs in June... unemployment down to 5.3% vs The civilian labor force declined in June by 432,000. Labor force participation rate is 62.6%, a 38 year low. Almost 94 million Americans are not working.

Populations of United Kingdom 64M, France 67M and Italy 61M.

WSJ 9Jul15: Harvard discrimination against Asian-Americans - can require Asian-American students to score 140 points higher than whites and 450 points higher than African-American's on their SAT scores to be considered for entry.

In 2014, 24 billion liters of wine produced and only 1% is considered to be of investable quality.

Sanctuary Cities in MA
•Cambridge, MA (Source: Boston Globe. First passed resolution in 1985)
Chelsea, MA (Added: 8-14-07 Source: Chelsea government website with
     text of sanctuary policy.)
Northampton, MA (Added 6-20-12 Source: City of Northampton Resolution
     dated 8-18-2011. Resolution limits cooperation with ICE but does
     not use the term "sanctuary.")
•Orleans, MA (Added 6/13/07 Congressional Research Service)
•Sommerville, MA (Added 7-23-12 Original resolution passed in 1987,
     later repealed and replaced with Safe City Resolution. Source:
     Sommerville News Blog, 10-15-2007)

Springfield, MA (Disputed)

Political demagogues fan the fictitious flame of class antagonism.

Blue Stocking Class? It is in the nature of mankind to hazard their peace
to secure power, and they know fools make the best slaves. Elizabeth
Montagu 1743

WSJ 22Jun15: Fifty years of debasing U.S. money - 23July is the 50th year
anniversary of Lyndon Johnson's Coinage Act of 1965 making legal tender
of base metal slugs in addition to the 12 billion silver dimes, quarters and
half dollar coins. From 1792 till 1965, the dollar was 0.77 ounces of silver.
By 1980 the value of a dollar was 0.02 Oz of AG and today it is 0.06 Oz of
silver.

In support of spending billions of dollars on pharmaceutical remedies
for drug addiction, modern liberals have determined that drug addiction
is a medical problem and not a moral one. The drug addicted are not
responsible for their addiction. It is like any other disease!

WSJ 25Jul15: Terrorist incidents between 2010 and 2014 total fatalities
worldwide - up roughly by a factor of 4. The number of incidents
quadrupled between 2006 and 2013 while the number of fatalities rose by
130%. Percent attributed to Muslim groups rose to 92% from 75%.

WSJ 29Jul15 - Only 0.9 percent of defendants sentenced for drug offenses
in federal court on 2014 were sentenced for simple drug possession.

Homeownership rate hits a 48 year low of 63.4%

Deportation: First: All who have committed crimes or have chosen to receive public assistance rather than work while here illegally. Illegal items such as creating a false identity, using a fraudulent Social Security number and knowingly filing inaccurate federal forms are felonies for Americans.

A college education in the liberal arts can NOT be based on contemporary political, race, gender or class issues.

> Ivy League colleges cap Asian students vs their curtailing Jewish enrollment in the 1920's.
> President Woodrow Wilson, a southern racist fought the integration of the U.S. military and as president of Princeton University denied talented African-Americans admission.
> Margaret Sanger's Planned Parenthood sought to focus abortions on minority communities.
> Supreme Court Justice Earl Warren, progressive icon, incarcerated Japanese-Americans in internment camps when he was California's attorney general.

WSJ 10Aug15: Dissolution of black families predates mandatory sentencing and indicates the "Missing (black) Men" theory is flawed.

single mother black births	black men admitted to state & Fed prisons
annually from 1960's and early 70's =	
1960 20%	20 to 27,000
mid 60's 24%	
1980 50%	53,063
2010 72.5%	257,000 in 2009

Note: Federal prison incarceration = more than half for drugs but Fed is only 14% of all prisoners. In the State system, the majority of blacks serve sentences for murder, assault etc than drugs.

Question: Would the men doing time be good parents?

Millennials: 1981 - 1996

Being white and male supposedly means enjoying innate and undeserved privileges. But NOW trans-elites reinvent themselves as females or minorities and have access to special advantages or privileges. Nature fighting culture. Racial identity is becoming no more biologically based than sexual identity. Progressives inuit we can be what ever we want to be but still push for racially based scholarships, female sports programs or affirmative action for women and minorities.

Radium: Takes 7 tons of ore to produce 1 gram = $68,000. Uranium has 14 daughters.

The U.S has 72,000 tons of nuclear waste with a half life of 100,000 years.

There are 4,200 oil tankers and 300 LNG tankers in the world's fleet.

Monetary police vs Fiscal policy

Fixed assets vs consumption

Crises response = 0% interest on money. We do not have a crises but we still have 0% interest!

Thomas Sowall: For every year from 1994 to the present (2015), black married couples have had a poverty rate in single digits.

Transporting oil in the U.S. in 2014: Pipelines delivered 3.4B barrels (58%), Boats 2.2B (37%), Rail 157M (2.7%),

Trucks 152M (2.6%). A large tanker can hold 84M gal, barge 1.3m gal, a truck 9,000 gal and a 100 car train 3M gal.

Oil from North Dakota to Gulf Coast or Atlantic Coast by rail, 5 to 7 days, by pipeline about 40 days.

WSJ 22Sep15: U.S. Economy is 4 times Germany and our energy consumption is 7 times.

Medicare WSJ 1Aug15: 3.1Million participants subject to higher Part B premiums. (couples above $170,000 income) Couples above $214,000 up from $146.90 to $ 223 (up 52%) in 2016. There are 9 million lower income whose premiums are paid by state medicaid programs.

5Oct15 - IBD: During September another 350,000 Americans of working age disappeared from the labor force, bringing the total over age 16 not working to a record 94.6 million. Participation in the labor market of 62.4% - lowest since 1978. The workweek shank again - to 34.5 hours.

Thomas Sowell: Back in the early 19th Century, an official of the Russian Empire reported that even the poorest Jews saw to it that their daughters could read and their homes had at least 10 books.

Milton Friedman supported open immigration but said as long as the U.S. wants to maintain a welfare state, a completely open immigration system would be ruinous.

Fox News, 16Oct2015 reports: "The Day of Rage is off to a good start, 7 stabbings and 2 people shot".

(Refers to Palestinian protests in Israel.)

WSJ 20Oct15 - Education: Academic year 2015-16, Colleges will enroll around 20.2M students and graduate 2M

with avg. debt $35,000. 50% of college graduates in jobs that require a high school diploma or less and 300,000 are working at minimum wage. By 2020, college graduates will rise by 19M and jobs requiring college degrees will rise by 7M. Since the 1980's: food up 151%, energy up 154%, Health care up 401%, education up 757%.

Student loans of $1.2T have 25% in default.

Soak the rich: Maryland raised the tax rate on people with incomes over $1M. The number of people in the category went from 8,000 to 6,000 and the projected increase in taxes of $106M became -$257M.

MA Sheriff: Mike Bellotti of Norfolk County for 17 yrs. (There are 14 sheriffs in MA.) Bellotti's budget is $33M with 300+ employees, 200 uniformed, 500 to 700 in custody. Avg hold 9 Mos with 2 1/2 yrs Max. 80% due to drugs/ alcohol. Jail in between Rt 128 N / S.

Islamic immigrants: Are they unassimilable and incapable of maintaining an American level of civilization???? Will Sharia wreak our entire structure, including urbanity, economy, language, government and culture.

Drug offenders sentenced by Federal courts 2014: Hispanics 48%, Blacks 27% and Whites 23%.

Fans of the Showtime series "Homeland" have been talking about the following opening of Season 5. Peter Quinn, a young CIA operative, had just returned from 28 months in Syria to report to a roomful of CIA executives.

CIA BOSS: Is our strategy working?

QUINN: What strategy? Tell me what the strategy is, I'll tell you if it's working. See, that right there is the problem, because they — they have a strategy. They're gathering right now in Raqqa by the tens of thousands. Hidden in the civilian population, cleaning their weapons, and they know exactly why they're there.

BOSS: Why is that?

QUINN: They call it the end times. What do you think the beheadings are about? The crucifixions in Deir Hafer, the revival of slavery, you think they make this (bleep) up? It's all in the book, their ... book, the only book they ever read. They read it all the time. They never stop. They're there for one reason and one reason only: to die for the caliphate and usher in a world without infidels. That's their strategy, and it's been that way since the seventh century. So do you really think that a few Special Forces teams are gonna put a dent in that?

perhaps falling into economic chaos as our own people become more irresponsible, more fractional, more insistent on "free stuff," eventually needing "someone strong" to keep order.

Taxes - Of American taxpayers, 54.7 percent (51.2 million out of 93.6 million returns) who reported adjusted gross income less than $50,000 during tax year 2013 legally did not pay any federal income tax (source: Internal Revenue Service, BTN Research).

Cut in Half - American spending on "National Defense" (stated as a percentage of the size of the economy) has fallen from 7.2 percent in fiscal year 1965 to 3.3 percent in fiscal year 2015 (source: Treasury Department, BTN Research). In 1968 it was 10% and in 1986 6.8%

Muslims read only one book - the Koran

Middle aged (45-54) white Americans death rates rise due to suicide, alcohol abuse, drug overdoses and chronic liver disease from 1999 to 2013.

The secular mind has a fatal attraction to the politics of impending apocalypse. China's one child policy, global warming, black lives matter, Occupy Wall Street,

In the U.S. 75,000 die due to infections acquired in hospitals per the Center for Disease Control

Close to 1M barrels of oil a day move across the U.S. on trains. One train can move 80,000 barrels. More than 10% originates in Canada. In August, we imported a record 3.4M barrels a day from Canada.

WSJ 5Nov15: Car-Loan balances reach a high of $968 Billion

German sausages: Germany has at least 3 sausage museums.

Cage fighters seek "psycho switch" - a capacity to go berserk "when they need it". Similar to the "Wolf Rage" sought after by ancient Greek warriors.

1 in 6 U.S. voters are Evangelicals.

The U.S. Supreme Court has historically been composed of Jews and Catholics.

In September 2015, there was no NFL player arrested. The first such month in the past 73.

Islam has nothing in common with Western civilization, not religion, not law, not language, not rights, not beliefs about the role of women in society.

S.P.Q.R. = senatus populusque romanus or "the senate and people of Rome".

Islam: The Major Crusades were between 1095 - 1291. Muhammed died 632.

Islamists call the "refugee resettlement" "hijra"! "Muhammad told his followers to migrate and spread Islam in order to dominate all lands of the world."

IBD 13Nov15: Income inequality:

Per the Washington Post - 5 of the top 7 are blue: New York, Connecticut, California, Massachusetts and Rhode Island. Lowest for inequality: Red Utah, Wyoming and Nevada.

By city: most 9 of top 10 run by Democratic mayors SFO, Boston, D.C., NYC, Chicago, LA and Baltimore.

Least 7 of 10 run by Republicans. Under Obama Incomes of the bottom 20% have fallen for the past 4 years and are now 8% below where they stood when Obama took office. While the incomes of the top 5% have climbed.

WSJ 10Aug15: Electricity from existing coal plants costs $38 per megawatt-hour; from new wind facilities, $106.

Currently, 115 Million people get energy assistance in the U.S.

The Islamic State has publicly vowed to use the refugee program to invade Europe and America, and allegedly has already infiltrated some 4,000 "warriors" among the flood of Syrian refugees.

In 2015, a family of 4 with household income up to $95,400 qualifies for health premium credit.

SNAP = Supplemental Nutrition Assistance Program. Roughly 15% of U.S. residents are on food stamps. Cost in 2014 = $70B with 46.7M participants. Average monthly food stamp benefit per person = $125. Buy all the candy, soda, cookies and ice cream you can eat.

Civilization, a society, culture and way of life of a particular area, in our case, Western civilization.

Shop from trusted sites you're familiar with, or at least make sure the site has secure sockets layer encryption installed (identified with an HTTPS:// instead of a mere HTTP:// in the URL).

European Union takes 800,000 mostly Muslim refugees. Can a civilization whose population is on the verge of decline fill its demographic void by taking in culturally incompatible people from elsewhere and still maintain its own unique culture and identity? The answer is NO! Europe's millennia-old civilization is in danger of being erased by a tide of people having very few things in common - not religion, not law, not language, not rights, not beliefs in the role of women.

Hunger in the U.S.: Liberal advocacy groups routinely claim that one in seven Americans are hungary - - in a country where the poorest counties have the highest rates of obesity.

Liberal racialism = affirmative action, diversity quotas, slavery reparations etc.

Climate Change = Job security for tens of thousands of people - EPA, wind turbine and solar panel manufacturers climate scientists, etc.

Population problems: from the 1968 "The Population Bomb"'s in the 1970's and 80's hundreds of millions of people will starve to death. vs In 2015 - the West can not populate it self!

Chickens to feed the future world: one breed can gain 1 pound for every 1.2 pounds of feed consumed.

Major Islamic Terror Strikes in the U.S. during Obama's 7 years: 7!

Obama has spent much of his time vilifying the private sector's banks, insurers, energy producers and utilities. The publics favorable rating of the Department of Justice is 46%!

Rush: There's a lot of terrorism in the world, and if it has nothing to do with Islam, where are Islamic leaders standing up and acting mad about it? If Islam's being perverted, where are the devout Muslim Islamists standing up and expressing their anger over it? I don't know about you, but if worldwide terrorism was being carried out by a bunch of people calling themselves Christians, I am pretty confident that mainstream Christianity would stand up and denounce it and join the hunt to track them down and get rid of them as soon as anybody else was trying too.

Where does "jihad" come from? Jihad is an Islamic concept. It's not something ISIS made up or Al-Qaeda made up. Jihad is an Islamic concept. Terrorists cannot have jihadist ambitions and then use Islam to explain it. The Islam comes first.

IBD 3Dec15 Mass Shootings:2015 France had 3, Norway's 67 dead. K-12 worst: 3 of 4 worst in Europe total 34 dead. When based on population since 2009 Norway had highest death rate Macedonia, Serbia, Slovakia, Czech Republic all higher than the U.S. @ 8th / 0.095 per million! In frequency of attacks the U.S. is 9th. All of Obama's advocated solutions are in force in Europe. His statement "Just doesn't happen in other countries" is a fabrication.

In 2015 the Russia army ceased recruiting in the Caucasus region due to a worrisome over reliance on Muslim troops.

WSJ 9Dec15: Under World Bank management, between 2011 and 2013, 2,000 houses were built by the Bangladesh Department of Disaster Management at the cost of $ 3M. Built without walls, the "open" design would help make the houses cyclone proof. Local comment, "This house isn't fit for my cows let alone my family" said Mr.Sarkar standing in front of the dark and damp one room building. The $10B Green Climate Money from wealthy nations should have NO conditions. 100 developing nations - "Have no time for rich country red tape" The developing countries "know best" how to spend the $10B

Uninsured in the U.S. down from 45M (14% of population) to 35M (11%) one half by expansions of Medicaid. Per a 2008 study in Oregon, Medicaid expansion had no significant effects on beneficiaries physical health.

Dec 15: 94.4M Americans are not in the work force, almost 1/3rd of the country and the government declares unemployment in only 5%. A $20T deficit means disaster but we continue with $500B annual deficits. Changes made without majority legislative decisions: Gay marriage, military women to join all combat units, presidential tacit end of border enforcement. If we express concern about impending financial catastrophe, the threat of radical Islamic terrorism, the sense that cultural and social stability has disappeared, they are declared of a thought crime.

During Obama's 7 years he signed 895 bills into law. During the same period, federal regulators issued 24,478 rules.

Climate Change: per UNFCCC's Executive Secretary Christiana Figueres, climate change "is not about the temperature. That is just a proxy. The discussion is about the de-carbonization of the economy." Three years ago at Doha, Qatar, she revealed that the goal of the whole process is a "complete transformation of the economic structure of the world." Earlier this year (2015) she said "this is probably the most difficult task we have given ourselves, which is to intentionally transform the economic development model, for the first time in human history." The EPS' Clean Power Plan basically eliminates coal-fired electric utilities and as it has turned out, it was developed by Green sources outside the Government and written to make it impossible for coal fired generators to comply! Congress should refuse to provide the $100B a year Obama has promised to the Green Climate Fund starting in 2020.

Defense 'USA vs Russia. Army personnel: US 539,450 vs Russia's 230,000. US Navy 326,800 vs 130,000

Air Force US 334,550 vs 148,000. Costs US $581B vs $70B a year.

Toilet paper: The U.S. consumes some $6B worth a year.

In 2013 gamblers in the U.S. lost $ 119B.

Visa Program EB-5 (Invest $500,000 and get Green Card) On Sept 30, 2015, 17,367 pending applications!

Solar: Net metering is regressive political income redistribution in support of a putatively progressive cause.

In Nevada, non-solar rate payers - who tend to be lower income - subsidize each solar user in southern Nevada to the tune of $ 623 per year. WSJ 29/12/15

"In the long sweep of history, this chapter is all pretty simple: The country actually switched from one dominant culture that was in charge for 240 years to one that's multicultural," said one Obama campaign veteran. "And that wasn't going to go easy. But now we're in the middle of it, so it seems chaotic and complicated.".

Hillary has allies in all the institutions that could potentially help keep the market propped up. She has received tens of millions of dollars in speaking fees from big Wall Street banks that have been implicated in market rigging schemes. She has the backing of some the world's most powerful billionaires, including Warren Buffett and George Soros. Her campaign has received more than $125 million in donations from hedge funds. Meanwhile, they have given Donald Trump less than $1 million. Of course, Hillary also has allies in the Obama White House and the Democrat-run Treasury Department.

But perhaps Hillary's most important backer of all is the Federal Reserve. The central bank doesn't appear on the list of official donors to her campaign. Yet by repeatedly backing off on vows to raise rates, the Fed helped push the stock market up into record territory this summer. Yellen and company seem poised to set the table for rising stock values and a positive social mood to help carry Hillary to victory.

This isn't to say that Trump has no chance to win. He still has a potential path to victory. But Hillary has overwhelming institutional backing from the financial, political, and monetary establishments -- plus near uniform support from the mainstream media. In previous years, no opposition candidate would stand a chance against such an establishment juggernaut.

Skin in the Game - Twenty percent of American workers today have health insurance that has an annual deductible of at least $2,000 (source: Kaiser Family Foundation, BTN Research).

Lowest Ever - Economic turmoil throughout Europe has driven global debt investors to the U.S. Treasury market. Increased demand for 30-year U.S. paper has pushed prices up and yields down. The closing yield on Jan. 23, 2015, for the 30-year bond was 2.37 percent, its lowest closing yield ever. The 30-year Treasury bond has been traded globally since 1977 (source: Treasury Department, BTN Research).

They Like Our Stuff - Of the $6.1 trillion of U.S. Treasury securities held by foreigners, $2.5 trillion are owned by residents of China and Japan, i.e., 41 percent of the total (source: Treasury Department, BTN Research).

US Embassies closed since the Arab Spring of 2011: Libya, Syria & Yemen.

Executions during the 345 years of the Spanish inquisition were less than half of the 6,832 Clergy executed in 1936 by the Spanish Republican Red Terror.

IBD 17Feb15 - Waste Management recycles almost 14 million tons of material a year. "Lower commodity prices are making recycling unprofitable"!!!!

France's left changes its approach to Islamic Terror from a policy based on multiculturalism and political correctness back to its longstanding principles of secularism and liberalism. They now reject the politically correct, value neutral approach that has failed. Now the principles of the Enlightenment and tolerance will oppose reactionary fanaticism.

China's cement production: Over 2013 & 14, 4.2 billion metric tons of cement was produced! More than the United States produced in the 20th century.

Muslims: The Mecca Muslims - not inclined to practice violence, where Muhammad started with his Religion of Peace, after 10 years of little progress, Spread the word with the sword = the Medina Muslims - see the forcible imposition of Shariah as a religious duty.

Iran (Shiite) vs (Sunni) Saudi Arabia, Egypt, Qatar, The United Arab Emirates, Bahrain, Kuwait, Morocco, Jordan, Pakistan, Sudan and Turkey.

The U. S. dollar is the official currency in El Salvador and Ecuador. Some 11 billion one-dollar bills are in circulation. Their average life is 5.9 years and cost about 4.9 cents to produce. The $1 coin costs 20 cents to produce and lasts 25 years.

Lifeline Program: Program subsidizes phone bills for low-income Americans. In 2014 cost $1.6B to provide discounts for 12.4 million phone lines. Phone companies receive $ 9.25 a month per phone line.

"We're leaving behind a sovereign, stable and self-reliant Iraq." President Obama 14Dec2011.

The key to the rise of Classical Greece: The citizens controlled their own destiny: no autocrat or foreign ruler imposed burdensome taxes or loaded the economic dice in his own favor.

IQ tests measure the kind of intelligence that makes you do well at school.

White privilege: Asian-American median household income = $ 68,636. White household income = $ 57,000. Did they win the Lottery? - "win" by chance???

Lack of academic integrity

The West = right of free expression, human rights, religious tolerance, constitutional government, independent judiciary, separation of church and state, free market economy, protection of private property.

Personal achievement does not equal "privilege".

A legacy of economic freedom forges long term incentives to build physical capital in the first place. It directly shapes the incentives that push countries to us existing capital effectively and productively. A large capital stock guided by market forces leads to high living standards; cronyism and central planning waste capital, eventually sapping consumption per capita.

California's problem??? the long term campaign by radical environmentalists using political pressure and profuse lawsuits in their quest to remove from production 1.3 million acres of farmland. Not solving the "water crisis"

Obama Care WSJ 24Jun15: Eight million enrollees, 74% satisfied, annual subsidy per enrollee $3,312 or $268 per month vs out of pocket $69. There are 12 million eligible who decline.

The Greeks & Taxes: There was a tax put on private swimming pools in response to the European Banking system's "austerity" program. In the North of Athens some 300 pools were registered for taxes. An airial survey identified some 16,000 pools in the area.

There are 59 million Social Security beneficiaries today, 2015. That number is projected to grow to 78 million in 2025 and almost 100 million in 2040 (source: Congressional Budget Office, BTN Research).

Roughly 2 million registered girls play soccer in the U.S. A.

Ratios of 2014 GDP and 2013 debt: Puerto Rico 66.4% and 2nd Massachusetts @ 17.9%. 3rd NY 10.6%, 4th Maryland 8.1% and Avg. U.S. state 7.2%.

WSJ 30June15: Obama's foreign policy: lofty in its pronouncements and rich in self-regard, but incompetent in its execution and dismal in its results.

Artifacts bring history to life.

MA 6.25% State Sales Tax only applies to the first $1,000 regarding collectible coins.

Black Economic Catastrophe (IBD 2Jul15): The sub-prime mortgage crises wiped out roughly half the net worth of black families. Clinton's Community Reinvestment Act of 1977 = a strict quota system for lending in low-income minority communities. From 1977 to 1991, subprime loans cumulatively totaled under $ 9B. In 1992 they jumped to $34B. Over the ensuing 16 years - HUD pressured Fannie Mae and Freddie Mac to lower standards and accept subprime loans while the Justice Dept sued banks to open lending offices in high-risk urban areas and actually "target" minorities for sub prime loans - right to the moment of the housing crash - they expanded to $6Trillion!

IBD 6Jul15 - Largest reduction in workforce participation = 16-24 age group: 1990's = 66%, 2005 = 60.8% and 2015 = 55.1%. Minimum wage increases are pricing the youth out of the workforce and the myriad of welfare programs are effectively paying the youth not to work.

IBD 7Jul15: Per Obama - "We created 223,000 jobs in June... unemployment down to 5.3% vs The civilian labor force declined in June by 432,000. Labor force participation rate is 62.6%, a 38 year low. Almost 94 million Americans are not working.

Populations of United Kingdom 64M, France 67M and Italy 61M.

WSJ 9Jul15: Harvard discrimination against Asian-Americans - can require Asian-American students to score 140 points higher than whites and 450 points higher than African-American's on their SAT scores to be considered for entry.

In 2014, 24 billion liters of wine produced and only 1% is considered to be of investable quality.

WSJ 22Jun15: Fifty years of debasing U.S. money - 23July is the 50th year anniversary of Lyndon Johnson's Coinage Act of 1965 making legal tender of base metal slugs in addition to the 12 billion silver dimes, quarters and half dollar coins. From 1792 till 1965, the dollar was 0.77 ounces of silver. By 1980 the value of a dollar was 0.02 Oz of AG and today it is 0.06 Oz of silver.

In support of spending billions of dollars on pharmaceutical remedies for drug addiction, modern liberals have determined that drug addiction is a medical problem and not a moral one. The drug addicted are not responsible for their addiction. It is like any other disease!

WSJ 25Jul15: Terrorist incidents between 2010 and 2014 total fatalities worldwide - up roughly by a factor of 4. The number of incidents quadrupled between 2006 and 2013 while the number of fatalities rose by 130%. Percent attributed to Muslim groups rose to 92% from 75%.

WSJ 29Jul15 - Only 0.9percent of defendants sentenced for drug offenses in federal court on 2014 were sentenced for simple drug possession.

Homeownership rate hits a 48 year low of 63.4%

Deportation: All who have committed crimes or have chosen to receive public assistance rather than work while here illegally. Illegal items such as creating a false identity, using a fraudulent Social Security number and knowingly filing inaccurate federal forms are felonies for Americans.

Random Thoughts 2016

Entitlements: 1964 "pensions and other payments to individuals" by the Federal Government amounted to 5% of GDP. By 1980 10% and today "payments for individuals" is 15% of GDP and 66% of the federal budget! At this level, no more talk about "outgrowing entitlements" - need serious reform.

Per Milton Friedman, "Open immigration is incompatible with the welfare state." Per Czech President Milos Zeman, the refugees are not normal - the old, sick and the kids. That's the image. but in reality they are overwhelmingly young unmarried men, the exact people who form invading armies and can change continents." It is Europe's vast welfare benefits, not arms and aid to fight terrorists in their homeland that brings them to Europe. They are culturally alien. Stop the flow or perish as free nations.

Per Bernie Sanders, "in the richest country in the history of the world, people shouldn't have to be working 50 or 60 hours a week to put food on the table." Actually, professionals average 50 hours or more while 25% of middle income over 50 . Workers in 1950 38 hrs vs 34 today. Thus the average worker has 217 more hours of leisure today. Plus roughly 100 million Americans want work but can not find jobs.

Muslims: Per Pew Research, 99% of Afghanistan's Muslims, 91% of Iraqi and 84% of Pakistani identify themselves as fundamentalists who favor Shari'ah law. In Pakistan, students in some schools routinely pray "May God annihilate America."

The Federal Government has placed some 30,000 Somalis in Minneapolis most prefer Shari'ah law.

From Garett Jones's Hive Mind: On average, smarter people are more patient and more interested in saving. National savings rates correlate with national IQ scores. Singapore tops with a 45% savings rate and an IQ of 108. "On average, nations with test scores in the bottom 10 percent worldwide are only about one eighth as rich and productive as nations with scores in the top 10 percent."

Americans 65 and older living in poverty was 4.6 million in 2014, up nearly 30% from 2010, Census figure show.

Number of "Incentives for Renewables and Efficiencies" programs in Massachusetts: Federal 28 and 71 Massachusetts = 99!!!!!!!!!!!

Navy: Under Reagan 594 ships vs todays 280 although the spending remains essentially the same. The problems: 1. Explosive growth of bureaucracy with civilian defense employees at 970,000, up several 100 thousand from the Reagan years. Roughly half of of all uniformed personnel serve on staffs. The Defense Department now has 17 independent Defense Agencies, 9 Unified Combat Commands and 250 joint task forces. 2. The procurement process, it now takes 22 years from start to first deployment of a weapons system.

Fear is wisdom in the face of danger

In Iraq 2005 - U.S. flew 9,000 missions and only dropped bombs on 15% of them.

Parents or Kids? - According to a July 2014 survey, 31 percent of U.S. households are providing financial assistance to adult children, a larger number than the 21 percent of U.S. households that are providing financial assistance to elderly parents (source: American Consumer Credit Counseling, BTN Research).

The total return of the S&P 500 over the past five calendar years (2010-2014) is 105.1 percent (total return). The best 12 trading days during the five years (i.e., 12 days out of 1,258 total trading days) produced a 53.7 percent gain. Thus, 1 percent of trading days over the past five years was responsible for 51 percent of the index's total return (source: BTN Research).

Does "Congress returns to work" cause a panic attack?

Early in his first presidential campaign, Barak Obama promised to "develop a strong international coalition to...eliminate North Korea's nuclear weapons program," through "sustained, direct and aggressive diplomacy - - the kind that the Bush administration has been unable and unwilling to use."

Christians do not believe in the divine inspiration of the Quran. Muslims do not believe that Jesus is an incarnation of God.

The Federal Government now runs more than 80 different antipoverty programs at a cost of $ 750 billion a year. Yet 46 million Americans are poor today, and the poverty rate has barely budged: from 19% in 1965 to 14.8% in 2014. We need to take the focus off intentions and put it on results.

Of the 193 countries in the UN, 50 have Muslim majorities.

The Obama administration has used its limited criminal enforcement resources to focus on clemency for convicted and imprisoned felons, the investigation of police departments, and civil rights cases. The latter two categories represent important work, but the Department of Justice lost track of one of its core missions of enforcing criminal law: prosecuting violent criminals, including gun criminals. Proof of this lack of enforcement is revealed in the decline of weapons-related prosecutions during the Obama administration. As data obtained from the Executive Office of United States Attorneys, through a Freedom of Information Act request, reveal, firearms prosecutions are down approximately 25 percent under the Obama administration versus the last year of the Bush administration.

The no-fly list is actually multiple lists, which are generated in secret and controlled by executive branch bureaucrats.

The total foreign-born population in the U.S. is at a record-breaking 42.4 million, having more than quadrupled since immigration caps were raised five decades ago. Excess labor supply has already helped drive down today's median household income more than $4,000 beneath levels at the turn of the century.

Gun carrying, private citizens who used firearms to stop criminal attacks saved at least 283 potential victims in a period between July 2014 and July 2015, according to a Daily Caller News Foundation analysis. While Obama quotes the more than 30,000 gun deaths in a year — omitting that 60 percent are suicides, 6 percent are gang related, 3 percent are accidents, and the vast majority of the rest occur in urban areas — A noteworthy number of kids, the elderly, and women successfully defended themselves against criminals by use of gun fire.

Five percent (5%) of cats are allergic to humans!

Quoting Pope Francis, deploring "the globalization of indifference" to the poor, refugees and other victims of "throw-away culture."

Public Debt is a Public Curse! The Fed bought 71% of U.S. debt recently.

Funding debt to pay debt! The U.S. debt is growing at $33,000 per second

One Million seconds = 12 Days
One Billion seconds = 31 years
One Trillion seconds = 31,000 years

4,000 babies are aborted in the U.S. daily.

Turandot: vincero = I shall win. Let your destiny be fulfilled. Ice princess. Hope, Blood. In the night that has no morning!

Hitler's Mein Kampf's copyright expired (1925 + 70 years) and is back in German bookstores. Banning books is a sign of fear and weakness done by dictatorships.

Chief among the schools of ancient philosophy were the Academics led by Plato, the Peripatetics by Aristotle, the Epicureans by Epicurus, and the Stoics founded by Zeno of Citium.

In 1840, Alexis de Tocqueville warned that once the majority of Americans discovered they could elect leaders who would buy their votes with other peoples' money, democracy would become a farcical bidding war. Welcome to campaign 2016.

How can a government that is bankrupt possibly act as spender, lender and guarantor of last resort?

Busing in Boston: Before busing you were Irish or Italian. After busing you were merely white.

60% of the prison population in France are Muslims

In the U.S. in 2015, more salsa was sold than ketchup.

Murder rates rise sharply in USA in 2015, 31Aug 2014 to 2015.

Milwaukee	up 76%
St. Louis	up 60%
Baltimore	up 56%
Washington DC	up 44%
New Orleans	up 22%
Chicago	up 20%

Iowa Caucus 2016: Bush spent $2,800 per vote ($14M) vs Cruise $156, Trump $82 and Rubio $280. Iowa picks corn, New Hampshire picks presidents. As goes Iowa, goes Iowa.

Obama sets new record: $1T debt in 13 months! The last two took 14 months each.

We need politicians who will "rise above principle".

2016 - The administration creates a new organization: The Interagency Working Group to Counter Online Radicalization to Violence, focused on anyone that subscribes to "Global warming is a myth" among other thoughts.

It requires an estimated 1 gallon of water to produce one almond!

We face a painful process of adjustment for having mistaken the spending of borrowed money for economic growth.

Lenin aspired to a Utopia, "organized on the lines of a state capitalist monopoly." Shortly before seizing power in Russia, Lenin declared his ambition "to organize the whole national economy on the lines of the postal service." He said "that the technicians, foremen, bookkeepers, as well as all officials, shall receive salaries no higher than 'a workman's wage,' all under the control and leadership of the armed proletariat — this is our immediate aim." = Bernie Sanders 92% tax over $200,000.

Ludwig von Mises: There is no means of avoiding the final collapse of a boom brought about by credit expansion. The alternative is only whether the crisis should come sooner as the result of a voluntary abandonment of further credit expansion, or later as a final and total catastrophe of the currency system.

Taxes - The top 10 percent of taxpayers in 2013 earned at least $127,695 in adjusted gross income (AGI), reported 45.87 percent of all AGI nationwide and paid 69.80 percent of all federal income tax (source: Internal Revenue Service, BTN Research).

In 2015, 45.3% of U.S. tax units have a "zero or negative individual income tax". We don't have income inequality, we have income tax inequality!

65% of gun fatalities are suicides. Since 2000, non-firearms suicides have increased twice as quickly as firearms suicides. IBD 1Feb16

In 2014, 50 children under 15 died from accidental gun shot most by an adult male.

Movements become Businesses that become Rackets.

IBD 11Mar16 - Pew Research Center estimates the share of household income going to middle-class families fell from 62% in 1970 to 43% in 2014, while the share for upper-income families (over $100K) rose from 29% to 49%.

According to the World Bank figures, we pay 25 times more than the Chinese do for health care. So that's something that the Chinese workers, even with their lower wages, don't have to truck with. And we pay, basically, ten times more for elementary and secondary schools than the Chinese do, and they have much higher test scores than we do.

GDP: A large and growing percentage of the GDP is based upon the government spending out of an empty pocket - deficit spending. Randy Degner observes, "Since 1980 the number of years with negative GDP growth jumps from 7 to 15, and the average GDP growth rate drops from 2.7% to an incredible MINUS 0.3% when deficits are deducted from GDP.

With more than 80% of the world's lawyers living within the U.S., the odds of a lawsuit are far greater than that of a lightning strike. In fact, more than 15 million tort suits are filed in the U.S. every year. And 55% of those are found in favor of the plaintiff.

"Socialism is a philosophy of failure, the creed of ignorance, and the gospel of envy. Its inherent virtue is the equal sharing of misery."
— Winston Churchill

"The problem with socialism is that eventually you run out of other people's money (to spend)."
— Margaret Thatcher

WHY does DHS need:

1.6 billion rounds of ammunition
• 7,000+ assault rifles

• 2,700+ armored assault vehicles

Only Cuba and North Korea do NOT have Coke a Cola. Until President Obama's Cuba policy checks in.

Per Rush Limbaugh: Establishment opposition to Trump is personal. The people I'm talking about, imagine they're Superman, and this is all kryptonite to them. Their power, their prestige, their positions, their futures, their present -- their reputations as opinion makers, their reputations as relevant people who matter in terms of Washington and policy -- all of that is threatened. Those people's positions exist because there is a Republican Party that is controlled and run by people like them" -Rush

Michael Snyder Economic Collapse March 4, 2013

Are we running out of time? For the last several years, we have been living in a false bubble of hope that has been fueled by massive amounts of debt and bailout money. This illusion of economic stability has convinced most people that the great economic crisis of 2008 was just an "aberration" and that now things are back to normal. Unfortunately, that is not the case at all. The truth is that the financial crash of 2008 was just the first wave of our economic troubles. We have not even come close to recovering from that wave, and the next wave of the economic collapse is rapidly approaching. Our economy is like a giant sand castle that has been built on a foundation of debt and toilet paper currency. As each wave of the crisis hits us, the solutions that our leaders will present to us will involve even more debt and even more money printing. And each time, those "solutions" will only make our problems even worse. Right now, events are unfolding in Europe and in the United States that are pushing us toward the next major crisis moment. I sincerely hope that we have some more time before the next crisis overwhelms us, but as you will see, time is rapidly running out.

The following are 12 things that just happened that show the next wave of the economic collapse is almost here...

#1 According to TrimTab's CEO Charles Biderman, corporate insider purchases of stock have hit an all-time low, and the ratio of corporate insider selling to corporate insider buying has now reached an astounding 50 to 1....

While retail is being told to buy-buy-buy, Biderman exclaims that "insiders at U.S. companies have bought the least amount of shares in any one month," and that the ratio of insider selling to buying is now 50-to-1 – a monthly record.

#2 On Friday we learned that personal income in the United States experienced its largest one month decline in 20 years...

Personal income decreased by $505.5 billion in January, or 3.6%, compared to December (on a seasonally adjusted and annualized basis). That's the most dramatic decline since January 1993, according to the Commerce Department.

#3 In a stunning move, Michigan Governor Rick Snyder says that he will appoint an emergency financial manager to take care of Detroit's financial affairs...

Snyder, 54, took a step he avoided a year ago, empowering an emergency financial manager who can sweep aside union contracts, sell municipal assets, restructure services and reorder finances. He announced the move yesterday at a public meeting in Detroit.

If this does not work, Detroit will almost certainly have to declare bankruptcy. If that happens, it will be the largest municipal bankruptcy in U.S. history.

#4 On Friday it was announced that the unemployment rate in Italy had risen to 11.7 percent. That was a huge jump from 11.3 percent the previous month, and Italy now has the highest unemployment rate that it has experienced in 21 years.

#5 The youth unemployment rate in Italy has risen to a new all-time record high of 38.7 percent.

#6 On Friday it was announced that the unemployment rate in the eurozone as a whole had just hit a brand new record high of 11.9 percent.

291

#7 On Friday it was announced that the unemployment rate in Greece has now reached 27 percent, and it is being projected that it will reach 30 percent by the end of the year.

#8 The youth unemployment rate in Greece is now an almost unbelievable 59.4 percent.

#9 On Saturday, hundreds of thousands of protesters filled the streets of Lisbon and other Portuguese cities to protest the austerity measures that are being imposed upon them. It was reportedly the largest protest in the history of Portugal.

#10 According to Goldman Sachs, bank deposits declined all over Europe during the month of January.

#11 Over the weekend, the deputy governor of China's central bank declared that China is prepared for a "currency war"...

A top Chinese banker said Beijing is "fully prepared" for a currency war as he urged the world to abide by a consensus reached by the G20 to avert confrontation, state media reported on Saturday.

Yi Gang, deputy governor of China's central bank, issued the call after G20 finance ministers last month moved to calm fears of a looming war on the currency markets at a meeting in Moscow.

Those fears have largely been fueled by the recent steep decline in the Japanese yen, which critics have accused Tokyo of manipulating to give its manufacturers a competitive edge in key export markets over Asian rivals.

#12 Italy is an economic basket case at this point, and the political gridlock in Italy is certainly not helping matters. Former comedian Beppe Grillo's party could potentially tip the balance of power one way or the other in Italy, and over the weekend he made some comments that are really shaking things up over in Europe. For one thing, he is suggesting that Italy should hold a referendum on the euro...

"I am a strong advocate of Europe. I am in favor of an online referendum on the euro," Beppe Grillo told Bild am Sonntag.

Such a vote would not be legally binding in Italy, where referendums can only be used to repeal laws or parts of laws, but would carry political weight. Grillo has said in the past that membership of the euro should be up to the Italian people.

In addition, Grillo is also suggesting that Italy's debt has gotten so large that renegotiation is the only option...

In an interview with a German magazine published on Saturday, Mr Grillo said that "if conditions do not change" Italy "will want" to leave the euro and return to its former national currency.

The 64-year-old comic-turned-political activist also said Italy needs to renegotiate its €2 trillion debt.

At 127 per cent of gross domestic product (GDP), it is the highest in the euro zone after Greece.

"Right now we are being crushed, not by the euro, but by our debt. When the interest payments reach €100 billion a year, we're dead. There's no alternative," he told Focus, a weekly news magazine.

He said Italy was in such dire economic straits that "in six months, we will no longer be able to pay pensions and the wages of public employees."

And of course government debt has taken center stage in the United States as well.

The sequester cuts have now gone into effect, and they will definitely have an effect on the U.S. economy. Of course that effect will not be nearly as dramatic as many Democrats are suggesting, but without a doubt those cuts will cause the U.S. economy to slow down a bit.

And of course the U.S. economy has already been showing plenty of signs of slowing down lately. If you doubt this, please see my previous article entitled "Consumer Spending Drought: 16 Signs That The Middle Class Is Running Out Of Money".

So what comes next?

Well, everyone should keep watching Europe very closely, and it will also be important to keep an eye on Wall Street. There are a whole bunch of indications that the stock market is at or near a peak. For example, just check out what one prominent stock market analyst recently had to say...

"Every reliable technical tool is warning of major peaking action," said Walter Zimmerman, the senior technical analyst at United-ICAP. "This includes sentiment, momentum, classical chart patterns, and Elliott wave analysis.

"Most of the rally in the stock market since 2009 can be chalked up to the Federal Reserve's attempt to create a 'wealth effect' through higher stock market prices. This only exacerbates the downside risk. Why? The stock market is no longer a lead indicator for the economy. It is instead reflecting Fed manipulation. Pushing the stock market higher while the real economy languishes has resulted in another bubble.

"The next leg down will not be a partial correction of the advance since the 2009 lows. It will be another major financial crisis. The worst is yet to come."

Sadly, most people will continue to deny that anything is wrong until it is far too late.

Many areas of Europe are already experiencing economic depression, and it is only a matter of time before the U.S. follows suit.

Time is running out, and I hope that you are getting ready.

Note: Time is still running out!

23Mar16 - Terrorist result: Grand European River Cruise - New Lower Prices - 2 for 1 plus additional savings up to $2,000 per couple & Free Air!

Until 1582, March 25 was New Years day.

From my book, Astonishing Conservative Thoughts, Facts and Humor, published in 2008, on page 131, in 2005 "There are 20 million Muslims in Europe." The 1 April 2015 Investors Business Daily records, "There are an estimated 44 million Muslims in Europe, or roughly 6% of the total population. That will rise to 58 million or 8% of the population by 2030, estimate made before the recent flood of newcomers." After more than 70 years of experimenting with bringing millions of Muslims into Europe to become Europeans, surveys find instead an implacable population of unassimilated, un-acculturated people who share few if any of Europe's Enlightenment-inspired beliefs.

80% of Americans had there net worth decline by 40% since 2007. In Spengler's view, democracy was synonymous with plutocracy. He declared, "In the form of democracy, money has won." Hence the heartaches and frustrations of the mass of voters who have turned toward Donald Trump because it has finally dawned on them that otherwise their vote "possesses in the end not the slightest positive influence."

Barry Shulsky, a life-long registered Democrat told The Financial Times: "All politicians are puppets — except for Donald Trump." Dr. G. Heath King, who formerly taught philosophy at Yale, hardly qualifies as "the man in the street." Yet he saw almost immediately, and announced that "Trump has rung the bell that awakened a nation in slumber."

People are not voting for Trump (or Sanders). People are just voting, finally, to destroy the establishment."

Donald Trump is now threatening the grandees of the Republican Party — by threatening to nullify the power of money exercised by special interests.

An economy that can expand only by growing debt can only go so far. At some point, the credit expansion reaches its natural limits where the debt-saturated economy can no longer service the debt. That's when a breakdown, economic collapse and depression, must occur to purge the debt — the rot — from the system.

In 2015 a reported 10,000 millionaires left France.

Companies pass taxes along in the form of lower wages and benefits to the work force, higher prices to the consumer and lower stock valuations for investors.

Social Security: Nearly one in four married beneficiaries and one in two single beneficiaries get at least 90% of their income from SS.

Money transferred to Mexico = $25B annually.

Researchers combining U.S. Census Bureau and Federal Reserve data found 38.1 percent of households are carrying credit card debt, with an average balance of $15,863.

Losing the Safety Net - On Friday, April 1, the first of at least 500,000 Americans (up to as many as 1 million Americans) were dropped from the Supplemental Nutrition Assistance Program (SNAP) also known as food stamps. A three-month limit on food stamp benefits that has been waived since 2008 was reinstated at the beginning of 2016 in 22 states (source: Center on Budget and Policy Priorities, BTN Research).

Triple - The total market capitalization of the U.S. stock market was $23.7 trillion as of March 31. At its bear market low on March 9, 2009, the country's total market capitalization was $8 trillion (source: BTN Research).

The Catholic Churches principle religious enemy for over 1,000 years was Islam! "A religion preached by the sword and violence without any element of persuasion."

In the 1830's the 70% of American's who worked in agriculture used a hand held scythe which took one person 14 hours to cut and bundle an acre of wheat. In 1840, Cyrus McCormick's horse drawn reaper could do the same in 90 minutes! Results: released workers for the industrial revolution and contributed to ending hunger around the world.

Since 2008, there have been 606 global interest-rate cuts, alongside $12.4 trillion in "quantitative easing" — all designed to fix a global economy that Smith's "invisible hand" was unable to correct.

- For every job created in the U.S. this decade, traded companies spent $296,000 buying back their own stock to push up their share price and maximize stock options held by senior executives. This came at the expense of investment in plant and equipment to produce goods and services and grow market share. There's no better illustration of the results of the pursuit of personal self-interest over the common good.

- Partly because of this orgy of speculative financial engineering, an investment of $100 in a portfolio of stocks and bonds since Q4 2008 would now be worth $205. Over the same time, a wage of $100 has risen to just $114. Cheap money has pumped up asset prices, not wages. Look no further for an explanation of soaring inequality.
- Quantitative Easing (QE) has produced the sort of liquidity that loves Wall Street, but hates Main Street. For every $100 U.S. venture capital and private equity funds raised at the start of 2010, they are now raising $275. But for every $100 of U.S. mortgage credit extended then, just $61 was extended in June 2015. Over the same period, U.S. prime commercial real-estate values have gained 168%, compared to 16% for residential property.

The lesson: Thanks to QE, there's plenty of money available to speculate on assets ... but for jobs and housing, not so much. As BofA put it: Zero rates and asset purchases of central banks have, thus far, proved much more favorable to Wall Street, capitalists, shadow banks, 'unicorns,' and so on than it has for Main Street, workers, savers, retail banks and the jobs market.

Gay couples - Joy of the Marriage Penalty. If each partner is making $ 150,000 per year they each pay 28% bracket but as a married couple earning $300,000 they pay 33% bracket also must choose to take either the standard or itemized deductions.

22Apr16 IBD: Philadelphia Fed's first ever survey on regulatory costs said that manufacturers are now spending more money on regulatory compliance than they do on data and network security, or on equipment and workers!

The average Boston School teacher makes $107,562 in salary and benefits — paid two grand a week and having the summer off.

Buried on page 49 of a recent IMF document, in layman terms, it says: "Tax those who have saved, and do it before they know what's coming." It doesn't stop there. Since taking office, Obama has increased taxes by 54%. And in a recent speech, Hillary Clinton didn't mince words, saying "We're going to take things away from you on behalf of the common good."

Per Warren Buffett, 2May: US trade deficit is $500B/yr or 3% of the GDP - would prefer to have it in balance. US exports = 12% of GDP.

Retire to a state with a low cost of living, affordable health care, plenty of cheap entertainment options and low property crime. States to target (in order of preference) are Florida, Wyoming, South Dakota, South Carolina, Colorado, Idaho, Texas, Montana, Nevada and Virginia. Those to avoid (again descending in order) are Rhode Island, the District of Columbia, Hawaii, Connecticut, Vermont, New Jersey, West Virginia, New York, Alaska and — alas — my home state of Maryland

Six of the top 10 worst cities for air pollution are in California. According to the State of the Air report.

Studies have found that Asian students enter college with combined math/ verbal SAT scores on the order of 80 points higher than white students and 200 points higher than black students. SAT scores predict later success as measured by college grades and graduation rates.

The first hotel to be air conditioned in the U.S. was in 1950!

The average man who earns $30,000 a year can expect to live to 78 while a man from the top 1% can expect to live till 87 collecting some $115,000 more from Social Security

Our historical "establishment" = The immense authority once exercised by the White Anglo-Saxon Protestant upper class, in an era when the influence of big Eastern corporations, railroads, investment banks and law firms pervaded politics and national development = privilege! For the first 200 years of the U.S. they did it alone. Not till the Irish potato famine in the 1840's did the Catholics arrive in any number.

Bach's religious notations: at the start of a composition "J.J." (Jesu Juva: help me Jesus) or "I.N.J." (In Nomini Jesu: In the name of Jesus). At the end of a manuscript "S.D.G." (Soli Deo Gloria: to God alone all glory).

In 2015 there were 80,000 SWAT raids on American homes. That's 80,000 times fully-armed police with assault rifles, flash-bang grenades and battering rams broke into civilian homes. All without a warrant.

Making Less - Manufacturing in the United States represented 21 percent of the economy in 1980, falling to 12 percent today. Manufacturing jobs in the United States represented 18.6 million jobs as of Dec. 31, 1980, a total that has fallen 34 percent to 12.3 million jobs as of April 30, 2016 (source: Department of Labor, United Nations, BTN Research).

Month After Month - Since finishing at a bear market low close on March 9, 2009 (i.e., approximately 86 months ago), the S&P 500 has gained 254 percent (total return). The stock index has gained just 1 percent (total return) in the past 12 months but has gained 15 percent (total return) over the past 24 months (source: BTN Research).

The National Debt - The U.S. national debt is 105 percent of the size of the U.S. economy today. Our national debt was 54 percent of the size of the U.S. economy in 1960 (source: White House, BTN Research).

Eleven Billion Each Day - The U.S. government is projecting fiscal year 2016 spending of $3.951 trillion, equal to $10.8 billion of daily outlays (source: Treasury Department, BTN Research).

Foreign students enrolled in U.S. colleges in 2014/15 = 974,927

Defense as a % of GDP	WWII	34.5%
	Korea	11.7%
	Vietnam	8.9%
	Iraq/Afgh	4.7%
	2001	2.9%
	2015	3.3%
Defense as % of Federal Spending:	WWII	80%
	Eisenhower 50%	
	Reagan	25%
	2015	16%
	2017	14.9% - projected

The unemployment rate — which has simply become a joke and which I'm certainly praying that policy makers aren't actually using to make important decisions — dropped to 4.7% from 5.0%. Of course, the main reason for the decline was due to 458,000 people leaving the workforce.

WSJ 4Jun16 - As of 2015, 18% of unmarried males and 23% of unmarried women ages 25 through 54 - people of prime working age - weren't even in the labor force. Just about all were already living off other people's money.

Weddings: In the U.S., 16% occur in June.

The ancient Greeks regarded weddings as potentially dangerous. In one version of the Trojan War narrative, Iphigenia, the daughter of King Agamemnon, walks to the alter dressed as a bride, unaware that she is about to be killed to appease the goddess Artemis, who had held up the warriors' voyage to Troy.

Religious preferences 2014:

	Democrats	Republicans
Catholic	21%	21%
Evangelical Christian	16%	38%
Mainline Protestant	13%	17%
Historically Black Protestant	12%	2%
Other Christian	2%	4%
	64%	82%
Non christian faiths	8%	3%
Unaffiliated	28%	14%

The U.S. actually provides arms and training to 180 of the planet's 196 countries.

The CPI-W (the monthly Consumer Price Index for Urban Wage Earners and Clerical Workers) significantly understates the decline in consumer purchasing power. In this respect, it is noteworthy that the CPI-W was explicitly chosen as the index for the annual adjustment of benefits paid to Social Security beneficiaries and Supplemental Security Income recipients.

The idea was that a low-ball inflation adjustment would save trillions as compared to a more accurate index. Social Security outlays would be approximately double their current level if inflation had been accurately measured.

8Jun16: Since 2007 the workforce has grown by 21 million people, while the number of employed has grown by only 5 million.

- The labor participation rate has plunged from 66.0% to 62.6%, the lowest since the 1970s.
- The number of Americans who have left the workforce, allegedly because their lives are so fulfilled, is 16 million. Meanwhile, enrollment for the food stamps and Social Security Disability programs is through the roof.
- The number of people over the age of 65 who are still working keeps growing as older workers try to avoid starvation and homelessness.
- Of the 5 million jobs added since 2007, only 2 million of them were full-time.
- Obama's success in destroying the mining industry is borne out in the 207,000 jobs destroyed in the last two years.
- The percentage of men aged 25 to 54 (prime working years) not working is at an all-time high.

Real median household income (using the official CPI, which is also highly manipulated for PR purposes) is still 1.3% LOWER today than it was in 2007. Wages continue to stagnate in the 2.3% growth range, while actual inflation for real people in the real world exceeds 5%.

Cultural appropriation is generally defined as taking something from someones else's culture - an image, a prop, a term - and degrading him or it by making that thing your own.

Homicides per 100,000 people: UK 0.06, France 0.6 & US 3.4!

Firearms per 100 people: UK 6.7, US 101

The richest person in Venezuela is Hugo Chavez's daughter!

Regular contact is the foundation of trust!

Millennial: ages 18 to 34, 92 million, buying 28% of autos and 35% of homes.

The French consume 40,000 tons of snails per year.

U.S. Charitable donations 2015: $373.25B, up 4%. Individuals = $264.58B. 60% of households make donations.

2013, Deaths by medical mistakes = 251,000. Twice total of suicides, firearms and car crashes.

One million dollars in $20 bills = 110# vs 22# in $100 bills. There are 11.1B U.S. $100 bills with 75% in other countries.

Food-Stamps: Supplemental Nutrition Supplemental Program (SNAP) costs $ 74 billion a year.

May 2016: Germany exports twice what it imports from the UK!

WSJ 29June2016 - Henry A Kissinger, from his article on the Brexit: "These vistas cannot yet be discussed at a geopolitical level, but the EU's leaders should be able to form discrete and discreet panels for exploring them."

discrete: individually separate and distinct.
discreet: careful and circumspect in one's speech or actions, especially in order to avoid causing offense or to gain an advantage

Martin Schulz, the president of the European Parliament comment on Brexit vote: let it be known that little people don't have any role to play in deciding what they do, Quote: "The British have violated the rules. It is not EU philosophy that the crowd can decide its fate."

4Jul16 - If other countries decide to leave, then that's that. The euro is kaput. You know, there's over $1.4 trillion worth of euros held in reserves across central banks around the world. They're already starting to divest out of it, and that's going to take some support away from the price of the euro.

A high dollar tends to be reflected immediately in lower commodity prices = deflationary!!!

July 2016 - We have now $11.7 trillion worth of sovereign debt trading with negative rates in the world.

Coal Country: In 2014, West Virginia's per capita income was $36,644, the lowest of any state save Mississippi. The suicide rates of West Virginia and Kentucky are among the nation's highest.

Alan Greenspan helped both Republican and Democrat administrations drive up the national debt from $2.4 trillion to $8.5 trillion in the years 1987-2006.

America's annual "contribution" to the UN is $8 billion.

Above ground: Silver 1B OZ, Gold 4 to 5B Oz.

Silver is the best natural biocide against some 400 viruses & bacteria.

Swedish economic model? A Swedish economist once boasted to Nobel Prize winner Milton Friedman that his country proved the efficacy of social democracy because "in Scandinavia, we have no poverty." To which Friedman acidly replied, "That's interesting, because in America, among Scandinavians, we have no poverty, either."

Gun Violence?: In 2014 long guns were used in only 3% of all homicides committed in the U.S. Reported gun ownership: Blacks 19%, Hispanics 20%, Whites 41% and in rural areas 51%. The gun violence is consistently concentrated among certain racial and ethnic groups, it is more likely to be a cultural problem - like attitudes toward established authority in general, and officials in the criminal justice system in particular.

FBI Director James Comey's statement on 5 July - "This is not to suggest that in similar circumstances, a person who engaged in this activity would face no consequences. To the contrary, those individuals are often subject to security or administrative sanctions." regarding his decision NOT to prosecute Hillary Clinton for mishandling classified information.

Women earn 60% of both undergraduate and master's degrees as well as 47% of law degrees and 48% of medical degrees.

The sperm count of the average young American male today is much lower than what his grandfather's sperm count was. Bone density is also declining. Due to: fast food diets, lack of physical activity, rising obesity levels????/

The average salary for a lawyer in the U.S. is $135,000 but the median salary is not much over $110,000. A welder can make that much!!

There is a current shortfall of 240,000 welders in the U.S.

Generation X (60's to 70's):

Sharia prescribes both religious and secular duties, a religious legal system.

The old joke in seminaries: What's the difference between a dissenting Catholic and a Protestant? The Protestant has integrity.

President Theodore Roosevelt I think stated it quite clearly and perfectly: "If you want to come to the United States of America through the legal immigration process you are welcome, but understand that you will have to adapt to our culture, to our language, and to our way of life." That's just good manners.

They're trying to create a situation in which individual people are losing their sense of a cultural identity, a regional identity, a historical identity.

Fraud in the Democratic primaries calculated to have cost Bernie Sanders 184 delegates. And what that comes down to is without the cheating, Bernie Sanders would have won the nomination. they're trying to pretend that Benghazi's not a factor, the private email server's not a factor, Travelgate, Chinagate, Vince Foster, all of that stuff is completely irrelevant; the only reason people are not supporting Hillary Clinton is they have this mental illness.

"The Federal Reserve in New York and JP Morgan and these other bullion storage vaults, got caught playing fast and loose with other people's gold. The German demand for repatriation kind of triggered it. And we actually covered this a lot in an episode of History Channel's 'America's Book of Secrets: The Gold Conspiracy,' in which the New York Federal Reserve was taking other people's gold to store for a fee, like a safety deposit box, then they were turning around and taking that gold and leasing it out the backdoor. And then they got caught because they couldn't get it back. And that's what led to that big stink about Germany only getting a tiny fraction of their gold back. It wasn't the original numbered and hallmarked bars, and assays showed it wasn't even anywhere near as pure. And so rather than risk a gold run, I'm certain that the New York Fed and JP Morgan and the U.S. Government as a whole are trying to get their hands on as much gold as they can to reassure the rest of the world that the gold they placed for safekeeping in these various vaults is in fact still there. That's another overlapping factor. One of the problems that the paper money is dealing with, it's estimated now that global quantitative easing is now running $180 billion per month. And that kind of inflationary pressure is going to have to push the value of the paper currencies down, and as a result gold and silver and other metals like platinum inevitably are going to rise. Emotional capital. This is very important. It doesn't do any good to be rich in all sorts of other areas if when a crisis comes you fold up your mental shop and shut down. Not good. We already see people doing this with increased rates of suicide, drinking, video game playing, other forms of numbing out because the reality is just not appealing.

Most Ever - National health care expenditures in the United States during calendar year 2016 are projected to reach $3.351 trillion, or $10,346 per person (source: Centers for Medicare and Medicaid Services, BTN Research).

2Aug16 - the top five contributors to Clinton's campaign efforts are employees or owners of private hedge funds, according to federal data. Seven Wall Street firms alone have generated nearly $48.5 million for her. The total for Donald Trump from those same sources? About $19,000.

U.S. CASH: $100 bills bound in mustard colored bands. $5M = in $100 bills is 100 pounds. A million dollars in $1 bills = 2,000 pounds Half to two-thirds of the $1.4T U.S. bills are overseas.

IQ = intelligence quotient. Only 40 to 50% of school achievement is related to IQ. The remainder to such qualities as motivation, determination and a desire to succeed.

Better off than 7 years ago? Recession ended June 2009! Poverty: 3.1M into poverty with rate up from 14.3% in 2009 to 14.8% in 2014. Household Incomes: top 40% up but bottom 60% down. Bottom 20% down 8.4%. Food Stamps: Up 8.7M. Labor dropouts: Unemployment down 7M while number dropped from statistics = 14M. Home ownership lowest in 51 years.

Catholic populations top 5: Brazil 171M, Mexico 110M, Philippines 83M, U.S. 72M, Italy 58M.

Muslim: "We saw the simplicity and the enlightenment of the religion but not the rigidity and dogma".

Underrepresented in Engineering: Women and URG (under represented groups), Hispanics, African Americans, Native Americans, Pacific Islanders, Native Hawaiians, persons with disabilities, veterans, LGBT. The Progressive views engineering as another institution of white, male privilege, exclusion and inequity.

The U.S.A. consumes 80% of the opiates in the world with 5% of the population.

Middle-class family spending 2007 - 2014: Health care +24.8% vs Total Food -7.6%, Housing -6%, transport -6.4% clothing -18.8%

WWII German "Sociological" military philosophy: emphasis on the effectiveness of an organization that allowed more initiative to "primary groups" - the smallest organizational units of the German Army - and so inspired its members to identify with their immediate comrades. Small unit cohesion!

The ongoing bull market for the S&P 500 (now in its 90th month) has achieved 118 all-time closing highs, the most recent occurring Monday, Aug. 15

Massachusetts Medicaid now makes up more than a third of state spending, up from less than a fifth in 2000. In the fiscal year that ended in 2001, there were 998,000 people enrolled in the program. Last fiscal year, officials estimate there were 1.85 million members....

The Federal Reserve and other central banks providing monetary welfare for the stock market.

Hillary speaks as a lawyer, only about regulations and laws, never about incentives.

Research by McKinsey Global Institute showed that a staggering 81% of American households saw flat or falling incomes over the past decade. This is why I expect Donald Trump be to elected president in November.

Roughly seven million men age 25 to 54 are jobless in America.

America's male ex prisoners and felons not behind bars accounts for one adult male in eight in the civilian population excluding those in jail now.

Asperger's syndrome makes it impossible to lie. Sees the world in absolutes. Usually a form of autism.

It takes 1,700 pounds of coking coal to produce one ton of steel.

Why we are not universally liked: In 2015 we sold Saudi Arabia $20B of weapons and bombs to be used in Yemen.

The mainstream media with all its bells and whistles, sensational sound bites and meaningless montages, is designed not to educate you, but to entertain you ... not to answer questions, but to question answers ... to detract and distract ... amuse and confuse ... paralyze and terrorize ... motivating investors to make decisions based on their emotions and not on logic.

September 2016 - The U.S. of A. is bombing 6 countries: Afghanistan, Iraq, Libya, Syria, Somalia & Yemen.

U.S. Foreign Aid = $38.5B or 1% of budget.

In 2014 45% of tax payers had an AGI less than $30,000 while 4% made over $200,000

In 2016 there were 2 million households with $3M or more in assets.

Clinton Foundation 2014: Spent $91.3M (34.8M salaries, 50.4M "other", 5.2M charity & .851M fund raising.)

Nothing is confirmed until it is officially denied.

The bigger the question, the more likely it is to be overlooked.

Some 43 million Americans collectively carry nearly $1.4 trillion in student debt, making it the second-largest source of household debt after home mortgages, according to the Federal Reserve. The federal government owns or backs more than 90 percent of it. More than 42 percent of federally owned student loans aren't being repaid as expected or on time.

Life Expectancy born 1935, White Male 61years,
        born 1938, White Female 66 years
At age 81: Life Expectancy (Female): 9.0 years
        Life Expectancy (Male): 7.6 years
        # Alive Out of 100,000 born: 53,732
        Leading Cause of Death: Cancer

DEMENTIA: Basically, the likelihood of dementia illness doubles every five years that we age. It starts out at tiny levels in the early 60s. But every five years that we age, the chance of having dementia doubles. By the time we get to our 80s, the likelihood of having dementia is about 20%. But it's a little worse than that, because dementia is a severe case of cognitive impairment. There's another diagnosis, which is called "cognitive impairment not dementia" (CIND), which describes a set of symptoms that are characterized by cognitive decline that is significant, but not so significant that we're into the realm of dementia. And about 30% of the population in their 80s has the symptoms of CIND. Now, those individuals are also in a very poor position, really an inappropriate position, to make important financial decisions. If you add up the two groups, 20% of those in their 80s with dementia and 30% of those in their 80s with cognitive impairment not dementia, then we're talking about, in total, half the 80-year-old population that is not in a position to make important financial decisions.

Private sector vs public: Facing up to the beneficiaries of the status quo, using facts and data to inform their recommendations, while the other side resorts to personal insults, bullying, hyperbole, and desperate publicity stunts.

In 1669, Louis XIV of France decreed that knives must be rounded at top, not threateningly pointed to stop people from using their knives to pick their teeth.

The rule is that the table is set with knife blades facing in. An obscure rule calls for the knife blade to face out during times of war.

From 2000 to 2010, U.S. multinationals shed 2.4M jobs while employing 2.4M overseas. GE's Jeffrey Immelt was chosen by Obama to head his Jobs Council while GE reduced U.S. employment by 34,000 jobs and increased jobs overseas by 25,000.

The young may, and the old will die! The shifting sands of time will separate you from things, therefore love people, use things - - not the other way around.

"If voting made any difference they wouldn't let us do it." Mark Twain

Libya — which was Hillary Clinton's great foreign-policy

accomplishment. She said: "We came, we saw, he died."

So she managed to kill Saddam Hussein—good for her—but then, what good did that do anybody? We have, I think, a really destructive aftermath of this, and the real reason it came out in the WikiLeaks that she wanted to get rid of Saddam Hussein is because of what?

Because he wanted to put an end to fiat money, that he was planning to create a gold dinar that he wanted to circulate throughout Africa to price the sale of

Libyan oil in gold dinars, and this was going to put the kibosh on this ridiculous fiat money system that we have, which is pulling the world toward disaster.

A record 4,279 U.S. citizens renounced their citizenship and moved overseas in 2015, a 20% increase over 2014, according to the Internal Revenue Service.

Death by first shot from handgun: 7%.

The "elites" got where they are by developing advanced survival skills.

Today, the top 1% of Americans earn nearly a quarter of the country's income and control an astonishing 40% of its wealth. At the same time, traditional ethnic groups are marginalized by a new demographic tidal wave of immigration. This, even as previously unheard of minorities are noisily asserting their rights.

As former New York Mayor Michael Bloomberg pointed out in his 2013 commencement speech at Harvard University:

"In the 2012 presidential race, according to Federal Election Commission data, 96 percent of all campaign contributions from Ivy League faculty and employees went to Barack Obama. Ninety-six percent. There was more disagreement among the old Soviet Politburo than there is among Ivy League donors. That statistic should give us pause -- and I say that as someone who endorsed President Obama for reelection -- because let me tell you, neither party has a monopoly on truth or God on its side."

The Progressive push for diversity is directed to doing away with borders and citizens and replaces rights and liberty with welfare and regulation as the objects of its administrative It will also dilute both American blood and culture. By 2040 whites of European decent will no longer be a majority.

Public sector "defined benefit" plans (Have essentially disappeared from the private sector) should be replaced with more transparent "defined contribution" plans, like 401(k)s which are fully funded, do not depend on wishful projections or actuaries for their soundness, and leave no opportunity for unfunded liabilities that are backstopped be taxpayers.

Inerrancy = Incapable of making a mistake, infallible

emendation = suggest changes to free text documents from errors, correct, improve

The rapturous bliss of oblivion!

China's four great inventions--paper, the printing press, gunpowder and the compass--were all developed more than 1,000 years ago.

Income: SFO #1, Wash #2, Boston #3! Boston 2015 income Top 25% = $122K, 10% = $193K, 5% = $260K, 1% $529K

Top 1% = 25% of national income + 40% of its wealth.

Top 10% have 90% of the national wealth!

Massachusetts 2016: Clinton 61% vs Trump 34%

MA house Dem 125 vs Rep 35. Senate Dem 34 vs Rep 6

Hillary Clinton's lead in the popular vote has topped 2.8 million, while Clinton's overall margin looks large and impressive, it is due to Clinton's huge margin of victory in one state — California — where she got a whopping 4.3 million more votes than Trump.

Progressives say, "Trump will wreck international trade with his 35% tariff." They appear to have missed Obama's Commerce Department's boosting the tariff on Chinese cold rolled steel to 522% in May 2016.

I attended an all men's college and one of my degrees is in Engineering - a profession recently labeled as a white mens institution of privilege, exclusion and inequality.

Islam is a culture and a way of life. A way of life completely incompatible with Western civilization on all accounts; religion, law, language, rights, beliefs re: the role of women.

Healthcare spending in the United States reached $3.2 trillion in 2015 (18 percent of the nation's economy), equal to spending $9,990 per person. In 1995, 20 years earlier, per person healthcare spending in America was $3,788 (source: Health Affairs, BTN Research).

End of Life - Total Medicare spending in fiscal year 2016 was $595 billion. Of that total, 25 percent ($150 billion) was spent during beneficiaries' final 12 months of life (source: Medicare, BTN Research)

Taxes Paid - The top 5 percent of U.S. taxpayers paid more in federal income taxes ($721 billion) than the bottom 95 percent of U.S. taxpayers ($511 billion) for the 2013 tax year (source: IRS, BTN Research).

A crisis is a period of resolution.

Roosevelt said Social Security would never be taxed. Only over his dead body - he died!

After eight years, we are now witnessing these facts:

1. 1The economy never grew more than 3% during Obama's years in office, the worst performance since the Great Depression.
2. For the first time in decades, business failures now exceed new start-ups in the United States.
3. Not a single new community bank has been formed since the passage of Dodd-Frank in 2010.

The United States has fallen to #12 among developed countries in terms of business startup activity. Countries such as Hungary, Denmark, Finland, New Zealand, Sweden, Israel and Italy all have higher start-up rates than America does

College admittances have been falling since 2012 as the first wave of millennial s that peaked in births in 1990 wanes until 2019.

Wall Street's surge has taken the S&P 500 to an eye-watering 27.9 times the corporate earnings of the past 10 years. This puts the market about the same level that it hit just before the crash of 1929. Remember sharp yield spikes — like that witnessed for 30-year Treasuries since the election of

Trump — have a history. They have preceded every major financial crisis over the past 30 years.

Federal courts will quickly sacrifice private bondholders, even though they have a clearly superior legal claim, in favor of public workers and retirees. This fight will play out in state capitols around the nation, pitting public employees against taxpayers and investors. It will get ugly.

Retail housing construction constituted 5% to 6% of the economy in the mid-2000s, but now sits around 3%. We're building homes at a rate consistent with previous recessions, not expansions.

The yield on the U.S. 10-year Treasury touched 2.62% on Friday 23Dec16, up from 1.78% the day before the election; a 47% jump in yield. This is a remarkable move! And then there was the breakout in the greenback. The U.S. Dollar Index (DXY) that trades against the other five major currencies in the world surged from 97.3 to 103.5, and is now at the highest level against the euro in over a decade. With the European Central Bank (ECB) telegraphing a continuation of quantitative easing (QE) well into 2017, currency speculators are predicting that the euro (currently 1.0435) will trade at parity, or 1:1, with the dollar as the next target.

Since the crisis began in 2008, corporate debt has grown by $3 trillion, the U.S. government has added $7.6 trillion to its debt. And households owe $1.2 trillion more, too, not including mortgage debt.

2017

Jan 17: It is hard to say who despises Trump more — the conservative columnist George Will or the left wing liberal economist Paul Krugman.

Consider this: Before the 1930 tariffs, the U.S. would export about 919,000 dozen eggs to Canada. After the tariffs, exports fell to less than 1% of the previous numbers — just 7,900 dozen. Real national income fell by 36%. And by the end of 1934, global trade had fallen by 66% from the 1929 level.

We're quickly morphing into a nation of service workers looking to retirees for a tip. In a sense, it's income redistribution through social protocol, instead of payment for services rendered.

Federal Government medical covers 8 million (employees and their dependents).

Per Kristin Armstrong: If you have a preference, voice it.

If you have a question, ask it.

If you want to cry. Bawl

If you need Help, Raise your hand and jump up and down.

Politicians should be changed often like diapers.

The past is history, the future is a mystery.

But at the end of the world, we're going to have a world dominated by machines. And so it becomes very important to do one of three things: It's either learn how to work with the machines, learn how to make the machines or own the machines. And if you can do one of those three things, then you'll probably be OK.

30% of all agricultural surfaces is used by cows.

The U.S.A. has a military presence in 140 countries.

Ron Paul was born 1935.

It takes 4 gallons of sea water to produce 1 pound of sea water salt.

In a stationary state (no growth economy), unfortunately, investment in exploitation may pay better than in progress. Boulding goes on to suggest that no-growth economies are likely to be "mafia-type societies in which government is primarily an institution for redistributing income toward the powerful and away from the weak."

Small Number, Big Dollars - National health care expenditures in the United States during calendar year 2016 were an estimated $3.4 trillion. Just 10 percent of Americans were the source of 65 percent of that total (source: Centers for Medicare and Medicaid Services, Kaiser Family Foundation, BTN Research).

Among beneficiaries 65 and older, 1 out of 5 married couples — and 2 out of 5 singles — receive at least 90 percent of their income from the Social Security program, according to the Social Security Administration.

Ups and Downs - The S&P 500 has gained 10.2 percent per year (total return) over the last 50 years (1967-2016) in spite of suffering through eight bear markets of at least a 20 percent decline each time (source: BTN Research).

Renters Soar - The 109.6 million households in the United States on Dec. 31, 2006, were split between 75.4 million owners and 34.2 million renters. The 118.6 million households in the United States on Dec. 31, 2016, were split between 75.6 million owners and 43 million renters (source: Census Bureau, BTN Research).

Studies showed that coffee intake can reduce the risk of oral/pharynx cancer, colon cancer, liver cancer, prostate cancer, endometrial cancer and melanoma by 31%, 13%, 54%, 11%, 27% and 11%, respectively. That's for the highest vs. lowest coffee intake.

Best place to live: For the seventh year in a row, Vienna, Austria, has claimed the No. 1 spot. The capital of Austria, Vienna has more than 850 parks and green spaces while being rich in culture and history. Filling out the top five spots are Zurich, Switzerland; Auckland, New Zealand; Munich, Germany; and Vancouver, Canada. In fact, the highest ranked U.S. city is San Francisco, which came in at No. 29, while Boston followed at No. 35 and Honolulu at No. 36.

Eight Years of Gains - The ongoing bull market for the S&P 500 reached eight years in length as of the close of trading on Thursday, March 9. Over the eight years, the index has gained 314.4 percent (total return), an average annual return of 19.4 percent (source: BTN Research).

Addiction: being that curious state of getting acute pleasure and acute anxiety from the same thing.

Off to College - Of the 3.14 million high school graduates in 2016, 2.19 million students began college in the fall of 2016, i.e., 70 percent of 2016 high school graduates went onto college (source: Department of Labor, BTN Research).

US workforce: 17% are foreign born, 27M.

The average two person, retired couple receives some $40,000 in benefits between Social Security and Medicare.

Debt: In 2015 government debt stood at $18.8 Trillion (104% of GDP) while private debt was $27.1 trillion (150% of GDP).

There are currently 60 million on Social Security.

Stansberry Digest, 26May2017: The main driver of liquidity over this past cycle was, incredibly, student loans.

That spigot is being slowly turned off as both losses soar and the political environment changes.

For example... yesterday James Runcie resigned from the Department of Education. He ran the office of Federal Student Aid, which administers a large portion of the federal student loan program. Under Runcie, the portfolio of student loans administered by the Department of Education grew tenfold, to $1 trillion. (Yes, $1 trillion.)

The federal takeover of student lending was accompanied by a correspondingly large increase in... fraud. (Shocker.)

It's hard to believe that the Obama administration turned a blind eye to the fact that billions and billions of dollars were being distributed via fraudulent Pell grants to poor families around the country. Poor families who just happened to be Democrats. Of course, I'm sure that had nothing to do it...

The Office of Management and Budget found that under Runcie's watch, more than a billion dollars in fraudulent grants (aka, "improper payments") were made in 2014 alone, about 4% of all the distributions made. Rather than admit this, the Obama Administration decided to retroactively change the audit methodology. (I'm not making this up...)

It reported an "improper payment" rate of only 1.5%. And a subsequent investigation by the government's Inspector General found that the Department of Education lied when it published these loss statistics. (Shocker.)

Called to testify to Congress about these and other abuses of the public Treasury, Runcie resigned... and blamed the whole mess on the new, incoming head of the Department of Education, Betsy DeVos. (Again, I'm not making that up.)

And the best part? Look at the media's reporting on Runcie's resignation. The media all blames DeVos too. The Politico headline, for example: "Top Education Dept. Official Resigns After Clash with DeVos."

Nothing about the billions and billions he distributed illegally to Obama's backers. Nothing about lying about it for years. Nothing about the hundreds of billions in losses that the loans he approved will cost taxpayers. And nothing about facing Congress this week if he didn't resign.

Nope... Just blame it all on Betsy DeVos. Obviously, it's her fault.

Roman numerals were used in Europe and most other regions of Western civilization until the adoption of the Hindu-Arabic numerals (devised between the 2nd and 3rd centuries by indian mathematicians, adopted by the Arabs in the 800's) during the adoption of the printing press in the mid 1400's.

To keep ObamaCare costs down, insurers raised up deductibles into the $6,000 range. "Pre-existing condition": before ObamaCare, the vast majority got their insurance through work or some other group plan, or directly from the government. The only ones who did not were the 7.5% who were in the individual market.

Under current law, around $100 B per year will be spent subsidizing the premiums and cost sharing of individuals on the ACA's exchanges. Only 2 million out of the 10 million on the exchange have pre-existing conditions, but 9 million are currently receiving subsidies.

Higher rates of taxation amount to a penalty levied on work and investment, for those who do not seek every possible deduction.

Goldman Sachs Asset Management and Vanguard Group oversee a combined $5 trillion.

Businesses serve as society's wealth generators.

The result of shareholders of the coal industry management's failure to combat its opponents was dramatic. The market value of coal companies declined from $69 billion in 2011 to $4.8B in 2016 - a 93% drop in 5 years. Oil companies wake up!!!!!!

The devil can quote scripture.

Per Michael Goodwin, "The Occupy Wall Street movement was a pestilence, egged on by President Obama and others who view other people's wealth as a crime against the common good."

From the "Imagine Boston 2030 Plan": The median net worth of white Bostonians is over $247,000, while the median net worth of "U.S. Black" Bostonians is $8. !!!!!!!!!!!!!!

Harry Dent "The greatest event in modern history occurred in 1776. That's when the brilliant Declaration of Independence was penned, hence our very festive holiday tomorrow, the 4th of July. Democracy was born. It was also the year that Adam Smith published the greatest economic book of all time, The Wealth of Nations. The Industrial Revolution began transforming economic progress with steam-powered factories and new manufacturing processes from the 1760s onward. The convergence of two opposite principles, democracy and free market capitalism, has driven the greatest long-term boom and productivity revolution in history.

U.S. Customs and Boarder Protection (CPB) can stop and search you and your possessions if you are within the zone extending from any U.S. coast to 100 miles inland! (2/3 rds of Americans live in the zone)

During the past 13 years, median household income increased 28%. But medical costs increased 57%, food and beverage prices jumped 36%, housing was up 32%.

July 17: Since Trump election, Mining jobs up 56,000.

Last 2 years of Obama: 7,000 rules & Regulations passed.

Cost of Solar down 80%.
2017 - Economists say Trump's two out, one in" policy has reduced corporate regulatory costs by about 5%. Regulatory paperwork hours have dropped by about 10%. -
Newsweek Oct 17.

Vacation Pay: 42% of employees get none.

For every $1 a barrel oil price movement, gasoline moves 2 cents a gallon.

WD-40 was invented in 1953 to lubricate NASA's umbilical connectors.

The average retiree gets $40,000 / year in Government benefits, primarily Social Security and Medicare.

Currently there are 60 million on Social security, in 2020, 80M!

In 2016, 17% of U.S. residents were foreign born, 27M.

Mental problems: 17% of Americans.

2017, first 7 months = International stocks up 42%!

Investor owned businesses:

2007	4,783
2017	3,982

Working Americans: 32% of Americans 65-69 are employed as are 19% of 70-74 year olds, up from 11% in 1994. 19% of people 65 or older were working at least part time in the 2nd quarter of 2017. This is the highest proportion of such people in the workforce for 55 years, even before Medicare and Social Security. Source: U.S. Jobs report released in July 2017. - - - most need the money!!!!!

The actual number of middle-class Americans has dwindled over the years. Today, "middle class" describes only 10% of U.S. households – the 10% just below the richest 10%. Per Smith... The "bottom 80%" are lacking essential attributes of a middle-class lifestyle that was once affordable on a much more modest income. Outside of income, he includes these criteria in his definition of middle class: good health insurance, 25%-50% equity in a home, the ability to save at least 6% of your income, lots of money in a 401(k) or IRA, the ability to cover your debt and expenses if one of your household's primary wage earners loses his or her job, reliable vehicles for each wage earner, no reliance on government assistance, "generational wealth" (in the form of heirlooms, precious metals, etc.) that you can hand down, the ability to invest in kids (education, clubs, training, etc.), and leisure time for physical, spiritual, and mental fitness.

Mr. John Brennan, per the retired NSA head, "The CIA is the largest employer of lesbians in America".

Since 1987, the high close for the S&P 500 index has occurred in December 16 times (source: BTN Research).

Average daily trade of the S&P 500:

2007	1,290.5 million shares
2016	642.2 million shares
2017	565 million shares

Concealed-carry permits: "Permit holders are about six times less likely to commit a crime than police officers are." Newsmax Oct 2017.

Food stamp use at lowest level in seven years with 1.1 million Americans dropping off the rolls.

Milk - Holstein cows milk (94% in America - produce more milk than Guernsey) contains 2 beta-casein proteins, A1 and A2. A1 linked to serious disorders! French Guernsey cows milk produce only A2. A2 only cows produce more fat thus more flavor, is this why France has 1,200 different types of cheese, butters and creams.

July 2017: In Afghanistan the US has 9,000 military & 26,000 contractors.

In Boston's Public Schools: Minority students 86%, Speak English as a Second Language 45%, Disabled 20% and Economically Disadvantaged 70%. Dropout rate 33% and teachers get lifetime employment after their 3 year probation.

Income to buy a home. National median home price $255,600 6/17.

Buffalo median home price $140,000 vs SFO $950,000.

Boston $469,900 need a salary of $98,519 with 20% downpayment.

Air Force One's hourly flight cost = $142,380.

Counterterrorism uses less troops and relies on helicopters vs Counterinsurgency efforts that use more ground vehicles.

Taxes on air line tickets = 25, on WiFi 21.

Maintenance costs per state-controlled mile in Massachusetts totaled $78,313 while the national average was $25,996. Administrative expenses costs per mile was $74,924 in Massachusetts while only $10,051 nationally. I asked, "Why doesn't the committee look into these exorbitant costs and unconscionable waste and come up with cost savings?

While Listening may be the sincerest form of flattery, Alert attention is the mother of intelligence.

Islam views blasphemy* as heresy and punishable by death. In Pakistan, the blasphemy laws apply to Muslims and non-Muslims with *Mandatory death penalty for using derogatory language about the Prophet Muhammad." There is no forgiveness for blasphemy and no punishment for anyone who kills a blasphemer. In this religion, there isn't any room for 'free speech'.

Shariah rules apply to marriage, divorce, alimony and child custody. It does not recognize wills, instead applying set rules for what proportions of an estate children and spouses receive. Sons are charged with caring for a family's women and inherit the majority of an estate. "Wills bring hatred and discord in the families," "It would be like giving a dead person the opportunity to intervene in the lives of those still alive." - Mustafa Imamoglu

State religion: 43 countries have official state religions, 27 are Muslim.

U.S. Market disruption recovery: 9/11 2001 terrorist attacks took 19 trading days to recover, Fukishima nuclear disaster 2011 took 9 days, Flash Crash 2010 took 5 days, Greek Debt crisis 2015, 11 days and Brexit 2016 took 10 trading days.

Dec17 - Between 2010 and 2016, investment bank Citigroup estimates that U.S. corporations bought back $3 trillion worth of stock (and paid out $2 trillion in dividends). Keep in mind, the S&P 500's total market value in 2010 was roughly $10 trillion. That's a lot of capital that has been plowed back into the stock market, which helps explain why stocks are relatively expensive (and why they've gone up so much).

The last three times that short-term (2 year) interest rates moved above 10-year Treasuries were in 1989, 2000, and 2007. Those were the last three recessions in the U.S. The rate hikes in 2000 and 2007 led to major stock market crashes.

THE END